MW00875505

Jack Burgess

Whispering Death

by

Lee Heide

An autobiography of World War II

Cover: Beaufighters over Grand Harbour, Malta

Book design, typesetting, graphics
Roy Diment
Vivencia Resources Group
Victoria, BC Canada

Note for Librarians: A cataloguing record for this book is available from Library and Archives Canada at www.collectionscanada.ca/amicus/index-e.html
ISBN 1-4122-0129-2

Printed on paper with minimum 30% recycled fibre. Trafford's print shop runs on "green energy" from solar, wind and other environmentally-friendly power sources.

TRAFFORD
PUBLISHING™
Offices in Canada, USA, Ireland and UK

Book sales for North America and international:
Trafford Publishing, 6E–2333 Government St.,
Victoria, BC V8T 4P4 CANADA
phone 250 383 6864 (toll-free 1 888 232 4444)
fax 250 383 6804; email to orders@trafford.com
Book sales in Europe:
Trafford Publishing (UK) Limited, 9 Park End Street, 2nd Floor
Oxford, UK OX1 1HH UNITED KINGDOM
phone 44 (0)1865 722 113 (local rate 0845 230 9601)
facsimile 44 (0)1865 722 868; info.uk@trafford.com
Order online at:
trafford.com/00-0051

10 9 8 7 6 5 4 3 2 1

Contents

By the Author (Lugus, Toronto)

Short stories
 Love in the Autumn
Novels
 If Freedom Fail
 The Avro Arrow Affair
 The Land God Forgot

Author's Notes:

1. Quotes from the book 'A Lighter Shade of Blue' by C. Foxley-Norris are made with the kind permission of Ian Hall Publishing, Surrey, England.

2. There are several versions of the song 'Lili Marlene'. While not the exact verse that we sang, I have chosen to quote the original version, obtained on the Internet. Source: http://www.ingeb.org/Lieder/lilimarl.html

Prologue

En route from Egypt to Malta, heavily laden with fuel and a torpedo, the Beaufort plodded along at a stately 140 knots. The ungainly aircraft was not known for its speed. It was a perfect summer day with wispy cirrus clouds on high, a deep blue sky and azure water below. It was a picture post-card of a Mediterranean holiday.

But it was no vacation. It was the last day of June, 1942, and the war was going badly for the Allies. Malta was under siege. Rommel's Afrika Corps had stormed across North Africa and were nearing Alexandria. He had promised Hitler to 'Serve Egypt up on a plate.' At the other end of the Med, Operation Torch, the U.S. invasion at Casablanca, was still many months away.

From my position in the nose I called Harry, my pilot, on the intercom: 'I've got Malta on the ASV . . . 40 miles . . . dead ahead.'

'All right,' he replied.

'Good thing you've got this new radar,' carped Taffy, from the rear turret. 'You'd never find this little island without it.'

'Up yours, too.' I replied. 'I could find it in the dark with no radar.' I wasn't so sure about that statement. With an astro dome and a sextant I could find it but the aircraft had neither. However, I didn't mind the three Brits kidding the 'Colonial' in their crew; it's when they stop kidding you that you are in trouble.

'I'll give Malta a call,' Harry said. But he couldn't raise them on the VHF so he said to Ginger, the radio operator: 'Give them a call on the HF.'

After a few minutes Ginger came on the intercom: 'I've got them . . . they say that there is an air raid going on . . . we are to hold off until further advised.'

'Shit!' Taffy groused, 'I suppose there's always an air raid going on.'

'I guess so,' Harry sighed, starting to circle. After about 20 minutes he called Ginger. 'Tell Malta that we can't circle much longer . . . we'll run out of fuel.'

'Okay,' Ginger said. Then, after a moment: 'They say to come in now . . . the air raid is nearly over.'

We swooped in over Valletta Harbour and landed at Luqa airport. Harry taxied around the potholes in the runway from the air raid, which workers were already filling and patching. We were guided to a stone revetment where we shut down.

After finding our quarters on the base, we looked around the nearby area. It seemed that every building had been damaged to some extent. Pieces of rock and rubble lined the streets and there was danger from over-hanging mortices and tenons falling.

'Ye Gods!' Ginger exclaimed. 'I wonder how long a tour of operations is in this damn place?'

'I dunno,' I replied. 'I'll ask the Adjutant.' Finding him in a crummy office, a lanky Scot with dark pouches under his eyes, I asked the question.

'I'm not sure, old chap,' he replied. 'I'll have to look it up. Nobody has ever done one.'

I was stunned. What road had led me to this gloomy forecast of death, injury or a Prisoner of War camp?

Chapter 1

Canada

When I was growing up in Vancouver I was aware, without actually being told, that people in B.C. were a little different from other Canadians whom we regarded with an air of genial superiority. The great barrier of the Rocky Mountains was like a good-neighbour fence; our thoughts often turned south rather than east and there were many members of a splinter political party that advocated joining Washington and Oregon as a U.S. state. There wasn't even a decent road through the Rockies!

Over the Rockies the land flowed flatly across the prairies to Winnipeg. Anything after that was always referred to as 'Back East.' We knew that laws affecting the whole country were made in Ottawa, usually to the detriment of B.C. like the Crows Nest railway rates.

During the spring and summer of 1940 there was quite a bit of war news in the papers and on the radio. I knew, for instance, that Neville Chamberlain had screwed things up and was not surprised when Winston Churchill took over. However, my girl friend wanted to see Gracie Fields in 'Shipyard Sally' and tickets were hard to get.

I knew that the war was going badly for Britain. On the other hand, 'Seabiscuit' was a favorite at Santa Anita and it was best to get some money down before the odds got too low.

The German invasion of the Low Countries was a shock. But my favorite baseball team, the Brooklyn Dodgers, had won 11 straight and had to be encouraged.

The stories of Dunkirk were amazing, with all those little boats sailing across the English Channel to rescue the soldiers. But I had a tennis tournament to prepare for which took a lot of practice and didn't have much time to read.

My father was an itinerant newspaperman who had a hard time

in the Great Depression of the 1930s. I was the oldest of three children and my mother's health was poor. There was no money for luxuries nor for my university fees but I was lucky in finding summer jobs. In the summer of 1940 I found work in a plywood mill at the foot of Fraser Street. It paid well and I had more than enough money to see me through the year.

So I was fat, dumb and happy on my way to register at UBC for my second year when I met a friend, Carl, who lived across the street and was in the same year.

'Are you coming to register?' I asked.

'No,' he replied, sadly. 'I've been called up.'

'Called up for what?'

'The Army, of course! I suppose you don't know that there is a war on,' he added, sarcastically.

'Oh, hell!' I swore. Carl and I were the same age – twenty. 'Do you think I'll be called up, too?'

'Of course.'

My heart sank. All I knew about the Army were the horrendous scenes from World War I of troops slogging through mud, rain and snow and getting killed rapidly – 20,000 in a single day at the Somme. 'The Army is not for me,' I said firmly. 'I've always had a hankering to fly. I'll join the Air Force.'

True to my word, I went to the RCAF Recruiting Office the next day. I was told that there was a short waiting list for aircrew. They took my particulars and asked me to return in a month.

Three days later my Army Induction Notice arrived in the mail. 'Ha . . . Ha!' I exulted to my parents. 'I sure fooled them this time!'

But it was not to be.

The grizzled old Warrant Officer at the Army Recruiting Depot on Hastings Street rummaged around his desk as I was escorted into his office.

'What's your full name?' he growled.

'Cecil LeRoy Heide.'

'Ah, yes.' He found the right piece of paper.

'Ahem,' I said, smugly, 'I've already applied to join the RCAF.'

'Did you sign anything?'

'No.'

'No . . . Sir!'

'No, Sir.'

'Stand up straight.'

'Yes, Sir.' I stood at what I thought was attention.

'It's Training Camp at Vernon for you. See the clerk on the way out.' He handed me a piece of paper. 'Give him this and sign your papers and get a bus warrant.'

'But what about the RCAF?' I wailed.

'If the Air Force wantcha, they'll come and getcha. Now, get going.'

My dreams were not shattered but they had taken a cruel blow.

I had been to Vernon a few years earlier to pick hops one summer. A small town at the top of Lake Okanagan, just north of Kelowna. I remembered it as hot, dusty and dirty. It hadn't changed.

The Army Camp, north of the town, was made up of single-story barracks for Privates, NCOs and Officers. Administration buildings formed two sides of a large, square parade ground. Everything was spotless.

The first blow was a haircut; my longish blond hair was reduced to stubble. We were issued with boots that didn't fit and clothing that was so hot and itchy that some of us rubbed the inside with pumice stone. After finding our bunks we were assembled outside in a loose formation.

'Attention!' shouted a Sergeant, and we all jumped. 'You shower of shits are now in my care for the next eight weeks. What I've ever done to deserve such a hopeless bunch of idiotic misfits, I'll never know!'

Suppressing a chuckle, I coughed.

In a trice, his face was inches from mine. Lined and weather-beaten, it looked like an old football. But his eyes were stones. 'You said something?' he snarled.

'No, Sir,' I replied, nervously.

'I'm not an officer. I'm a Sergeant and you will address me as that.'

'Yes, Sergeant.'

'What's your name?'

'Heide, Sergeant.'

'Should be Heidi,' he smirked, 'you look more like a girl than a soldier.'

So mine was the first name that he knew and he never forgot it.

He walked back in front of us. 'My name is Sergeant Lennox. You can have the rest of the day off.' Since it was well past 1800 hours, this was no great concession. 'Tomorrow . . . breakfast at 0600 hours . . . form up here at 0630 hours and I'll try to do something with you stupid, scruffy lot. Dismiss!'

The others were as green as I in Army matters. We got along well but I never made a close friend. I took this occasion to change my name. I had always hated 'Cecil' and its diminutive 'Cece', so I told everyone that my first name was 'Lee'.

So it was Drill – March – Drill, most of it at double time. My legs were in good shape from playing tennis so I didn't suffer much but the pack grew heavier and heavier and my shoulders ached. Some guys stuffed their packs with paper but that was 'old hat' to the NCOs who could spot an errant pack at 20 feet and always resulted in punishment. We cursed at the obstacle course with its ladders, barriers and ropes; I was the only one not to fall in the mud and water below.

We were issued with elderly Lee-Enfield rifles and taken to the firing range where we also fired a brief burst from a Sten Gun.

In the Army

Given gas masks we were pushed into a small hut which contained a weak mixture of mustard gas. About 30 seconds before leaving we had to take the mask off and emerged coughing and hacking.

What I hated most was rushing at a make-believe body with a bayonet. I knew that I could never stab a living person like that.

So the weeks passed while I fretted and worried. Would the RCAF really come to my rescue? I decided that if I got stuck in the Army it wouldn't be in the ranks and applied for Officer's School.

Friday was inspection and parade day. It started with us standing to attention by our bunks with our kit placed exactly on our blanket. Sgt. Lennox and a Corporal took us to task for any infraction. But on this day, five weeks into the course, a vision appeared in the doorway. Six feet tall, ramrod straight, boots mirrored, puttees exact, leather burnished to a soft glow, buttons shining, hat square on his head with the peak one inch above his eyes, swagger stick under his arm. This paragon was the Regimental Sergeant Major, Mister Dawson, a Guardsman, whom we had only seen before from a distance.

We all stiffened up. Trailed by Sgt. Lennox he fixed us with a steely glare, gesturing at the slightest infraction which the Sgt. entered in his note book. We slowly exhaled as he left. But he was a devious sod, as I'll relate shortly.

The Friday routine was as follows. After the barrack inspection we formed up on the parade square. Each platoon Sgt. inspected his men. RSM Dawson arrived and took over, inspecting one platoon of his choice while the others stood at ease. Then the Adjutant, a Captain, took over and ordered the officers to 'Fall In'. He turned the parade over to the C.O. – a Major – who put us through our paces. Sometimes a visiting dignitary took the salute.

All of this usually took over an hour. Since it was blistering hot that August an ambulance waited at the rear to collect those few who fainted. (Sgt. Lennox had shown us the trick of relaxing while still standing to attention).

On this day when RSM Dawson took over he stood everyone at ease except our platoon. He had already inspected us in our barracks – why did he want to do it again?

Being tall, I was at the end of the front rank. As he approached, the RSM dropped a coin on the tarmac. Silly me – I looked down to see what had made the 'Tinkle'.

Dawson had me! 'That man!' he roared.

'Who, me?' I croaked.

'Yes, you! Head up . . . eyes front . . . stand up straight! Sgt. Lennox, give this man 'Clean-up' for tomorrow!'

'Yes, Sir,' Sgt. Lennox replied.

I noticed that RSM Dawson didn't pick up the coin; he probably had more in his pocket.

On the next morning I was given a pointed stick and a gunny sack to pick up any debris around the camp. In the afternoon I was given a pail of white creosote and a brush and ordered to re-paint the stones around the Admin building. I didn't mind; it broke the routine and I could work at my own pace.

Towards the end of week seven Sgt. Lennox ordered me to see the Adjutant.

'Oh, God!' I muttered. 'What have I done wrong now?'

'Stand easy, Private,' said the Captain as I stood in front of his desk. He shuffled some papers. 'It appears as if the Air Force feel that they can't win the war without you.'

My heart leaped.

'Here are your transfer papers,' he handed them to me. 'Report to the RCAF Recruiting Office in Vancouver on Monday. That will give you a week-end at home. See the Corporal in the office for a clearance form and a travel voucher.'

'Yes, Sir!' I said happily.

'For what it's worth,' he gave a brief smile, 'Sgt. Lennox approved your application for Officer's School.'

I was nonplussed. 'Thank you, Sir.' I had obviously misjudged Sgt. Lennox. Still, I was over-joyed to be rid of him and the whole Army that went with him! I sang all the way to Vancouver.

The Air Force Recruiting Officer in Vancouver was named Flying Officer Goldberg. He was in his forties with a fleshy face, generous nose and black hair combed straight back. He had a kindly, avuncular attitude and said: 'How nice to see you again, young man. Do sit down. How did you like Army Boot Camp?'

'I hated it,' I replied, easing on to a hard chair.

He chuckled. 'Good thing we brought you back, then. Now, you have two things to do tomorrow. Since you are applying for aircrew, you must have a medical exam in the morning. In the afternoon you will take an aptitude test.'

'Okay,' I agreed.

'Fine.' He stood up. 'Report back to me at 1100 hours on Wednesday, the day after tomorrow.'

'Right.'

The medical exam was very thorough but I was in top condition and there were no snags. The aptitude test was not difficult but quite long; it took over an hour to complete.

Promptly at 1100 hours the next day I was back in F/O Goldberg's office. I sat down while he looked at some papers on his desk. 'Your medical was fine . . . no problems.'

'Yes.' I waited.

'Your aptitude test shows you to be strong in Maths and Physics and very suitable to be a navigator.'

'I hoped to be a pilot.'

Goldberg steepled his fingers under his double chin. 'Flying an aircraft is much like driving a car and we have many people who can do that. What we don't have are good navigators. The key man in any crew is the navigator . . . he tells the pilot what to do. Most of us believe that the navigator should be Captain, like they are in the Dutch Air Force.' He paused. 'If you want to serve your country in the best capacity that you can, you should train as a navigator.'

I was being soft-soaped and I knew it. Still, I didn't have any strong preference one way or the other, so I said: 'All right . . . I'll be a navigator.' I never regretted the decision.

'Good . . . good!' Goldberg rubbed his hands together like one of his ancestors who had completed a profitable deal. 'Go and have some lunch and be back here at 1330 hours. We'll have your papers and rail warrant ready . . . we want you on your way tomorrow.'

'Where to?' I raised my eyebrows.

'Oh, sorry. Initial Training School in Winnipeg and then on to Navigation School.'

So I bid a hasty 'Farewell' to my parents and to my younger brother and sister and left Vancouver for places unknown. I had no idea of the anguish that I would put them through at a later date.

The CPR Trans-Continental arrived at Winnipeg station around noon. Parked outside was a blue bus with a sign: 'RCAF – ITS'. As

I walked towards it, carrying my suitcase, I was joined by several others. There were about 20 of us from points west, all looking as if we had just lost our best friends.

The ITS was in an old Armory building. The large floor area was divided by plywood panels into four separate places, each with about 20 iron beds, mattresses and lockers. We were later organised into prospective navigators, pilots, radio operators and air gunners. A Sgt. took names as men (boys?) filtered in and shouted: 'Go to Stores,' he gestured, 'and get sheets, blankets and a pillow . . . take any bed . . . we'll sort you all out tomorrow.'

The atmosphere was easy and casual, so different from the Army that I had just left.

I didn't fall for the sucker cry after the lights were out that night. 'Anybody here from the West?'

Some guys fell for it. 'Yes!'

'Fuck the West!'

In the morning we were issued our shoes, caps and uniforms with no badges; we were lowly AC-2. Aircraftsman Second Class. We were just getting organised by trade when a Sgt. shouted: 'Aircraftsmen Heidy!' (I was quite used to this mispronunciation of my name).

'Here,' I replied.

'Report to the office.'

'Yes, Sergeant.'

In the office I found a middle-aged Warrant Officer with a harried expression. 'What now?' I wondered.

'Stand at ease,' he ordered. 'I see by your documents that you almost completed Boot Camp in the Army.'

'Yes, Sir.'

'Good! I'm desperately short of drill instructors. You are now an acting, unpaid Corporal . . . get a couple of stripes from Stores and report to Sgt. Rawlings . . . he'll show you your squad.'

'Yes, Sir.' I was somewhat bemused.

My squad turned out to be 18 other hopeful navigators. Sgt. Rawlings watched me drill them on the parade ground for a while and then departed, satisfied that I knew what I was doing. We were at ITS for only two weeks. One day the Sgt. ordered me to: 'Take them for a route march . . . two hours . . . ten minute rest after the first hour.'

Since the Armory was in the city, the route march was in built-up areas. The end of the hour found us in front of a Dairy Queen. The ten minute break escalated into half an hour as we scoffed ice cream. I was quite popular.

In the bed next to me was a fellow from Newfoundland named Giles Bugden, always of course called 'Bugs'. He was to become a staunch friend until our ways parted in England.

In our time at ITS I seldom saw an officer. Thinking back to the Army as well, I realized that it was the senior NCOs who were the backbone of the Armed Forces. In some 23 years of service in the RCAF, I was never to change my mind.

The two weeks passed quickly. We were inoculated against some foreign diseases that we had never heard of and had sore arms for a few days. A lecture on venereal disease was followed by a film on female genital parts that was so graphic that I was almost sick. We were warned about little creatures called 'Crabs' that could infest our private parts. We had a 'Short Arm' inspection.

In those days navigators were called 'Observers'. Thus we reported to No. 7 Air Observer's School in Portage la Prairie. The school had not been open long; we were Course number five. Also based there was a pilot training school called EFTS – Elementary Flying Training School. We had no idea that Portage was just one of many bases formed under the Commonwealth Air Training Plan that would turn out some 28,000 aircrew a year for the war.

Since we were two to a room, Bugs and I teamed up. We were a study in contrasts. I was six feet tall, slim, blue eyes and blond hair. Bugs was five feet, seven inches tall, stocky, dark hair and brown eyes. I was quick off the mark and inclined to put my mouth in motion before engaging my brain. Bugs was slow and thorough but once absorbed, info was never forgotten. In common, we both had a sense of humour and liked a practical joke, dressed casually and hated people who were arrogant or condescending.

On the first day in our new classroom we stood to attention as an officer entered. 'Sit down,' he ordered.

He looked us over like the Lord of the Manor surveying his serfs, sure that we had some nefarious plot in mind that he would have to counter. 'My name is Flying Officer Cooke.'

He was about 30 years old with sharp features, shifty eyes and thin, pursed lips that rarely saw a smile. 'I will be your Navigation Instructor and also your Den Mother. Any problems, personal or otherwise, you may bring to me.'

I hoped, probably along with the rest of the class, that I wouldn't have any.

'The Course is four months long. It starts with three weeks of ground school on Maths, Geometry and Basic Navigation. You will then start to fly in Anson aircraft. There are mid-term exams after which some of you will be gone.' He said this with great satisfaction, as if his job might be barely tolerable after that point.

'Other subjects will be Maps and Charts and Airmanship, which I will teach, Meteorology, Wireless, Compasses and Instruments.'

'We will now proceed to stores where you will draw log books and note books, pens and pencils, compasses, dividers, protractors, rulers, slide rules and other arcane equipment.'

Bugs and I sat in the canteen that evening drinking a watery beer which was the only alcohol allowed. 'Well, what do you think?' I asked.

'We're gonna have trouble with Cooke,' he sighed.

'How so?'

'You can see him just waiting to jump on us for the slightest mistake.'

'Then we'll just have to be careful,' I remarked.

'YOU will have to be careful and not open your big mouth at the wrong time.'

'Who, me?' I said, innocently.

'Yes, you,' he confirmed.

F/O Cooke did most of the lecturing during the first weeks. He knew his subjects well but he was a poor instructor. He droned on with no slides, illustrations or examples to break the monotony. And of course no humour.

My seat was beside a window. I looked out one day when Cooke was talking and saw a Tiger Moth from the EFTS. It was suspended, in my view, between two power lines and didn't appear to be moving at all. I realised that it had a head wind almost equal to it's air speed and thus it's speed over the ground was almost zero. This was quite interesting. My reverie was broken by Cooke's shout: 'Heide . . . Heide!'

'Yes, Sir.' I came back to awareness.

'What did I just say?' he demanded.

'I don't know, Sir . . . my mind was wandering.'

'Well, your body can start wandering, too . . . go to the Chief Instructor's Office and tell him why I sent you.'

'Yes, Sir,' I sighed as I rose from my seat. Bugs had been right - we were gonna have trouble with Cooke.

F/O Cooke announced that the top five students would be commissioned as Pilot Officers; the rest would be Sergeants. I reckoned to make the top five with a reasonable amount of work but we knew that Bugs would have to concentrate just to graduate because of his academic weakness. I spent an hour or so every evening coaching him.

It quickly became apparent that Meteorology was a most important subject. This was taught by Mr. Jones, a civilian on loan from the Federal Met Service. (More on him later). In the absence of weather one could draw a line on a map from A to B and, with a good compass, fly the aircraft along this track. But of course there was always a wind to push you off course not to mention such things as rain, hail, sleet, snow, turbulence, lightning and that bane of all aviators - ICE!

F/O Cooke caught me again. He put on the blackboard for us to solve, a long equation which would take a full page to solve by algebra. I did it in six lines of calculus and handed it in.

'Heide!' he stormed. 'You're always such a smart-ass! Maybe you would like to teach this course?'

'No, Sir.' I kept a straight face.

'Your week-end pass is cancelled.'

We usually spent our week-ends in Winnipeg since the town of Portage did not offer much for us young blades. Since buses were infrequent, we crammed five people into a taxi and shared the cost. There was always a party in the Marlborough Hotel, often with Army troops from Camp Shilo.

Since I was confined, Bugs stayed in camp also and we did some studying. We also discussed F/O Cooke.

'Did you notice,' Bugs asked, 'that our classroom is always open but there is a key on the inside of the door?'

'No.' I raised my eyebrows.

'Suppose that Cooke came to work on Monday morning and the door was locked and there was no key?'

'He would have a fit,' I smiled.

And Cooke did. We all stood in the hall with faces of pure innocence as he raged around the building, finally finding a janitor with a pass key. He kept glaring at me and Bugs. He knew!

Things improved greatly when we started to fly and hence spent less time in the classroom. We flew three times a week, first with a partner and then alone. The Anson aircraft were twin-engine, slow and drafty. Since it was now November, with snow on the ground, the drafts were bone-chilling. The pilots were all civilians, mostly from the United States, who, I supposed, were here for the money. We gradually honed our navigation skills both by day and night and flew about 100 hours in total.

I loved flying from the start, even in the creaky Anson. Here was a new world where none could trouble you with the cares and problems of daily life, where you were immune from the dubious challenges of a make-believe society. Yet it was a most demanding world where a single mistake could have dire consequences. I liked to fly at night. With no visible reference to the ground the aircraft seemed suspended in space. Above the industrial haze the stars, soon to have names and be my friends, shone with a pristine beauty and clarity not seen by earth-bound mortals.

Bugs was much more capable in the air than in the classroom. He had an instinctive feel for the job and needed no help from me; he was a happy camper now.

I often flew with an American pilot named Al Husted. He was a tall, lanky Texan with crows-feet at the corners of his eyes from squinting into the sun in southern climes. The training flight this day was over a triangular route which brought us back near Winnipeg at the end. It was late on a Friday afternoon.

Husted came on the intercom: 'Heide?'

'Yes.'

'Watcha doin' this weekend?'

'Nothing much.'

'Do ya have it off?'

'Yes.'

'Wouldja prob'ly be goin' to Winnipeg?'

'Most likely.'

'Look,' Husted said, 'I got a heavy date in Winnipeg tonight and I'll be late if we fly to Portage and then I have to drive all the way back to Winnipeg again.'

'So?' I queried.

'So what say we land in Winnipeg now?'

'Okay by me . . . but how?'

'I'll show ya.' Husted turned sideways in his seat, lifted his right leg and drove it through a side window panel. 'Ah surely cain't fly with that wind comin' in.'

'Winnipeg Tower,' he called on the VHF, 'this is Anson 6494 outa Portage . . . you readin' me?'

The reply was quick. 'Anson 6494, this is Winnipeg Tower . . . go ahead.'

'6494 . . . Ah'm declarin' an emergency because of a broken window . . . Ah need to land right away.'

'Roger . . . what is your position and altitude?'

'About ten miles east . . . 4,000 feet.'

Winnipeg Tower obliged with a straight-in approach. After landing, Husted phoned Portage to get them to send a technician with a new window.

We both had a nice week-end.

The Avro 'Anson' Advanced Training Monoplane

We missed our families at Xmas. We had the day off but otherwise it was training as usual. F/O Cooke was disappointed that only one student was dropped at half-time.

Mr. Jones, the Government Met man, was in his forties with a bald head and grey tufts, and twinkling blue eyes. He had a sense of humour and was our favorite instructor. Ten days before the final exams he did something that I have never seen done in many years of education - and it was smart. He gave each of us three exam papers, saying: 'One of these will be your final exam.'

We were delighted, studied the papers in great detail and all got good marks. But the three papers included every formula, every weather map and every theory that Jones had imparted over four months. We sure knew our Met!

Four days before the end of the course, all exams written, I got into trouble again - and this time it was serious! Bugs and I were standing just inside the classroom door when I said: 'Hooray! A few more days and we are rid of that arrogant, sanctimonious prick, F/O Cooke!'

Cooke came through the doorway just in time to hear my bleat. His face blanched white. 'I demand an apology for those words,' he said.

'Well, you won't get it from me,' I said, stubbornly.

Without another word, he turned and stamped away. On the next day I was in front of the Chief Instructor, a Squadron Leader, on the charge of 'Insubordination'.

'There is no excuse,' he said grimly, 'for your remarks about F/O Cooke. He tells me that you have been a troublemaker all through your course. You will finish first or second on your course and would normally be commissioned. However, I am delaying that by a year and you will leave here as a Sergeant. There will be a formal 'Reprimand' on your file.'

Under my breath I said: 'Oh, shit!'

Aloud I said: 'Yes, Sir'. And marched out.

'Now, will you learn to keep your bloody mouth shut?' Bugs was mad at me, although me being a Sergeant would keep us together.

'Yes,' I promised. I kept my word. I was never again in trouble. For that.

So we put up three stripes and half-wing with an 'O' called by other aircrew a 'Flying Arsehole'. (This was later replaced by a double wing with a globe in the centre).

On 1 Feb 41 we arrived at No. 3 Bombing and Gunnery School at Macdonald, Man. There was little ground school which suited Bugs. All flying was done on elderly Fairey Battle aircraft. The pilots were mostly civilians. For gunnery we fired .30 calibre machine guns at ground targets and at a drogue pulled by another Battle. For bombing we dropped 25 lb practice bombs from both low and high level. Bugs and I usually flew together and swore it was not us whose practice bomb went through a farmer's barn roof and damaged a cow.

We flew about 30 hours in bitterly cold weather, the mercury dropping to -35°F. The aircraft were drafty and our numerous layers of jackets, coats and mittens made it hard to move around. However, we survived and both passed the course albeit with only average marks.

By a Fairey Battle

'The basis of astronomy is the spherical triangle formed on the celestial sphere between your meridian, the hour circle and the vertical circle through the object.'

I saw Bugs' face fall at the opening words of F/O Wilkes in the first lecture at No. 1 Advanced Navigation Course at Rivers, Manitoba. It should have been named 'Astro Navigation Course' because that was what it was all about - finding your position by the Sun, Moon, Planets and Stars.

The academic work concentrated on solving the spherical triangle by spherical trigonometry and the use of logarithms. It was hard

work for Bugs and I had to keep my wits about me in order to help
him out. But, as usual, when we got to the practical use of the
sextant, he was fine.

The Anson aircraft now had an astro dome, with a card showing
the refraction of that piece of glass in various quadrants. We soon
got used to our favorite heavenly guides. Sun and Moon always, if
they were out. Polaris for latitude. The bright giants - Aldeberan,
Capella, Arcturus, Antares, Vega and Sirius. I liked Betelgeuse and
Rigel, so easily found in Orion's belt.

But it was bitterly cold that winter on the prairies. The pilots, all
civilians, refused to fly when the mercury dropped to -40°F. In four
weeks we managed only 25 hours of flying. It was too cold to shoot
outdoors on the ground because the sextant wheels froze up. We
shot a lot of stars through the classroom windows.

'I know exactly where we are,' Bugs said.

'Yeah . . . where?'

'Twenty miles north of Chicago.'

I laughed. 'Well, fudge the window refraction until you get the
position lines where you want them.'

But the torture finally came to an end and we both passed and
were posted to Halifax to go by ship to England, after two weeks
leave at home. We sat in the canteen, drinking beer, on our last
night.

'What's the name of that town you come from?'

'Corner Brook,' Bugs replied.

'Where is it?' My knowledge of Newfoundland was sparse.

'On the west coast of the island.'

'Will your family be there?'

'I guess so. I've got two brothers and two sisters . . . all older than
me.' He took a swallow of beer and grimaced. 'I'll sure be glad to be
rid of this horse piss that they call beer and get a decent drink.'

'Like what?'

'Like Screech.'

'Screech? What the hell is that?'

'It's Newfie rum . . . from the bottom of the barrel.'

'Strong?'

'You bet!'

'Look . . . we'll meet in Halifax in a couple of weeks . . . bring some Screech so I can try it out.'

'Okay.'

It was not to be one of my better suggestions.

The weather in Vancouver, although rainy, was a tonic after the prairies. I entertained my family with stories of my experiences. They assumed that we all graduated with the rank of Sergeant and I didn't tell them any different. I had been home for a week when a telegram arrived from the Air Force:

'POSTING CHANGE. REPORT TO RCAF STN, DORVAL, P.Q. FOR FERRY COMMAND BY 22 APRIL.'

I was both delighted and sad. Delighted at the prospect of flying the Atlantic Ocean but sad because they had cut my leave short and I would not see Bugs again.

The train to Montreal was my third trip across the country. I was learning the ropes. How to get a lower bunk by faking a bad leg. Carry my wallet in an inside pocket and put my valuables under my pillow at night. Not to get in a poker game because of con men. Always go to the first sitting in the dining car before all the good food runs out. Don't order strawberries. There were always strawberries on the menu but if you asked for them, the waiter would say: 'We are all out of strawberries but we do have prunes.' Ever after, prunes were known as 'CPR Strawberries'.

Chapter 2

Trans-Atlantic Ferry Command

Dorval was a busy place. There was an air of hustle-bustle with men and machines on the go. I found the Adjutant and reported in. He was a harassed-looking Flight Lieutenant whose desk top could not be seen for paper. 'Heide . . . Heide,' he muttered as he searched for the right piece of paper. 'Ah, yes . . . there are no quarters free here. Go to the Queens Hotel in Montreal . . . they have a room for you.'

'Okay.'

'Now check with the Dispatcher . . . I think he has something for you.'

The flight line was crowded with aircraft and handling equipment of various sorts. I found the Dispatcher in a small building. 'Sgt. Heide, Sir,' I said.

'Yes.' He was another weary-looking man - a Flying Officer. 'You are to fly a Hudson aircraft over-seas but it won't be here for a couple of weeks. Meanwhile,' he searched for a manifest, 'the day after tomorrow you collect a load at Presque Isle and take it to Goose Bay.'

'Where's Presque Isle?' I had visions of an exotic Caribbean island.

'In northern Maine.'

'Oh. And where's Goose Bay?'

He looked at me with pity. 'In Labrador.'

'Who is the pilot?'

He looked at the manifest. 'Mr. Pangborn.'

'And the aircraft?'

'A Liberator.'

'How big a crew?'

'Four - pilot, co-pilot, WOP and you.'

'Where's the aircraft?'

He waved vaguely with one hand. 'On the tarmac.'

I was unhappy. I didn't know where these places were and had never seen the aircraft. I had a full set of navigation instruments including a sextant, air almanac and star tables but no maps.

'Take off is 0900 hours the day after tomorrow . . . be here an hour before.' The F/O interrupted my reverie.

'I'll be around here tomorrow,' I said.

He shrugged.

At the Queens Hotel I found that I shared a room with another Sgt. named Rene LaBlanc. He was a Wireless Operator. He spoke French but didn't know Montreal well.

After getting unpacked I went down to the lobby and, lo and behold, in limped Giles Bugden, a suitcase in either hand. His posting had also been changed. After a hand-clasp and a couple of back-pats, I said: 'It's great to see you, but why are you limping?'

'I'm not. It's just that this case,' Bugs gestured to his right hand, 'is so heavy.'

'Why?'

He gave a sly smile. 'It's full of Screech.'

'Oh, Boy!' I said. Little did I know.

After Bugs got settled, we gathered in my room. The Screech bottles had no label of any kind.He poured a generous portion, saying: 'It's best to add a little water.'

This we did and clinked glasses.

'A.r.r.gh!' I wondered if the lining of my throat was still there.

'Sacre Bleu!' Rene wheezed.

'Good stuff, eh?' Bugs showed no effect.

I had very little experience with hard liquor and things got a bit fuzzy. I remember going to a Chinese restaurant for dinner and then to a night club. After that, I could only remember trying to get my bed to stay still so that I could get into it.

To say that I had a hangover the next morning would be a massive under-statement. I vowed to take Screech in small doses thereafter. But I recovered enough to take the bus to Dorval in the afternoon.

I found maps in a small room near the Dispatch Office and took

'Bugs' and I in Montreal

those that I needed. Presque Isle was about 300 nautical miles from Dorval, in a built-up area with many radio aids and would be easy to find. Goose Bay, about 600 miles north from Presque Isle, was at the end of a long fiord from the sea into which flowed the Churchill River. It would be easy to spot if the weather was clear. But I was dismayed to see the whole of Labrador marked 'Unexplored' with no physical features shown.

I measured tracks and distances and made a rough flight plan. Then I went out on the tarmac to find a Liberator. There were two but the doors on both were locked. I sighed. At least they had an astro dome.

When Mr. Pangborn arrived, shortly after 0800 hours the next morning, I had checked the Met and completed my portion of the flight plan. He was a tall, thin American in his fifties with greying hair, crows-feet at the corners of his eye and a nice smile. Clyde Pangborn was an aviation pioneer the likes of Amelia Aerhart and had many records world-wide. I didn't know this.

The co-pilot was another American, named Tom Ulmer. A slight man in his thirties, he too seemed very friendly. The radio operator was my room-mate, Rene LaBlanc.

After introductions, Pangborn said to me: 'What does the Met

C-87

man say?'

'At Presque Isle there is overcast at 3,000 feet but little wind and good viz. He doesn't know anything about Goose Bay. There is a stratus layer between three and six thousand feet over most of Quebec.'

'You've got the winds?'

'Yes, Sir.'

He smiled sweetly. 'My name is Clyde.'

We completed the paper work and he led the way to the aircraft, explaining as he did the external check: 'This is not a Liberator, it's a C-87, the military version with Pratt and Whitney engines instead of Wrights . . . much better . . . not so much vibration.' Pangborn was the only one of us to have flown in the aircraft. 'It's a docile beast,' he looked at me, 'but it can't carry enough ice to make a good cocktail and above 20,000 feet it flops about like an injured whale.'

The navigator's position was very good. A large table on which to work, read-outs of vital info like airspeed, altitude, heading, outside air temperature; there was a drift meter and even a clock.

It was an easy flight to Presque Isle, a bucolic town near the New Brunswick border. The USAF base was crowded with aircraft and supplies for it was a major MATS terminal. We found our cargo to be construction material: heavy beams, both wood and metal; doors and windows; concrete; sand and much more.

With its heavy load the C-87 used up most of the runway before Pangborn eased it into the air. (I could never call him Clyde). We climbed through cloud to our assigned altitude of 9,000 feet where it was warm and sunny.

I set course for Sept Iles, on the north shore of the St. Lawrence river; it was slightly off our direct track to Goose Bay but it had a radio range and would give us a good fix before starting over 'Unexplored' Labrador. None of us had been to Goose Bay.

Leaving Sept Iles we still had cloud below. I gave the pilot a heading. The compass was wandering all over the place with a variation of over 35 degrees. Once we ran out of range of the Sept Iles beacon there was no other navigation aid but the sun. I got out my sextant. The position line from the sun would be at right angles to our track and thus give a ground speed check but no help for heading. I decided to use a technique called a 'Leading Line'. The procedure

ON FERRY SERVICE—
Sergeant Observer C. L. Heide, son of Mr. and Mrs. A. J. Heide, 1317 East Fourteenth, leaves tonight to report to bomber ferry command at Montreal. Sergeant Observer Heide has spent a week at home on leave after graduating with the rank of second in the class of astral navigation.

was to advance a sun line through Goose Bay, set course to the west of the base and then turn east on reaching the line. I explained this to Captain Pangborn.

'Sure,' he agreed. 'I've flown to one side of a place before today . . . at least you know which way to turn. By the way, did you know that Goose Bay has a radio range?'

'I didn't know that.'

'Nor did I but it's marked on my let-down plate . . . says intermittent operation.'

As things turned out we didn't need the leading line. Just before it came time to turn the cloud below broke up and we could see the Churchill River and the co-pilot picked up the radio range. But I was pleased to see that the leading line would have been spot on.

There was still snow at Goose Bay. The single runway was gravel but covered with packed snow. On the north side of the field was a partially-completed hangar and three other buildings; a Canadian flag flew. On the south side were eight buildings, one finished hangar and another being built; an American flag flew.

The few buildings looked rather pathetic in the bleak, semi-arctic surround. We had no idea that Goose Bay would later house some 3,000 people, both RCAF and USAF, and be a major terminal for trans-Atlantic air operations.

We taxied to the south side. We were met by the C.O., a USAF colonel, who was irritated to find that our cargo didn't include any alcohol. We found beds as we would stay overnight.

That evening Tom, Rene and myself had dinner and then sat in the Mess over a beer. Pangborn was having dinner with the C.O. Tom said: 'Do you know that our Captain is a famous flyer with many records around the world?'

'No,' I replied, raising my eyebrows.

'Mais, non,' Rene added.

'Well, he is . . . he's right up there with Wiley Post, Kingsford Smith and Lindbergh. We'll have to get him talking about some of his experiences.'

A few minutes later Pangborn strolled in.

'Hi,' Tom said. 'Would you like a beer?'

'No, thanks . . . I just had a large dinner.' He sat down.

'I've just been telling Lee and Rene that you are a world-famous aviator.'

'Hardly a household name,' Clyde smiled.

'Tell us about your flights,' Tom urged. 'What was the most memorable one?'

'Well,' Pangborn thought for a moment, 'I guess it has to be flying the Pacific Ocean non-stop from Japan to the States in 1931.'

'You flew across the Pacific?' I was amazed. 'It's huge . . . twice as wide as the Atlantic. You surely weren't alone?'

'No . . . I had a friend named Hugh Hendon with me.'

'Talk!' Tom ordered.

'Well,' Clyde started, 'in Japan I had first to get out of jail. I was taking pictures and they accused me of being a spy. The American Embassy got me out after a couple of days. I had a single-engine monoplane called a Bellanca CH-200 with a fixed under-carriage. The fuselage was so full of gas tanks that there was only a narrow aisle. I knew that we would never make it with the drag of the under-cart so we took it off and put it back on again with explosive bolts, activated by a wire to the cockpit. After take-off I dropped the gear into the sea. We took off from a place named Samushiro, about 300 miles north of Tokyo.'

'How did you navigate?' I asked.

Clyde chuckled. 'I just pointed her nose east and let her go . . . we couldn't miss the whole of North America.'

'Fantastique!' Rene remarked. 'Where did you land?'

'Near Wenatchee in Washington state . . . in a plowed field.'

'How long were you in the air?' I asked.

Clyde smiled. 'Forty-one hours and thirty-one minutes.'

'Good Lord!' I exclaimed. 'Is that the longest flight for a single-engine aeroplane in the history of aviation?'

'I dunno,' Clyde shrugged. 'It surely felt like it.'

'Tell us some more,' Tom urged.

'Not tonight,' Clyde stood up, 'I'm a lot older than you youngsters . . . I'm tired and going to bed.'

On the return flight to Dorval the cloud dispersed and we saw the 'Unexplored' terrain. It was not impressive: small, ice-covered lakes, rocks, scrub trees, no signs of any habitation. I thought that it might as well stay 'Unexplored'; there was nothing to find here anyway. Mile after mile with no change; it was as if the aircraft was standing still over a carpet of desolation. I gave a little shudder; this would be a bad place to come down in.

The steady drone of the four engines was comforting and I resolved to fly in such aircraft in the future. But that was not to be.

Bugs and I had a nice time for the next week or so. We checked daily with the Dispatcher but he had nothing for us. Rene left and Bugs moved into my room. We explored Montreal, saw the sights and had some great meals in the Old Town. I took my Screech in small doses.

We spent a day at Dorval planning our trans-Atlantic flight. The route was to Gander (I didn't know where that was but Bugs did). Then to Prestwick in Scotland (neither of us knew where that was). The flight was to be made at night because Astro was the only means of navigation. So we got maps, plotted a tentative flight plan and looked up in our Air Almanacs to see which stars would be the most visible.

'I guess we're ready,' I said, at the end of a long day.

'Yeah,' Bugs agreed. 'What happens when we get to Scotland?'

'We go to a Holding Depot at a place called Bournemouth.'

'Where's that?'

'I dunno . . . down south somewhere.'

'So I guess we'll meet there?'

'Yeah. The first one to get there books a double room.'

'Okay.'

It turned out that Bugs' flight left two days before mine so he got to Bournemouth first, but they paid no attention to his request for a double room.

I met the pilot and the radio operator on the day prior to our trans-Atlantic flight. Both were civilians. The pilot was a slim man in his thirties with dark, aquiline features, quick movements and a ready smile. His name was Bill Chouteau and he came from Maine; I was sure that there was some French-Canadian in his background. The radio operator was named Paul Frame and he came from Toronto. He had served as such on CPR ships for many years. He was also dark-featured but short and stocky. They had both made one crossing.

On the morning of 5 June 1941, we walked across the tarmac towards our aircraft. 'That's our Hudson, is it?' I asked.

'It's not a Hudson,' Bill replied, 'it's a Ventura, the military version with 2,000 horse-power Pratt and Whitney double Wasps. I took it up for a flight test yesterday.'

'Ventura'

'Oh.' I thought it odd that aircraft never turned out to be what they were supposed to be. 'We don't have a co-pilot?' I asked.

'No . . . pilots are scarce.'

Although I didn't know it then, the lack of a co-pilot was to be a blessing.

The navigator's position was in the nose with good visibility, a comfortable table and instrument read-outs of all pertinent info. It had a throat mike for crew intercom that I hadn't seen before.

The flight from Dorval to Gander was routine and took us about five hours. Two other Venturas took off shortly after us; one of them limped into Gander with both engines running rough and back-firing. The exhaust stacks had been stuffed with oily rags, obviously intended to start a fire in flight. A clear case of sabotage.

We refueled, had a rest and went for our Met briefing. Take-off time was 1600 hours. The forecaster, a cheerful, voluble fellow, said: 'You should top all clouds at about 10,000 feet . . . above that it will be clear and smooth and good for your astro.'

Although admittedly he didn't have much to work with, mainly reports from other aircraft en route, this was about the worst forecast I ever received in many years of flying. It was akin to a time in later years when a Met man in Ottawa said: 'There is little chance of rain', while water poured down the windows.

We filed our flight plan for the Great Circle route to a landfall in Ireland and thence to Prestwick. We were advised not to place any reliance on radio beacons from the British Isles because the Germans had a habit of bending them and two aircraft had ended up in France. Position reports were to be sent at certain Longitudes and Paul was instructed to work Gander on H/F until about half-way and then switch to Prestwick.

We were in cloud immediately after take-off. Still in cloud at 12,000 feet, Bill said: 'We'd better go on oxygen, fellas.'

It was then that I made the disturbing discovery that there was no oxygen outlet in the nose. 'Shit!' I cursed to myself and reported the fact to Chouteau.

'There's one in the co-pilot's position,' he said. 'You'd better come here.'

Someone had foreseen this problem for there was a table folded up against the fuselage. It wasn't very large but I would have to 'Make do'.

At 16,000 feet we were still boring through cloud and the speed started to fall. I pointed to the Air Speed Indicator and looked at Bill.

'I know,' he said. 'We are starting to pick up ice.'

Just then there was a loud 'Crack' and I almost jumped out of my seat. 'What was that?' I asked, shakily.

'It's ice thrown off by the wing de-icers,' Bill replied. He turned on the landing lights and we could see sleet forming rime ice. 'It's not too bad.'

I wasn't sure that I agreed with him.

At 19,000 feet Bill remarked, in his calm voice: 'She's starting to wallow, Lee . . . won't go much higher.'

I just nodded. I didn't know what to say.

Then JOY! We broke out into the clear and a myriad of stars filled the sky! The de-icers had removed most of the ice but the airspeed was still a few knots low.

'There you are,' Bill said, 'you can get busy with your astro now.'

'Great!' I responded. I picked up my sextant and started for the astro dome which was about half-way down the fuselage near a large auxiliary gas tank. When I got there my heart sank down to my boots. There was no oxygen outlet there, either!

I gave the bad news to Bill and added: 'Keep her steady for a bit . . . I'll do the best I can.' I picked out Vega, nice and bright, and took a shot. At the end of the two minutes that it took I was gasping for air like a salmon fighting up-stream. I staggered back up front and flopped in my seat.

The normal procedure to get a 'fix' was to shoot three stars at roughly 60 degree angles; the position lines would intersect to form a triangle called a 'cocked hat' - the smaller the better. After a brief rest I took another shot and so on. It took me almost 30 minutes to finally plot a fix and I was exhausted at the end.

When the time came for a position report to Gander I gave the Lat/Long, time and altitude to Paul and said: ' . . . and tell that stupid forecaster what the weather is really like.'

This routine kept up for another six hours until the cloud broke up. I was one tired flyer! Bill let down to 7,000 feet and we thankfully discarded our oxygen masks. The ice melted and, having used up a lot of fuel, the air speed increased to a respectable 175 knots. Things were looking up!

The sun rose and all cloud dissipated. It was going to be a nice, sunny day.

Approaching the Irish coast I unfolded my topographical map to look for our landfall - Galway Bay. As we got closer Bill pointed ahead: 'We're coming in between two large Bays. The one to starboard is narrower and extends further inland.'

'That's Shannon Bay,' I said gleefully. 'The one to port is Galway Bay.' We were only about 15 miles from our landfall.

'Nice work, Lee,' Bill commented.

'You bet!' added Paul, who had been looking over our shoulders.

I accepted their compliments but I knew that 'Lady Luck' had been with me. What I didn't know was that she would be my constant companion.

It was a short hour to Prestwick. Flying over Ireland I could see why it was called the 'Emerald Isle' - sparkling green fields bordered in hedges, trees and other foliage in multi-coloured green. We landed at Prestwick without incident, having been 10 hours and 40 minutes in the air. Here we parted company as Bill and Paul would return to Canada for another crossing. Bill got paid $1,500 for the flight; Paul got $750; I got my daily pay as a Sgt. - $4.25!

Chapter 3

England

In Bournemouth the RCAF had taken over a large hotel on the waterfront as a Reception Depot. It was fine accommodation but crowded. Being a resort town there were two movie houses, a stage theatre and several Pubs. The beach area was closed off with barbed wire and skull-and-crossbone signs warning of mines. So of course swimming was not allowed.

I found Bugden without trouble and, after we shook hands, asked: 'How was your trip over?'

'Piece of cake,' he replied. 'How was yours?'

'A proper bitch . . . I'll tell you about it.' Which I did.

After my story was told, I asked: 'What do we do here?'

'They say that there is a four or five week wait for an Operational Training Unit. We are to say whether we want Bomber or Coastal Command.' The RCAF bomber squadrons had not yet been formed so we would be flying with the RAF.

'I'm opting for Bomber Command,' Bugs said. 'How about you?'

'Coastal Command,' I said. In my mind's eye I pictured a large, stately, four-engine Sunderland flying boat on patrol over the vast Atlantic with me, the navigator, in complete control of the mission. I would give the pilot his instructions in a clear but firm voice, perhaps suggesting that he watch his heading a bit more carefully. The radio operator would send out position reports which only I could produce. The gunners would rely on my advice whether or not to be alert for enemy aircraft. I might stroll back to the galley where the engineer would make me a cup of coffee and a sandwich. HA-Bloody-HA!

Bugs and I were given ten days leave. Of course we went to London. So did everyone else. Canadians stayed at the Regent Palace

Hotel in Trafalgar Square. There were no rooms left when we arrived so they put us in the Annex across the street. Our room had two narrow beds, two hard chairs, a small dresser with two worn towels on top and a wardrobe so tilted that the doors wouldn't close. The Water Closet (toilet, to you) and the bathroom were down the hall and always occupied. When I finally got into the bathroom, the water was tepid and there was a six-inch line painted around the tub.

We walked to Buckingham Palace and saw the Changing of the Guard; to Green Park and to Regent Park. In the latter, the swans were accomplished beggars and would eat out of your hand. Bugs went up to a large male with his fist out-stretched. The swan craned his neck for the food. Bugs unfolded his empty hand, laughed and turned away. The swan nipped him in the ass! I laughed and took a picture of the swan.

We went to the Tower of London, the British Museum and St. Paul's but everywhere the queue was an hour or more long. The pubs and restaurants were crowded with a wide variety of uniforms from many countries. If we did get served, the beer was watery and the food inedible.

The air raid siren sounded every night at about 2200 hours. That meant an hour or two in a bomb shelter. Crowded, children crying, drunken servicemen, a smell of unwashed bodies and fear, arrogant wardens. We hated the places. At the end of four days we were fed up.

'I've had it with London,' Bugs complained.

'Me, too,' I agreed. 'What'll we do . . . go back to Bournemouth?'

'No . . . let's go to Scotland.'

'Scotland!'

'Yeah. I've always wanted to go there . . . my people came from there. If we go to Glasgow maybe I can find some Bugdens in the phone book.'

'Okay,' I agreed, 'it can't be worse than this.'

We got a railway schedule and, in our complete ignorance of rail travel in war-time England, arrived at Charing Cross Station about 20 minutes before departure. We almost didn't get on. Every compartment was long occupied and the aisles were crowded with servicemen sitting or laying on their packs. We squeezed in.

The train left at 2200 hours and was a 'Milk Run', stopping every hour or so at a blacked-out station. By 0600 hours the next morning my back was so sore and my spirits so low that I said to Bugs: 'The next time this train stops, I'm getting off and I don't care where it is. We can make our way to Scotland some other way.'

'All right,' Bugs sighed.

The train stopped at the small town of Penrith in the Lake District, not far from the Scottish border. At 0700 hours on a Sunday morning, the place was shuttered and barred. We knocked at the door of a medium-sized hotel until the manager appeared in his dressing gown, not happy at being rousted out of bed. But he gave us a nice room (with running water).

We dropped thankfully into bed and slept until noon.

Rested and refreshed after a bath, I suggested: 'How about a walk and then a pint and some lunch?'

'Only decent idea you've had in a month,' Bugs carped.

We found the town quite charming: gardens bursting with flowers, narrow streets with houses of different colours, churches with high pointed steeples, a small park with a carpet of blue bells, a stone bridge over a stream, blue-grey hills around.

After our walk we entered a pub on the main street called the 'Queen's Head' and stopped dead in our tracks - stunned!

'Do you see what I see,' I croaked, 'or am I dreaming?'

'I think I've died and gone to Heaven,' he sighed.

The large room was stuffed with girls, some in uniform but most in civvies. There were tall ones and short ones, fat ones and thin ones, dark ones and blond ones, homely ones and pretty ones. The town had a training school for the Women's Land Army.

In no time we were in a circle of girls, all of whom seemed to have questions about Canada. A pretty brunette asked me: 'Do you know my cousin, Hariette Roberts . . . she lives in Star, Alberta?' I told her I barely knew where Alberta was. They seemed to be delighted with two wandering airmen from Canada and we were delighted, too. We stayed in Penrith until our leave was over.

Shortly after returning to Bournemouth Bugs and I parted company - he to his Bomber Command OTU and me to Coastal Command. We promised to keep in touch but it was not possible as we went our separate ways. I never saw him again. I hope he survived the war.

Just east of Blackpool, Lancashire, are the resort towns of Lytham and St. Annes on a wide estuary of the Ribble River. Sandy beaches run for several miles and tourist hotels dot the waterfront. Blackpool itself draws a large crowd to games, rides, theatres and shops but it is scorned as 'tawdry' by Lytham residents. There is no dividing line between the two towns which are usually named together. Once every several years they jump into prominence when the British Open is held at the Royal Lytham-St. Annes Golf Course.

It was here, to an airport called Squire's Gate, that I was sent to No. 3 General Recce School. The aircraft used was the Botha - an overgrown cousin of the Anson. The course was three months long. Aside from a couple of search techniques I learned nothing new. I was bored. But I found a lovely diversion.

The barracks at Squire's Gate were full so six of us, including two other Canadians, were sent to the Fairhaven Hotel in Lytham. It was small but set on the waterfront and near a park which had a swimming pool and tennis courts. In the bar area was a snooker table. I was playing on it one Saturday afternoon when two girls came in, carrying their racquets, just off the courts.

One was blond and the other dark. The dark one was pretty but the blond was beautiful; tall, long legs, wavy hair to her shoulders, sparkling blue eyes, a wide mouth given to smiling and a peaches-and-cream complexion without a blemish. I winked at her and she smiled. My heart flipped. You may think it corny to say that it was love at first sight but the romance lasted almost 50 years.

I kept an eye on their drinks and when they were low walked over to their tables. 'Can I buy you a beer?'

'Thanks,' replied the blond, 'but it's not beer - it's a 'Shandy'.'

'What's a 'Shandy' when it's home?'

'Half bitter and half ginger ale.'

'Oh.' I collected their drinks and a pint for myself and joined them at their table. 'My name is Lee Heide.'

'Mine is Mary Fletcher,' the blond beauty said, 'and this is my sister Joan.'

'How do you do,' I said as we shook hands. I had been told that English people like to be properly introduced. 'How was the tennis?'

'Fine,' Joan replied, 'but quite warm.'

'I'd love to have a game,' I sighed.

'Are you a good player?' Mary asked.

'I'm a Junior Champion from British Columbia,' I replied, with false modesty. This was the truth but not the whole truth. The Open tournament that I had won was played on the hard courts in Stanley Park. But at this time all the good players belonged to private clubs with clay courts and would never lower themselves to play on asphalt.

Mary

'Would you like a game tomorrow,' Mary asked.

'Sure would . . . but I haven't got a racquet.'

'I have a spare,' she said, 'I'll bring it and another player and we can have a foursome.'

'Great!' I exclaimed.

'Two o'clock?'

So lost was I in those lovely, sky-blue eyes, that I could barely croak a 'Yes'.

The other person was a beauty named Sheila, so I played with three charmers but only had eyes for one. In later years Mary, who was my partner, swears that she said, before we started, 'What do you want me to do?'

Tennis Anyone?

'Just stand around and look gorgeous,' she says that I replied. But I wouldn't have said that. Would I?

There were problems with courting a girl in war-time England. There were many servicemen about, lots of whom were officers, and Mary had no lack of suitors. With double daylight saving time, it didn't get dark until 2300 hours and we couldn't find a place to cuddle apart from the rear row of the movie house which was in great demand.

Another obstacle was Mary's father. He had another daughter named Veronica and was very concerned about their behaviour with so many temptations around. Mary had to be home by 2200 hours and if we were later than that, he was standing by the front gate looking at his watch. I tried very hard to win him over but he was cool and not at all enchanted with his youngest daughter dating a wandering Canadian.

Until the night that he fell into the flower bed.

Mr. Fletcher drank little and then only beer. But one night his cronies led am astray at a reunion. He came home soused to the gills, opened the front gate and then fell into some rose bushes. He couldn't get up so he threw some small stones at the front window.

Mrs. Fletcher, the three girls and I were in the living room.

'TINKLE, TINKLE'.

'What was that?' Mrs. Fletcher said.

'I dunno,' I replied. 'Probably just some kids going down the street.'

'TINKLE, TINKLE'.

I stood up. 'I'd better have a look outside.' There I found poor father laying in the rose bushes. 'What are you doing in there?' I asked.

His reply was unintelligible.

'Come on.' I helped him to his feet, brushed off his clothes and half-carried him into the house where he was immediately assaulted by four indignant females.

'Robert!' exclaimed Mother.

'Father!' shouted all three daughters simultaneously.

I defended him as best I could (although it was hard to keep a straight face) pointing out that this was a totally rare occasion and a man is entitled to one small misdemeanor.

My stock with father went up.

The family was musical. All four females played the piano and father played the violin with the Manchester Symphony Orchestra. One night when I was waiting in the hall for Mary, I heard him practicing in the living room. He was playing one of the few operas that I recognized so I went into the room. 'Carmen, eh?' I ventured.

'Yes,' he replied.

'When do you perform?'

'Next Saturday. But I have a new version.' Then, to my surprise, he began to sing:

'Tor-ree-a-dor-a,
Don't spit on the floor-a,
Use the cuspidor-a,
That's what it's for-a.'

We laughed together. Perhaps I wasn't such a bad bloke after all.

The Fletcher house was one of a row, with both neighbors attached, made of brick. The houses were of superior quality and faced a large park which had tennis courts and a walking trail. It was just a short distance to Lytham town centre, with many shops and several pubs which fronted on the Ribble estuary over a green swath. There was a Light House - no longer in operation - and one movie theatre. Mr. Fletcher worked for a company in Manchester that made bond paper and commuted daily by train.

The summer weather was perfect; it was now late September and the days were sunny and warm. Mary and I saw each other every evening if I wasn't night flying or she working late at the District Bank. On weekends I rented a bike: we roamed through the lovely country-side and explored small villages untouched by war. Many evenings were spent singing around the piano. In addition to the five Fletcher voices (I was a dud) we often had the two young Proudfoot brothers, both RC priests. Donald Proudfoot was to help us greatly in later years.

Joan

On Sundays we went to church. My mother was very religious and I was accustomed to going to church. Mary's family were Catholic but I found the Service little different from my close-to Anglican. The Fletchers had their own pew, second from the front, with a small door bearing their name. If father thought the Priest was droning on a bit too long, he would take out his pocket watch and hold it up in plain sight. The sermon came to a quick end.

(In later years when I was instructing I would say to my pupils: "I don't mind if you look at your watches now and then but please don't shake them to see if they are still running.")

But all things come to an end and so did my time at No. 3 GR School. A few days before graduation the Chief Instructor, a Squadron Leader named Grass, had each of us in for an interview. Mine wasn't pleasant.

'Sgt. Heide,' he opened.

'Yes, Sir.'

'Did you enjoy yourself while you were here?'

I wasn't sure what he meant. 'Yes, but I found most of it a repeat of what I had taken at Navigation School.'

'Well, I'm sure you had a good time because you did precious little work.'

'My Course Average was 72.6%, Sir,' I said hotly.

'It should have been 95%. Let me read the comment by your Course Leader: "An intelligent student who put very little work into the Course . . . results disappointing."'

I didn't know what to say, so I kept quiet.

He glared at me and picked up a paper from his desk. 'I have here your posting.'

I brightened up. 'Yes, Sir.'

'You are to proceed to RAF Station, Turnberry, for operational training on Beaufort torpedo bombers. You will crew up there.'

My spirits sank. I had barely heard of a Beaufort aircraft but I knew that torpedo bombers had a short life. 'Oh, hell!' I said to myself.

S/L Grass seemed to enjoy my discomfiture. 'Anything to say?'

'No, Sir.' I wondered if he had deliberately arranged what might be a short career for me.

I explained it all to Mary that evening. We had agreed to marry but hadn't set a date. This posting threw all our plans awry. 'We'll have to wait,' I sighed, 'until I've done a tour of operations. I can't leave you a young war widow with, probably, a bun in the oven.'

I pulled her close to me, kissed her neck and nuzzled into her long, blond hair that always had such a fresh and enticing smell. I could feel her heart beating.

'How many children shall we have?' she whispered.

'Four,' I replied, firmly. 'Two boys and two girls.'

'It won't be easy.'

'What won't be easy?'

'Not having children before we are married.'

As usual, she was right.

Since I was not a golfer (at that time) I didn't know that Turnberry was a celebrated Scottish name, the Links Course second only to St. Andrews and the home of more than one British Open. Turnberry is 15 miles south of Ayr and has spectacular views including Robert the Bruce's castle in the distance. A British golfer, Sandy Lyle, said: 'Of all the great Scottish links, the Ailsa Course at Turnberry is the most dramatic, the most spectacular and the most compellingly beautiful.'

Had I been a golfer, I would have been appalled because the runway for the RAF Station ran right through the centre of the course with taxi strips, aprons and two small hangars taking up most of the remainder. The damage was considerable but, after the war, the course was restored by a man with the improbable name of Frank Hole.

Adjacent to the course, on a rise, was the luxurious Turnberry Hotel, now providing quarters for the staff and students of No. 5 Operational Training Unit. It, too, had to be refurbished after the war. No distinction was made of rank and officers and NCOs shared the same Mess and facilities. This was because we were left to form our own crews as we got acquainted and made friends.

There were 40 airmen on our Course - ten putative crews. There was a sprinkling of Officers among the pilots and navigators but the radio operators and rear gunners were all NCOs. Apart from three Canadians and one Aussie, all the rest were British. For the first few acclimatization flights on the Beaufort we changed crews each time. I quickly spotted a Flight Sgt. who was a bit older than most of us and who probably had more experience. I waylaid him in the bar.

'Hi,' I opened, 'would you like a beer?'

'All right,' he agreed. We chatted for a bit and then he said: 'Like the other half?'

'Sure,' I replied. After a few sips, I stuck out my hand: 'Lee Heide.'

'Harry Deacon,' he responded. He was of average height with a pale complexion that suggested he seldom went out of doors, thinning brown hair, brown eyes that bulged slightly and a bit bandy-legged.

I told him of my background and learned that he came from London, was 28 years old, married with a baby boy.

'I see you've got a pip more than the rest of us,' I said. 'Have you been in the RAF for a while?'

'Yes . . . three years. I've been instructing but asked to go on operations.'

'How many flying hours do you have?'

'About one thousand.'

Since I had a grand total of 200 hours, this sounded great to me. If I wanted him for a pilot (and I did) I would have to act fast before someone else snapped him up. 'Do you have a navigator?'

'No . . . not yet.'

'We seem to get on,' I put some warmth in my voice, 'what say we team up?'

'All right.' Harry put out his hand and we shook on the deal.

'Do you have any thoughts on a radio operator and a rear gunner?' I asked.

'No . . . do you?'

'No . . . let's keep our eyes open.'

I found our radio operator and Harry found our gunner.

Watching a dart game in the Mess one evening I was struck by the unerring accuracy of a rangy red-head who was picking out 'Doubles' like plucking cherries. More than that, he was animated, cheerful and full of fun. I could see that he would be an asset to any crew. When he finished the game I went up to him and said: 'You know, it's a sign of a misspent youth to play darts as good as that.'

'Eh, by Goom,' he replied in a thick Yorkshire accent, 'tha' may be right.'

I laughed. 'How about a beer?'

'Great idea!' He turned out to be a prodigious beer drinker but one who never got drunk.

I ordered us a pint. 'My name is Lee Heide.' We shook.

'You're a Canuck, eh?'

'Yes. I heard that they called you 'Ginger' because of your red hair. What's your real name?'

'Fred Jones . . . but never call me Freddy, I hate it.'

'Join me,' I chuckled. 'My name is Cecil LeRoy and I was called Cece until I joined up when I changed it to 'Lee'. I always hated Cecil.'

'Are you crewed up yet?' I asked.

'Nay . . . are you?'

'Well . . . I've got a pilot with 1,000 hours.'

'You have!' Ginger's eye brows shot up. 'What's his name?'

'Harry Deacon . . . do you know him?'

'Nay.'

'He's a Flight Sergeant, one of the few around.'

'I've seen him,' Ginger nodded. 'Do you think I could join you?'

'You're in,' I smiled.

He put out a big paw and we shook. Over another beer I discovered that he was 20 years old, single, born and bred in Yorkshire, had finished grammar school and was working in a feed store in Bradford when he was called up. I liked him at once and quickly found out that he was a great mimic and could speak in almost any British dialect.

Two days later Harry introduced me to a slim, dark-haired Welshman whom he had asked to be our gunner. His name was Stafford Evans but he was called 'Taffy.' I never found out if it was some kind of generic Welsh nickname or not. He was nineteen years old and had some acne scars on his thin face. He had joined the RAF straight from school and, of course, was not married. His movements were quick and darting. His wit was caustic; I found out later that he liked to 'rib' me but was not too keen when I returned the favour.

I rounded up Ginger from the dart board and we had our first get-together as a crew. We all explained where we came from and Harry told us of his wife and small son, named John. They were very interested in Canada but had only a superficial knowledge of the country. I spent some time on the geography of the large Dominion.

Ginger, Harry, Taffy, Me

After a couple of beers, the conversation somehow turned to railways and I complained how bitterly cold the English stations were because they were open to the weather and how you had to carry your own luggage up and down stairs to change platforms.

Ginger held up a big hand, like a policeman stopping traffic. 'There was this lady who stopped a porter pushing a loaded trolly at Wigan Junction. 'Porter,' she said, 'where do I get a train for Blackpool?"

Ginger put on a broad Lancashire accent. 'It's t'other side for Blackpool.'

'You mean, it is the other side for Blackpool?'

'Aye, lady . . . t'other side for Blackpool.'

'I have to cross the bridge?'

'Aye lady . . . cross t'bridge.'

'But porter, I've got a tin trunk!'

'Ah don't mind whether tha's got brass boobs . . . it's t'other side for Blackpool!'

We broke up at Ginger's story and relaxed as we got better acquainted.

It is time now to look at the Bristol Beaufort Mk 1, the outstanding torpedo bomber of the war. All-metal construction, it was powered by two 1,130 hp Bristol Taurus engines which gave it a top speed of 265 knots and a cruising speed of 145 knots. The aircraft had a range of about 1,000 nautical miles and could carry a load of 1,500 lbs, made up of one Mk 12 torpedo or the equivalent in bombs, usually two 500 lbs and two 250 lbs. While the armament varied, our aircraft had two .303 Vickers machine guns in the nose and two more in the rear turret. The Beaufort could take a lot of punishment and still remain in the air; its weakness was poor performance on one engine especially when loaded and especially in the heat of the Western Desert. It 'flew like a brick' on one engine.

The crew of four were nicely positioned in the aircraft. There was just one set of pilot controls as the entrance to the nose was to his right. The navigator had an excellent view through the perspex nose; he usually sat in a jump seat next to the pilot for take-off and landing. The wireless operator was seated directly behind the pilot, separated by armor plate. The rear gunner had a power-operated turret protected by armor plate. The fuselage was broad and the crew could move around easily, and, luxury of luxuries, the plane had an Elsan (a toilet, to you).

Bristol 'Beaufort'

The training at Turnberry consisted of conversion to the Beaufort plus bombing and gunnery; torpedo training would come later. While I had learned the essentials of these skills at McDonald, the bombsight and the machine guns in the Beaufort were different. I dropped singles and sticks at both fixed and moving targets on the practice range. I fired the machine guns at ground targets and at a drogue towed by another aircraft; the guns threw me around so much and made such a clatter that I was never very accurate with them. Also, I had to learn how to use a large, hand-held camera, supposedly to record results of a strike on operations.

Our first flight as a crew came about half-way through the course. We were all a bit nervous, wanting things to go right. Harry did his external check carefully and we all kicked the tires. I sat in the jump seat. Harry gave a 'thumbs-up' to the airman with a fire extinguisher near the port engine, started it up, and did the procedure again with the starboard engine. They grumbled and coughed into life. Harry went through his cockpit check as I read the items to him, paying special attention to the magnetos for any drop in revs. He taxied out to the end of the runway.

'Taffy, you ready for take-off?' Harry asked.

'Yes, Skipper.'

'Ginger?'

'All set, Harry.'

Harry looked at me and I nodded.

'Here we go.' He pushed the throttles forward and, with no armament load, the Beaufort responded nicely. Control column forward to bring up the tail wheel. Ease back and lift the nose. Come unstuck. 'Wheels,' he ordered; I brought the gear up. 'Brakes.' I tapped the lever to stop them from rotating as the doors closed over them.

We climbed at 500 feet a minute to our assigned altitude of 6,000 feet for our familiarization flight. I went into the nose and gave Harry the first heading; it was a simple triangular route north of Glasgow. The weather was clear and we watched the countryside unfold beneath us. I was not impressed with the bleak scene and remembered the remark of a Canadian traveller who, asked his impression of Scotland, replied tersely: 'Bare hills and damp sheep.'

We continued with our navigation, bombing and gunnery exercises as a crew, both by day and by night. We were all busy except for Ginger whose radio set was familiar to him. He passed the time by listening to the BBC.

The course finished just before Xmas, 1941 and we were given ten days leave with instructions to then report to RAF Station,

Abbotsinch, Scotland, for torpedo training. The other three went home and I went to Lytham with a rail pass provided by Mary's father.

```
┌─────────────────────────────────────────┐
│                                         │
│      LYTHAM ST. ANNES CORPORATION       │
│         TRANSPORT  DEPT.                 │
│                                         │
│              ─────────                   │
│                                         │
│         WORKMAN'S  REDUCED               │
│         FARE  CERTIFICATE                │
│                                         │
│              ─────────                   │
│                                         │
│    Available only until MARCH 31st, 1944│
│                                         │
└─────────────────────────────────────────┘
```

Xmas in Lytham made a nice break. I arrived two days prior having not bought any presents. So Mary and I shopped on the twenty-fourth and had lunch in the Queens Hotel on the waterfront. She had a 'Shandy' and I had a pint of bitter. 'It's funny,' I said, 'how beer differs around the country. In London it wasn't worth drinking but in Scotland its full and robust.' I took a large swallow, 'This is just average.'

'I think it has something to do with the water,' she remarked. She was not an authority on beer. 'Tell me about your crew.'

'Well, speaking of beer, I've seen Ginger drink six pints without showing any effect.'

'Where is he from?'

'Yorkshire.'

'Oh, well,' she said, scornfully, 'that explains it.'

I raised my eyebrows. Was the War of the Roses still on? 'But he's a tonic . . . full of fun and a great mimic.'

'What did he do before he joined the RAF?'

'Worked in a feed store in Bradford.'

'Hmm . . . ' Mary was not impressed. 'What about your pilot?'

'Harry is a little older than the rest of us . . . 28 years . . . and is married with a baby boy.'

'Is he a good pilot?'

'Yes. He has been instructing for a while and has about 1,000 flying hours. He's a bit of a perfectionist and if anything goes wrong it's never his fault.'

'And the gunner is from Wales?'

'Right. Taffy is a moody soul but seems to know his job.'

'How old is he?'

'Nineteen. Right out of school.'

'Where and what is this next course you're going to?'

'Oh, God!' I complained. 'Am I ever tired of being 'trained'! Do you know that, counting the Army Boot Camp, this will be the eighth consecutive Course I've been on? Anyhow, it's at Abbotsinch, which is a suburb of Glasgow, and it's to teach us how to drop torpedoes.'

'And then you'll go to a squadron?'

'I reckon.'

'Where will that be?'

'I think they are all down south someplace.' It never occurred to either of us that I might be sent overseas.

Rationing was strict but Mary's mother had found a goose and made all the trimmings for Xmas dinner. We all ate too much and then gathered around the piano. (I was improving; only off-key about half of the time).

There was no snow in Lytham but the raw, damp, seaside cold penetrated every bone in my body. The house did not have central heating. There was a fireplace in every room but, with coal severely rationed, they were used sparingly. Doors to the rooms were kept closed and the halls were freezing. Being accustomed to central heating, I was always leaving doors open. Then father would say to me; 'Put plug in't hole, lad . . . put plug in't hole.'

I must now describe my encounter with the Water Closet (a toilet, to you). The principle was simple; there was an over-head cistern with a hanging chain - pull and flush. So I did. Apart from a small trickle of water, nothing happened. I tried again - Nil. I stood on the toilet seat in an effort to have a look at this arcane mechanism but it wasn't high enough. Maybe a hard tug would work; it didn't and I was afraid of breaking the chain. Perhaps surprise was the answer; I turned my back as if to leave the room and then whipped around and pulled. Nothing. Finally, I pulled the chain and held it down for a few seconds while I thought. Eureka! A good flush!

Mary was in the hall when I came out. 'What took you so long?'

'We had a personality conflict,' I replied.

She looked baffled.

Two sisters doubled up so that I could have a bedroom. The fire in that room was never lit. I have never, before or since, been in a room so cold. I broke all records in shedding my clothes and diving under the covers. Mary brought me a hot water bottle and we had a few minutes to cuddle but she could never stay long lest father rapped on the door.

So we had a peaceful Xmas (except for some bright lights on the horizon that meant Liverpool was being bombed again) and parted with hugs, kisses and 'see you soon'.

We had no idea that it would be almost three years before we met again.

RAF Station, Abbotsinch was small and located at the end of the electric trolly from Glasgow. There were eight Beauforts on strength. Living quarters were austere in wooden huts with spasmodic heaters. The C.O. was a pilot, Squadron Leader Oland, who said a few words of introduction after which we rarely saw him. The ten crews at Turnberry had dwindled to eight; we never found out where the other two had gone.

The course started with four days of ground school after which we flew (weather permitting) on alternate days for formation flying and 12 torpedo drops against both fixed and moving targets.

We started in the hands of Warrant Officer One, Mr. Austen, a technician about forty years old who was very tolerant with us. At the front of the room, on a wooden trestle, was a torpedo with cut-away sections so that we could see the interior.

'This is a Mark 12 torpedo,' Austen opened. 'It is a self-propelled weapon driven by an engine which operates two props in the tail.' He pointed them out. 'These props rotate in opposite directions to keep the torp horizontal.'

'How fast will it go!' a Sgt. asked.

'The engine is a semi-diesel type and will drive the torp at about 40 knots.'

'For how long?'

Austen peered over his bifocals. 'About 2,000 yards, after which it will sink.'

'Now,' he continued, 'steering is done by vertical and horizontal rudders in the tail controlled by a depth gear and a gyroscope.'

Moving to the sharp end, Austen said: 'This is the war-head and behind it the pistol which fires the charge on contact but not immediately or it would explode on hitting the water. The torp must run some distance before it is armed. All clear?'

Thirty-two heads nodded.

'This chamber,' Austen pointed, 'contains the compressed air to drive the engine and depth gear to keep the torp running at a pre-set depth depending on the target. Finally, at the tail,' he pointed to a wooden device, 'is an air tail to control the torp during its flight in the air; it breaks off when hitting the water.'

For two days W.O. Austen described every part of the torpedo while we looked and fingered. He was a very patient man who answered every question even if some of them were inane.

Ginger came into the Mess one evening and found me idly throwing darts. He shook his head. 'You'll surely need some lessons if we are to win us a few pints.'

'We are?' I threw another dart.

'Nay,' he said, scornfully. 'You don't throw them over your shoulder like a bloody baseball!' He took a dart. 'Hold it gently between your thumb and fore finger, like this.'

I tried a couple; it was more comfortable.

'You see this line on the floor?'

I nodded.

'That's the throw line . . . you can't go over that. Put your left foot just behind the line and bring your right foot back a little . . . turn your body a bit.'

I did that and threw a few darts; most of them missed the board.

'For God's sake,' Ginger said, 'don't close one eye . . . it isn't a bloody rifle you're using.'

I threw a few more and managed to hit the board.

'Most games are 301 points and you have to start and finish with a 'Double'; that's the wee outer ring. The inner ring is a 'Triple' and the bulls-eye is 50 or 25 points. But you don't have to worry about that.'

'I don't?'

'Nay . . . all you have to do is to score as many points as you can.
I'll take care of the 'Doubles'. The easiest large number to hit is 19
. . . you see it there?'

'Yes.' It was at the bottom of the board.

'Throw at it,' Ginger ordered.

'Okay.' I threw two darts and missed the whole board.

'Ye, Gods,' Ginger lamented.

But after a few hours of practice I could put two out of three
darts in number 19 and occasionally got a 'Double' or a 'Triple'.

Ginger reckoned that we were ready. We challenged a few teams
in the Mess for a beer and won every time. Soon they would not
play against us. 'We'll have to go to the local,' Ginger said.

The local pub was called the 'Pig and Whistle'. After watching
for a bit, Ginger announced that he and his 'Colonial' friend, would
be willing to play for a pint.

There were several takers. But after a few games with no losses
the competition disappeared. We had to move to another pub.

Our instructor for flying operations was a pilot named Flight
Lieutenant Inglis who had done a tour on Beauforts with No. 22
Squadron at Chivenor. He was a thin fellow with a Scots burr and,
we discovered later, little sense of humour.

'Now that you know how a torpedo works,' he opened, 'I'll tell
you how to drop it and you will make dummy drops at a small
merchant vessel off the coast which has photographic and measuring
gear on board; they will assess your mission and tell us what you are
doing wrong.' He seemed to take it for granted that we would make
lots of mistakes. He was right.

'Torpedo ops are done at low level,' he continued. 'About 50
feet. The reasons are obvious: the camouflaged aircraft are hard to
see against the ocean by both enemy ships and fighters; most heavy
guns on capital ships cannot be lowered to this elevation; and, of
course, the torp has to be dropped at 75 feet.'

'Exactly 75 feet?' someone asked.

'Plus or minus 15 feet,' Inglis replied. He looked around for
other questions but there were none.

'Now, the torp must be dropped in straight and level flight at 75
feet and 140 knots. Too low or too great a speed and it will ricochet;
too high or too fast and it will dive to the bottom. Range from the

target must be between 1,000 and 1,500 yards.'

'Oh, shit!' I mumbled.

Inglis looked at me. 'Did you say something, Sgt.?'

'You mean that we have to fly straight and level, at only a thousand or so yards, with every gun in the convoy firing at us?'

'I'm afraid so,' he replied.

'Nothing like a short and happy life,' Taffy growled.

'What if the ship we are after takes evasive action?' I asked.

'I'll get into tactics later but it may take several torps to get one ship.'

'Range is very hard to judge,' Inglis held up a small sighting device. 'This is for the pilot's use. It assumes a range of 1,000 yards and he sets the estimated speed of the ship on it.'

I looked at Harry but he didn't react.

A couple of days later we had our first practice flight. Abbotsinch airport was always covered in industrial haze from Glasgow but take-off was not a problem - that would come in landing. Navigators were to look for a huge rock jutting out of the sea just off the Ayrshire coast called Ailsa Craig. The target ship would be near it.

We found the small freighter and did a couple of practice runs before dropping our dummy torpedo. Harry was an excellent pilot, calm and careful, who did things by the 'Book'. He quickly found out the 'quirks' of this particular Beaufort and flew her with ease and skill. Now, he admonished Taffy to: 'Keep the turret still and centered on the run in . . . it acts like a rudder, swinging me off course, and I have to compensate . . . I have enough to think about without that.'

Our final run looked good and Taffy reported the torp to be running well. The ship would send our results back to base by wireless.

Returning to Abbotsinch, I said to Harry: 'Did you get the drill for landing in the smog?'

'Yes . . . Inglis told me.'

Just to be sure, I repeated them. There was a large Gasometer rising above the smog north of the airfield. 'Cross over the Gasometer at 500 feet,' I said, 'on a heading of 200 degrees and let down at 200 feet a minute.'

It worked like a charm; we broke out right over the end of the runway.

Analysis of our flight revealed that our height and speed were okay but our range was too great. Harry and I discussed this at length. Obviously, the sighting device he had been given was not very accurate and it was also hard to use. I made a scale of ship's lengths as they would appear at 1,500 yards and fixed this to the perspex in the nose; it was of some help but still not very accurate.

'I guess it will only come with practice,' I said.

'I suppose.'

'Just wait until the ship is turning and we have to estimate its speed and angle on the bow.'

'I can hardly wait,' Harry said, dryly.

We went into the city of Glasgow only once during out time at Abbotsinch. We found it to be dirty, drab and suffering badly from bomb damage. The Germans had singled out the Rolls Royce aero-engine works for destruction and several Luftwaffe squadrons were trained with a new radio direction device aimed solely at this target. Although damaged, the factories never shut down. Also, the nearby, extensive docks at Greenock were the terminus of many trans-Atlantic convoys and hence got much attention from Herr Goering.

After several more flights, with the ship moving and taking mild evasive action, we were reasonably proficient and hit it maybe two times out of three. But we were keenly aware that our operational targets would not look anything like this little vessel and that no one was shooting at us. Also, while we did some formation flying, we never did a formation attack.

As the course neared its end we were all hyped up about our next posting. The strangest thing then happened. Flt Lt Inglis gathered all eight crews in the briefing room, saying: 'The C.O. wants to speak to each crew individually. Just wait your turn . . . it won't take long.'

Nor did it - the first four crews left at about five minute intervals and did not return. Then we waited. A half-hour passed before Inglis stuck his head in the door and said: 'Just hang on, chaps . . . the C.O. will be with you in a minute.'

The minute turned out to be twenty before he strode in, followed by Inglis. 'I'm sorry about the delay,' Sqn Ldr Oland smiled, 'but we had to get the other crews on a bus and away to No. 22 Squadron. You fellows have a different posting and its all very hush-hush!'

He had our total attention.

'You will board a ship in two days. In the hold of that ship, in crates, are four new Beauforts. That's all I can tell you right now. You are confined to the base until you leave for the ship; telephone calls and letters are prohibited.'

There was instant consternation. Everyone had something to say and they all said it at once. I looked at Harry; his face was white. It was bad enough for the other three of us but he had a wife and a small son.

Sqn Ldr Oland held up his hand for silence. 'I know this is hard but, as you will find out, there is a valid reason for this secrecy. I suggest you write a note to your families, saying simply that you have been posted over-seas and that you will write when you get to your destination; give these to Flt Lt Inglis and he will post them when you are on your way . . . unsealed, please.'

There was much grumbling.

'One more thing,' Oland went on, 'I know that you will be discussing this among yourselves but make sure that you are out of the hearing of such people as bartenders, batmen, waitresses and so on. That's all for now. As soon as I can tell you more, I will.'

Oland and Inglis marched out, leaving 16 airmen stunned, confused, and some of them hostile.

That evening I found Harry at a table in the corner of the lounge, nursing a beer. His head was down, his whole body a picture of dejection. I put my hand on his shoulder and said: 'Nil Carborundum Illegitmus.'

He looked up. 'What does that mean?'

'Don't let the bastards grind you down.'

'Oh.'

I sat down. 'Where do you think we're going?'

'The Far East somewhere . . . the Med is closed by the Italians and the Germans.'

Ginger and Taffy arrived, carrying their beers. Taffy looked up at Harry and said: 'Hey, cheer up, mate . . . it isn't the end of the world.'

Harry grunted.

'He's sad about his wife and kid,' I said. 'What about you guys . . . any romantic attachments?'

'I've got a girl in Cardiff,' Taffy responded, 'but we aren't engaged or anything.'

'Not me.' Ginger tried to push his unruly red hair into place. 'I'm playing the field.' He paused. 'I've got an idea. We'll have a pool on where we are going . . . each put in five pounds . . . winner gets it.'

We all nodded.

'Harry, you start,' Ginger said.

'The Far East,' Harry said. 'India . . . Karachi or Bombay.'

'Ceylon.' I put in. I had read of a large military build-up for the island.

'Around the Cape of Good Hope to Egypt.' Ginger said. 'Belay that . . . our Beauforts will be assembled in Cape Town and then we'll fly up the east coast of Africa, stopping to refuel at Madagascar and Kenya and places that are still under British control.'

'We're going to attack the Japanese Navy in Singapore Harbour,' Taffy said, glumly. 'A suicide mission . . . probably from some airfield in Burma.'

We scowled at him. In the end, nobody won. We were all wrong.

I wrote Mary a letter saying how sorry I was to be leaving for some indeterminate time and promised to write soon and often.

But the smooth, siren voice of adventure beckoned. Ulysses may have filled his ears with wax and lashed himself to the mast but all my senses were open to her summoning finger and her seductive plea of: 'Come . . . Come.'

Chapter 4

The Trans-Africa Route

At mid-afternoon on the 3rd March 1942, our bus with the four crews aboard arrived at Greenock. It was a drizzly, chilly day with the clouds below the tops of the hills. The docks and the roadstead were crowded with ships, both Merchant Marine and Royal Navy.

Somebody whistled as our bus drew up alongside a sleek-looking passenger liner. This was the Walvis Bay, out of South Africa, 25,000 tons of luxury liner, converted to a troop ship for the war. Larger cabins had been partitioned with bunks added as had part of the lounge; but we were two to a cabin because, as we found out later, the ship had only about 300 passengers and was almost in ballast. In the remainder of the afternoon we explored to find a first-class dining room (the only one), a luxurious bar room (only beer), a games room (with a gym) and a small swimming pool.

As soon as dusk fell the Walvis Bay eased out of its dock and into the main channel. We were on deck. None of the other ships were moving.

'I guess they are not our convoy,' Harry remarked.

'We'll probably pick up ours north of Ireland,' I said.

'Hey,' Ginger said. 'I told you that we were going to South Africa . . . that's where this ship is from.' But he was still wrong.

So we had a beer or two and went to bed. In the morning, en route to breakfast, we went on deck. Our ship was alone! No land was in sight and no other ships! Walvis Bay was knifing through the rough water at a great rate.

After breakfast we were all rounded up by an RAF Officer in Intelligence, who called himself Flying Officer Smith. (We were sure that wasn't his name). He herded us into a corner of the lounge where had had pinned up a map of Africa. He looked like a college professor, with large, horn-rimmed glasses, middle-aged, no wings, ribbons or other insignia on his tunic.

He gestured for silence. 'I guess you have a few questions.' He smiled.

There was a barrage of vocal noise as 16 voices all spoke at once, each with a different question.

'Settle down,' Smith ordered, 'and save your questions for later. Now, I'm sure that you have realized the need for ultra secrecy prior to leaving England and your confinement to camp. We are travelling alone and unescorted. Our speed of 30 knots is enough to avoid an attack by a wandering U-Boat. But it would not stop an ambush by a pack of U-Boats if they knew our route and were waiting for us. Nor would our speed elude an attack by a surface raider if she knew our route, and we believe the German cruiser 'Hipper' is in these waters. So you see the need for secrecy.'

'Where are we going?' someone asked.

'I'm getting to that,' Smith replied, extending a metal pointer as he moved to the wall map. 'Our first stop is Lagos, Nigeria.' He pointed. 'From here your aircraft will be taken by truck to Takoradi where they will be assembled by RAF technicians. The reason for this round-about route is because the dock at Takoradi is not large enough to take the Walvis Bay. There is a good airfield at Takoradi with hangars and machine shops.'

'Then what?' I asked.

'Then you will fly the Trans-African Staging Route. Because the Med is virtually closed, because the route around the Cape of Good Hope is so long and because shipping is so scarce, we have established a series of airfields across the heart of Africa from Takoradi to Khartoum and down the Nile Valley to Cairo.' Smith used his pointer. 'These bases are four or five flying hours apart and there are RAF technicians to service your planes. And fuel, of course.'

'Were those landing strips already there?' some one asked.

'In some cases, yes. In others we had to carve the runway out of the jungle from scratch.' Smith paused. 'Now you see why we didn't tell you this in England. We are not sure the Axis know about this route but we want to keep it a secret as long as possible.'

'What happens when we get to Egypt?' Harry asked.

'You are to join No. 39 Squadron, now at an airfield named Shallufa, near Cairo.'

Taffy, ever the pragmatist, asked: 'What about tropical kit?'

'We have some for you,' Smith replied. 'Now, that's all for today. I want a session with the Navigators tomorrow to go over the route in detail. The weather will be improving as we go south . . . relax gentlemen, and enjoy yourselves.'

The sea became smooth, the sky cloudless and the temperature soared. We sun bathed, swam in the pool and enjoyed our luxury cruise. The crew put on a real act when we crossed the equator. Leaving the wardroom after lunch we were 'captured' by four burly sea nymphs in seaweed skirts and bound with slack ropes.

Led to the deck by the swimming pool we were confronted by Neptune himself, seated on a wooden throne with a gold crown and a Trident in his hand. 'Who dares enter into my Kingdom?' he roared.

The sea nymphs forced us to our knees. 'Four traitors who scorn the sea for the sky,' they shouted.

'Guilty of treason!' Neptune snarled. 'Their punishment is death by drowning.'

Upon which the sea nymphs threw us into the swimming pool clothes and all. Of course, the ropes fell away and after we climbed out of the pool we were given towels and slapped on the back.

Our other three crews got the same treatment.

I got a map of our route and the crew gathered around as I pointed out the features. The exotic names flowed by: 'Takoradi, Kano, Maiduguri, El Fasher, Khartoum, Luxor, Cairo, Shallufa.' A tour across the heart of Africa and down the famous Nile River.

'The only place, apart from Cairo, that I've ever heard of is Khartoum,' Ginger said. 'You know . . . General Gordon, Whirling Dervishes and all that stuff.'

'I've heard of Luxor,' Taffy said, 'Isn't that famous for its pyramids . . . Valley of the Kings?'

'We'll never come this way again and we'll have to keep a record of these flights and places,' Harry said. He was a few years older than the rest of us and this extra maturity was a bonus that appeared often in our lives. 'I want to tell my son about this when he is older. Does anyone have a camera?'

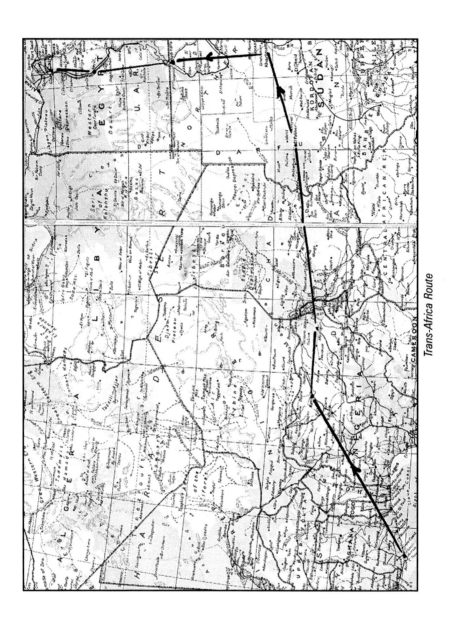

Trans-Africa Route

We all shook our heads. NO !

'Then we'll buy one in Lagos.' Harry turned to me. 'Lee, you're
the official recorder.'

'Okay. Lagos was one of the main ports for the slave trade. Maybe
there's still something to see there.' I thought for a moment. 'We'll

have time to look around en route. Take-offs are scheduled for 0600 hours and we're finished flying by about noon, so we'll have the afternoon and early evening free.'

'Why so early?' Taffy asked.

'Because the aircraft get too hot if they sit around after the sun is up. Except for Takoradi, and maybe Khartoum, there are no hangars in any of these places.'

Our ship docked at Lagos and our four crews went by bus to Takoradi. It was hot. The RAF Base was well organized with ample housing, a mess and recreation building and a large hangar without sides in which a production line had been set up to assemble our Beauforts. The C.O. was a Flight Lieutenant named Valley, a technical officer with a brusque, no-nonsense manner. Of course, our first question to him was 'How Long?'

'The first aircraft in seven days,' he promised, 'and the others at 10, 13 and 16 days.'

'Who gets what aircraft?' someone asked.

'I have the schedule somewhere,' Valley answered. 'I'll look it up and let you know.'

By the luck of the draw, we got the last aircraft and even that was delayed, as I'll recount shortly. With nothing to do at the base, we made plans to explore Takoradi, its close neighbor Sekondi, and Lagos.

In Takoradi we rented a car for two weeks at a garage whose owner had obviously never done this before and didn't know what to charge. The town is laid out with a circular Market Place in the center, streets extending like the spokes on a wheel. Shade trees line the streets. Two break-waters enclose the harbour where a ship was loading bauxite while another was discharging oil.

We had lunch at the Zenith Hotel, an old but well-maintained building with a central court yard; good food.

On the eastern outskirts we found the Pra River entering the ocean. Nearby was a beautiful, sandy beach with low breakers rolling in.

'Stop!' Ginger ordered. It was hot and the sight of the cool water was enticing. It was glorious both in and out of the water.

So we formed a habit. In the morning we would watch the Beauforts being assembled (which was interesting) or we would sight-see, before it got too hot. In the afternoon we would go swimming.

Ginger had to be careful not to take too much sun on his very fair skin; his freckles multiplied. The rest of us tanned up nicely. Taffy would stretch out on his towel and say: 'Ah . . . I wonder what the poor people are doing today.'

Takoradi was the railway terminus for Ghana and we took a day trip to the Tarkwa gold mines which had produced much money but were now nearing their end.

It was eight miles to Sekondi along a coastal road with the sea crashing into surf only a few yards away. Sekondi is older than Takoradi and the 'European Town' has many Colonial-style houses in various stages of disrepair. Fort Orange (now a lighthouse) was built by the Dutch in 1640, seized by the Ashanti in 1694, abandoned in 1840 before being taken over by the British in 1892 and turned into a trading post. The Market seemed to be 'manned' solely by women.

It was more than a one-hour drive from Takoradi to Lagos. We decided to stay for a couple of days, since Lagos is the major city in Nigeria. Lagos was a Yoruba city, with 80% of its people belonging to this tribe. The topography is dominated by canals, sandbars and lagoons; it sprawls over four main islands - Lagos, Iddo, Ikoyi and Victoria, which are connected to each other by bridges. Lagos is the most important island and here we checked into the Wayfarers Hotel. It was a bit expensive but had comfy beds and private baths. We found a bank and changed some money; bought a camera and several rolls of film; had lunch in a small restaurant where fans circulated the hot, humid air.

We inspected the Oba's Palace, the former traditional home of the king of Lagos, built in the 18th Century of mud with bronze pillars and a red tile roof. In the commercial quarter we saw a multitude of petty traders, tiny shops, shacks and houses with open drains.

Sitting in the hotel bar in the evening over a cool drink, Harry remarked: 'We know that Lagos was the centre of the slave trade in the last century but we haven't seen a single sign of it.'

'You're right,' Ginger said. 'Maybe they are ashamed of it.'

'I would be,' Taffy added.

'I wonder,' I said, 'if the man at the hotel desk knows anything? I'll go and talk to him.'

I walked into the lobby. The man behind the desk was a middle-aged black man with glasses and a round, friendly face. 'Can you help us,' I started, 'to find out something about the slave trade in the last century? Are there any buildings still around where they were kept?'

'The person you want to talk to,' he replied, 'is Mr. Manson at the 'Bookworm' bookstore on Victoria Island. He is an Englishman who has been here for many years and has written a book on the slave trade.'

'Thanks very much,' I said.

It was Taff's turn to drive and Harry's to navigate. Ginger and I sat in the back to kibitz, which we did when they crossed the wrong bridge and ended up on the wrong island. But they managed to find the 'Bookworm'.

Mr. Manson was a thin man in his seventies with a leathery skin, sparse hair and glasses. He was delighted with our enquiries, turned the store over to his assistant and took us in the back where he made a cup of coffee so strong that I was afraid the spoon would melt. 'Now,' he said, 'you want to hear about the slave trade in this part of the world, do you?'

'Yes,' I responded. 'We believe that you are the authority.'

'I guess I am,' he said, modestly. 'Well, the slave trade was at its height in the 18th Century and in Lagos until 1861. Probably three million slaves were taken from Africa, two million to British America alone. Many family fortunes in England were based on the slave trade.'

'What happened in 1861?' Taffy asked.

'The British 'annexed' this part of the coast by invading Lagos and blockading the coast in order to stop the slave trade. This was not as altruistic as it sounds. They wanted to open up Nigeria for trade, especially for the cotton that flourished here and was needed for their factories. Missionaries also put on some pressure.'

'Did the slave boats come right into Lagos?' Ginger asked, 'and what was their barter - guns?'

'Yes. They would anchor just off shore and send in a ship's boat. The barter was guns, liquor, cloth and iron bars like this one.' Manson reached behind him and picked up a bar about the size of a stair rod. 'The natives had no source of iron so it was prized; the going rate was 60 or 70 rods per slave.'

'The slaves were badly treated?' Harry asked.

Manson reached for his book. 'Let me read you a passage.' He adjusted his glasses and found the page.

'Few Europeans knew what conditions were like in the interior. They may be imagined by describing a 'coffle' or a train of slaves. Coimbra (a mulatto trader) arrived with a gang of 52 women tied together in lots of 17 or 18; some had children in their arms, others were pregnant, all were laden with huge bundles of grass-cloth and other plunder. These poor women, weary and footsore creatures, were covered with sores and scars showing how unmercifully cruel was the treatment received at the hands of the savage who called himself their owner. To obtain these 52 women at least ten villages had been destroyed, each having a population of one or two hundred. They are brought by tying them by the neck with leather thongs about a yard distance from each other. Some slavers made a practice of kidnapping children, who were always in great demand.'

Manson paused for breath. 'One reason,' he continued, 'that you don't hear much about slavery in Lagos is because many families had slave children for domestic duty.'

He paused again. Like most experts on a subject, he was easy to get started but hard to stop.

'How about some lunch,' I suggested, brightly.

This was agreeable to all and Manson took us to a nearby cafe. The temperature was 92° F and it was humid. Two ceiling fans moved the heavy air around to no effect.

'Is there a slave museum?' I asked.

'Yes and no,' Manson replied. 'I have a building on the waterfront which was used by slave traders. I have many things there but it is not ready to be open to the public. Would you like to see it?'

We all said 'Yes' but a couple of us wished later that we had said 'No'.

There were handcuffs and thumbscrews. Chains with shackles for both arms and legs. Wooden yokes that fit around the neck. Whips of various shapes and sizes. Baskets for women to carry on their heads. Branding irons both large and small. Sacks in which children were stuffed. Hooked and serrated knives carried by the slavers.

We drove Mr. Manson back to his store and thanked him profusely. But the car was very quiet on the drive back to the hotel.

A few days before our Beaufort, now labelled 'J' for Johnny - Harry's son - was ready for flight test we were called together by Fl/Lt Valley. 'Do you know,' he said, 'that your Beaufort is to be fitted with an experimental type of radar called 'Air to Surface Vessel'?'

'No,' Harry replied. 'What is it?'

Harry

'As the name implies it is used mainly for the detection of ships but it is also good for coastal waters because the land/sea contrast is excellent. A transmitter irradiates the surface in front of the aircraft; the returns are picked up by a pair of Yagi aerials in front of the aircraft and displayed on a screen in the navigator's position.'

'Sounds very useful,' I remarked.

'Yes,' Valley grimaced, 'if only we could get it to work! We have never seen it before and have only the manuals to go by. Corporal Kirby,' he gestured towards a plump airman, 'is our electronic specialist. He is doing his best but you may be delayed a day or two.'

'Lee,' Harry said, 'since this gear will be your responsibility you had better work alongside Cpl Kirby and learn as much as you can about it.'

'All right,' I agreed.

So I spent several days with Cpl Kirby until we finally got the radar working. I could see that it would be a great operational tool. I wondered why our aircraft had been selected to carry it.

We took off from Takoradi for Kano early in April, 1942, at 0630 hours. The temperature was already 80° F. There was not a cloud in the sky as we climbed to our assigned altitude of 6,000 feet. Lightly loaded, the Beaufort made a true airspeed of 160 knots. The winds were light and variable. The flight would take just over five hours. I gave Harry the first heading.

My topo map described the area over which we were flying as 'Savannah'. I fished my Pocket Oxford from my flight bag and found out that it meant 'a grassy plain with few or no trees in tropical regions.' Right on. I could see the borders of some farms scattered about.

Just over halfway in the flight we intercepted the railway line from Lagos to Kano. 'Okay,' I said to Harry, 'just follow the railway . . . our ETA is 1345 hours.'

I called Ginger: 'Are you working Kano yet?'

'Not yet,' he replied.

'Well, here's a position and ETA when you do get them.'

But he never did because at that moment his radio set went dead and so did several of Harry's instruments.

'Balls!' Harry swore. 'Ginger . . . what's the problem?'

'Just a minute,' Ginger replied. A moment later the power came back on, only to go off again. 'There's a short somewhere from the port generator,' Ginger reported, 'and it's popping the circuit breaker. I don't think I can find it in the air.'

'Well, have a try,' Harry ordered.

'Okay. Are you missing any essential instruments?' Ginger asked.

'Not as long as the weather stays like this,' Harry replied.

Ginger could not find the fault but the weather stayed perfect and soon the weird towers of the old, historic, walled city of Kano came into sight.

A long runway was being further lengthened by several hundred workers. Harry greased the Beaufort down with barely a rumble. The RAF detachment was using the civilian facilities. As we taxied in I could see that there were several buildings that looked like workshops but no hangars.

After lunch, Ginger and the RAF techs started work on the

electrical problem but by the end of the day they had not found it. This meant a day's lay over. This was all right with us because we had been told that Kano was one of the most historic old cities in Africa and we wanted to have a good look at it.

Over dinner, Harry had a brain wave. 'You know, what we need tomorrow is a guide, otherwise we'll miss a lot of the good sights.'

We nodded.

The C.O. of the RAF group was a Flying Officer named Nesbitt, who had been there for several months. When Harry asked him about a guide, he said: 'Yes, there's a young Hausa man here who speaks English. I think we can line him up tonight.' Which we did.

The next morning, the three of us (Ginger had to work on the wiring problem) plus our guide took a taxi to Kano. The guide was named Ethan. He was a serious, black man in his twenties whose English was precise and rather stilted. He had been educated at a Missionary School. He wanted to be a teacher and was saving his money to attend College in Lagos. We paid him well for his day's work.

'Kano,' he said in the taxi, 'is the main city in northern Nigeria. It was founded about 1,000 A.D. People always think of Timbuktu as the destination of the great camel caravans across the Sahara from Tripoli but it was not. Kano was. And still is. It has always been a manufacturing city with a great deal to offer the traders.'

'What's the population?' Taffy asked.

'About 120,000,' Ethan replied. 'More at times when the peasants come in.'

Approaching the city, Ethan said: 'You can see that the wall is crumbling in places. It was built about 1,000 years ago. It is 17 kms long and has 16 gates; we will enter at Sabuwar Kofar. The old city is within the walls and the new city is outside.'

We paid off the taxi and continued on foot. The houses were all jammed together like one continuous building; most were one story high, made of red mud, and fronted directly on to the street. The odd house was stained dark maroon by using pods of the Dorowa tree. The trim on some houses was painted white or cream. Occasionally, a pattern had been made on a wall before the mud set.

Narrow alleys twisted between some buildings with Palm and

Acacia trees. Several Mosques rose above. Lepers and blind beggars, some with open sores, sat against the buildings with their monotonous whine for charity. Donkeys and oxen roamed freely, many showing signs of abuse.

We heard a gabble of young voices and turned to see an open school with small boys crouching over their wooden slates, open books of the Koran nearby. 'They write with ink,' Ethan explained, 'made of water, charcoal and gum arabic. They must memorize all 114 chapters of the Koran. By reciting verses in a ceremony during adolescence a boy becomes a man in the eyes of the Muslim elders.'

There was an Arab quarter where the lighter-skin faces contrasted sharply in the black man's city.

I saw a line-up of men in front of a building marked 'Clinic' and asked Ethan about it. 'It's for circumcision,' he replied. 'The prostitutes will only take men who have been circumcised.'

Suddenly there was a piercing cry from a Minaret as the Muezin called the faithful to prayer. This was a Muslim city. Everything stopped. It was like an old movie when the reel got stuck. Prayer mats appeared as if by magic as the men faced east towards Mecca, dropped to their knees and bowed, chanting.

'What are they saying?' Harry whispered.

Ethan replied: 'There is no God but Allah and Mohammed is his Prophet'. Over and over . . . five times a day.' He paused. 'I am a Christian.'

As soon as the prayers finished the city came to life again as if the movie reel had been fixed. Men with bicycles had pirated cassettes and radios for sale; a woman on a corner cooked balls of flour in relish; a man skewered gobbers of meat over a slow fire; others cut paper-thin slices of meat to dry in the sun for travelers to take on long journeys (like Canadian pemmican).

In the late morning a brisk, dry wind sprang up and my throat was parched. I indicated to Ethan that I would like a drink. 'Ah, yes,' he said, 'the wind off the desert is bitter with dust, it cracks your lips, skins your face, chaps your hands, inflames your eyes and dries your throat. But the rainy season is only a few weeks away. Come, we will go to Sabon Gari, the New Town, which is outside the wall and which has some foreigner's restaurants, for lunch.'

Harry and Taffy instantly agreed. Sight seeing must be punctuated by rest and sustenance.

We ate curried chicken for lunch in an outdoor cafe, waving off the ubiquitous flies. We would have liked a beer but strict Islamic law meant no alcohol. Talking over lunch, Harry asked Ethan about the economy in the area.

'In the countryside,' Ethan replied, 'cattle, ground nuts and cotton; peanuts grow well here and many tons are exported each year. In Kano are soap factories, oil and flour mills, cotton weaving and shoes and tiles.'

'Do camel caravans still come here?' Taffy asked.

'Oh, yes . . . regularly.'

'What's the name of that tribe with the blue robes?'

'Taureg,' Ethan replied. 'They also make up their faces with powdered stone which is amber or red.'

'Do you see them here?'

'Yes, the indigo dye for their robes is made here.' Ethan stood up. 'I have been saving the Karmi Market, in the heart of the Old City, for this afternoon . . . come.'

Covering 16 hectares, the Karmi Market is the pulse and hive of Kano. The interior is filled with stalls of bamboo, laid out in regular streets. The number and variety of items for sale is astonishing. One cigarette or one needle; a truck load of scrap or camel parts; spices such as cinnamon, ginger, kohl, salt and antimony; cloth of silk, satin, cotton, calico and Moorish dresses; charms and jujus of amber and gum arabic; bronze and silver bracelets; pewter rings; herbal remedies and medicines.

The food stalls bulged with produce. Rice, black-eyed beans, meat, nuts, dates, corn and vegetables of all kinds. Garden tools such as rakes, shovels and hoes. Livestock included goats, chickens, donkeys and sheep.

Artisans worked with gold, silver, bronze and iron producing knives, scissors and jewelry. Tanners were busy with saddles, bags and sandals.

And over all the crush of people and the noise. Men in their blue-and-white gowns. Women covered from head to toe in their chadors. Children shouting. A small band of musicians paraded up and down. Disco music blaring. Old beggars calling their blessings.

There was no mistaking Harry, Taffy and myself for anything

but wide-eyed tourists, gaping at the sights before us and plying Ethan with non-stop questions. 'If you buy something,' he advised, 'be prepared to bargain for that is considered a large part of the sale.'

Each of us bought a souvenir of Kano but we didn't bargain to the extent that Ethan would have liked. We returned to the airport tired and foot-sore but excited at all we had seen.

'I suppose you all had a good time swanning around Kano,' Ginger remarked, when we caught up to him in the evening, 'while I had to stop here.'

'It was a great day,' Harry replied. 'We saw some sights that few people ever see.'

'Well,' Ginger grumbled, 'it took all day to find the wiring fault and the temperature must have been 125 degrees inside that kite. My clothes were stuck to me like glue.'

'Ah-h-h,' Taffy mocked. 'Sympathy for Ginger!'

We all chanted: 'P-o-o-o-r Ginger!'

'All reet, ye daft buggers,' Ginger growled. 'I'll get me own back one day.'

But Ginger was inherently incapable of staying cross for very long and in a few minutes he was his usual cheerful self.

On the following day we had a short flight of just over two hours to Maiduguri. Situated in the far north-east corner of Nigeria, Maiduguri was the center of a large area that comprised the former provinces of Bauchi, Adamawa plus the old Trust Territory of Sardauna. The majority of the people are Kanuri.

The short flight got off to an inauspicious start. I was using the drift meter in the nose when the ground disappeared, as did the horizon. Underneath was a sickly, brown pall. 'Harry,' I called on the intercom, 'what's going on?'

'It's called the 'Haboob', he replied. 'F/O Nesbitt warned me about them. The wind picks up the desert sand of a million square miles round and sometimes carries it as far as the sea. Most depressing.'

'How long will it go on?' Taffy asked.

'Don't know,' Harry replied. 'I'll see if we can climb above it.'

But at 10,000 feet we were still in the 'Haboob'.

Ginger came on: 'What will happen to the engines, ingesting all this sand?'

'Don't know,' Harry repeated.

'Well, it won't do them any good,' I said. 'Pity the poor souls down below on camels or whatever.'

About an hour later we broke into the clear. We all gave a sigh of relief as the two Bristol engines purred smoothly along.

The runway at Maiduguri was short and rough and had been hacked out solely for the Staging Route. Harry did a circuit to look things over and then landed without any trouble.

The first thing that happened was what I later called the 'Vulture Incident'. I made a trip back to the aircraft to collect something I had forgotten. Two young RAF men were re-fuelling the Beaufort from 55-gal drums of aviation fuel. They wore only slouch hats, shorts and gloves. The gloves were necessary because, although the aircraft had been on the ground for only a short time, one could get burned from touching the metal. They were caustic with their condemnation of Maiduquri which they called: 'The asshole of the world.'

Walking back, on the outskirts of the base, I saw a vulture sitting on a post about five yards away. I had never seen anything so ugly and revolting in my life. We wore side arms, so I pulled out my pistol. I was no marksman but could hardly miss at this short range. I had just drawn a bead when a black mess boy came running up, shouting: 'No . . . no shoot! Sir . . . sir . . . no shoot!'

It turned out that the vultures were protected because they kept the camp clean. Too bad. I never got another chance, either.

We found the town to be depressing with its mud huts and many lepers in the streets. Ginger tried to buy some stamps in the Post Office but the black lady behind the counter said: 'No stamps . . . no stamps.'

However, on the outskirts of the town we found a nomadic group of cattlemen. (Later, we found out that they spent the rainy season here and then went to the vicinity of Lake Chad for the dry season). They were friendly and showed us around although we couldn't communicate. Their huts were made of wooden poles and straw with a bed on a raised platform of branches and a canopy of straw mats. In the circle of space between the bed and the walls, the animals were tethered at night.

The RAF Station was spartan, to say the least. Two of us in a room with only beds and a wash stand, the water brought in by a black mess boy. The food was mostly tinned, although we had seen fruit for sale in the town. We were glad to leave the next day.

En route to El Fasher, five hours flying time from Maiduguri, the savannah gave way to trees and then to jungle. Beneath us was a solid canopy of green, mile after mile without a break. I wondered what was underneath and if the sun ever shone there.

El Fasher was a revelation! My map showed an elevation of 5,000 feet. There was a long, paved runway near the town. In its glory days, Imperial Airways had used El Fasher as a route stop to the Far East and had built a palatial rest house with every amenity including a well-stocked bar. The small RAF contingent lived in luxury, waited upon by soft-spoken Sudanese.

The town was crowded and apparently this was normal, for it was on the route to Mecca - the 'Hajj'. According to Muslim belief, the pilgrimage should be made by every Muslim at least once in his lifetime. For centuries, groups of believers have set out from all parts to walk or ride to the shores of the Red Sea. The mid-African route starts on the Atlantic coast and runs through Kano, Fort Lamy, Abeche, El Fasher and Khartoum. As many as 10,000 people may be on the route at any given time and many stop for up to a year to earn enough money for the next stage.

The whole of Central Africa rings with the chanting of: 'At thy service, My God, at thy service'. They know that they will find at Mecca the most holy places in the Muslim world - the plain of Mina where Abraham intended to sacrifice his son; Mount Arafat where the Koran was given to Mohammed; and, most of all, in a shrine called Ka'aba, the Black Stone, a huge cubic structure covered with 1,000 pounds of black silk.

We spent a few hours in the town but saw nothing of great interest. We were surprised, on returning to the base, to find an invitation to dinner from the local Chief. Given a Land Rover and instructions, it was a twenty-minute drive to his home.

The house was a raised, wooden bungalow with a few steps up to a veranda which extended across the full width. The Chief, with three young men, was waiting in front when we arrived. He was an imposing figure. Over six feet tall, his arms and legs were the size of my thighs. A loose, flowered shirt only partially concealed an enormous belly. I judged his weight to be around 300 pounds. Around his neck was an exotic necklace of carved icons in wood and ivory; rings on most of his fingers and silver bracelets on his arms. His head was bare except for a jeweled brooch.

We were astonished when he greeted us in an upper-class English accent. 'Good evening, young gentlemen. I am Chief Kala Mbulu. These are my sons.'

Introductions were made.

He continued: 'You are on your way to the Middle East, I know, where the war is not going well for Britain or her Allies.'

The Chief spotted my Canada badges. 'Ah, I see that one of her Dominions is represented.'

I nodded.

'Do you follow the war closely?' Harry asked.

'Yes. We listen to the BBC World Service every day. I was educated in England and wish her to be successful against her enemies.' He turned towards the house, saying: 'Come . . . let us have dinner.'

A lengthy table was set along the veranda with gleaming cutlery and glasses. Although I could see lights on inside the house, and hear the hum of a generator, illumination on the veranda was provided by torches mounted on each of the upright posts. We were seated alternately with Harry and I flanking the Chief and Ginger and Taffy to the right and left. The Chief was knowledgeable and articulate. His sons' English was heavily accented but understandable.

Each of us had our own personal waiter. None were less than six feet tall, coal black, naked from the waist up with oiled bodies and three diagonal scars on each cheek. These were warriors of the Nuer Tribe, their spears and shields mounted on the wall behind us. They were renowned not only for their fighting prowess but for being proud, loyal and very honest. No glass or dish was ever empty.

In the soft African air, the torches flickering, the bejeweled Chief, the exotic waiters, it was a scene straight from 'Arabian Nights'.

I don't know what we ate but it was delicious and helped by local wine and a potent fruit brandy. I could hear Ginger and his companion laughing - at one of Ginger's stories, no doubt. Taffy was telling his companion about Wales. It was an unforgettable evening.

We drove home in a bemused state to find the RAF group and some Sudanese sitting in the sand and watching a movie with Roy Rogers and his famous horse.

We had been briefed at Takoradi to land and re-fuel at Khartoum but this had been changed and we were now instructed to proceed to Wadi Halfa, some 60 miles north. About two hours after take-off from El Fasher we approached Khartoum, its position unmistakable at the junction of the two Nile Rivers. The Blue Nile was a light blue but the White Nile was a muddy brown.

I came out of the nose with my topo map and said to Harry: 'Circle around and let's have a look at the place.' Ginger and Taffy came up to stand behind us.

'There's two cities here,' I said. 'That's Omdurman across the river.'

'Isn't that where General Gordon fought?' Ginger asked.

'I think so,' I replied. My knowledge of English history in the Sudan was sparse to say the least.

'They've got a large airport,' Harry pointed. 'Look to the east of it . . . there are a lot of camels . . . probably a Camel Market.'

We flew around for a few minutes longer and then set course for Wadi Halfa. 'Hey, guys,' I said, as we proceeded, 'there's a railway here . . . maybe we can get back to Khartoum this afternoon.'

The runway at Wadi Halfa was just hard-packed sand with oil drums to mark the threshold and the port side. We landed, had lunch with the C.O. - a F/O McGinn - and spoke to the RAF technicians about servicing the Beaufort. Then we took the train to Khartoum.

At the station, hawkers of food and porno magazines thrust their goods in our face. Children begged for 'Baksheesh', and ran after the train, shouting at the carriage windows, their tiny legs trying to keep up.

The train was hot and dusty but not crowded so we had a compartment to ourselves. Harry opened a 'Guide to Khartoum' and started to read.

'Where did you get that?' Taffy asked.

'McGinn loaned it to me.'

'Well . . . fill us in,' Taffy ordered.

'Give me a few minutes,' Harry said, ' and I'll try to summarize it for you . . . it's quite detailed.' He read on for about 20 minutes and then said: 'All right.'

'General Gordon didn't really fight a battle. The Foreign Office decided to evacuate the Sudan and leave it to an Islamic leader named Mahdi who was a religious fanatic and who was whipping up the people for a holy war against the Egyptian Governor, Raouf Pasha. So Gordon was sent to Khartoum and did evacuate 2,500 women and children. But then he defied his orders and dug himself in, refusing to leave. This was in 1884. But he was surrounded by Mahdi and his Dervishes.'

'He didn't fight them?' I asked.

'No, he was badly outnumbered. A relief column under a General Stewart ran into the Dervishes and was wiped out. After a siege of ten months, Gordon surrendered but when he and his men came out of the palace they were murdered on the steps by the Dervishes.'

'Oh, boy!' I exclaimed. 'Did that make the British mad?'

'Yes,' Harry replied, 'but it was 14 years before a large force under General Kitchener got their revenge. The Mahdi had died by then and his successor, a man named Khalifa, was not a fanatic and obviously not a military genius. He decided to attack Kitchener's force at night. The Dervishes were armed with swords, spears that had savage fish hooks on them and some ancient rifles with which they were poor marksmen.'

'And they screamed,' Taffy said.

'I imagine so,' Harry replied. 'Anyhow, it was a massacre. About 14,000 Dervishes attacked Kitchener's gunboats over open terrain. The British gunners simply mowed them down. By dawn, 7,000 were dead and 2,000 wounded. By the end of the day, 12,000 Dervishes lay dead. British casualties were 48 soldiers killed. This was the Battle of Omdurman.'

'Wow . . . what a slaughter,' I remarked.

'Kitchener was brutal,' Harry continued. 'He killed all the wounded Dervishes because they had a trick of pretending to be dead or wounded and then would jump up and stab you, But it hardly seems likely that they would lie doggo for 24 hours and the British were still killing them the next day. Kitchener desecrated the Mahdi's tomb, digging up the body and throwing the skeleton in the Nile. He used the Mosque for his Headquarters.'

By the time Harry had finished our history lesson on The Sudan, the train pulled into Khartoum.

Our time there was limited by the railway schedule back to Wadi Halfa. The train station was in North Khartoum, across the Blue Nile from Khartoum itself. Since this was close to Omdurman we visited the site of the battle, observing the 'killing fields' from a low hill called Jebel Sirkab. In Omdurman, the Khalifa's house is now filled with relics of the battle, including the Dervish spears with their deadly fishhooks.

General Gordon's palace in Khartoum has a plaque to commemorate his murder on the steps. 'Why was he called 'Chinese Gordon?' Ginger wondered.

'Because he spent so many years in China, you dolt,' Taffy replied.

We tried to visit the National Museum but it was closed for the day. We sat on a bench over-looking the Blue Nile and observed the 'Melik' - one of Kitchener's gunboats now used by the Yacht Club.

Harry looked at his guidebook. 'The name Khartoum means an 'Elephant's Trunk' in Arabic.'

'Now there's a really useful piece of information,' Taffy scoffed.

'The original name,' Harry continued, 'was Ghartum which came from the sunflower seeds used to cure the wounds of the soldiers.'

'Jeez!' Taffy threw up his hands. 'By the time you finish I'll have a degree in trivia!'

'It's no use,' Ginger said loftily, 'trying to educate an ignorant Welshman.'

'Cwmru am Byth,' Taffy responded. 'Wales forever!'

We just had time to visit the 'Souk' - the market - and to purchase some momentos. Ethan would have been pleased at the way we bargained.

At Luxor, three hours flying time from Wadi Halfa, the RAF were using the civil airport, about 7 kms east of the town. We spoke to the technicians about serving the aircraft and had lunch with the C.O. - F/O Thompson. We questioned him about what we should see in Luxor in the afternoon.

'This is a prime tourist area,' Thompson said. He was a man in his forties with a thin face and rapidly departing hair. He spoke precisely, like a professor. 'But the war has brought everything to a halt. Many shops are closed and hotels are virtually empty. I suggest that you spend your time on the east bank of the Nile.'

'Why?' Harry asked.

'Well, the Valley of the Kings, and Queens, and the tombs of the Nobles, are all on the west bank but that area is only open at certain times. But the Karnak Temple, near Luxor on the east bank, is open and is so striking that you could spend a whole day there.'

'Do we take a taxi into Luxor?' Ginger asked.

'Yes,' Thompson said, 'you can get one in front of the civil terminal.'

The taxi driver spoke English and was glad to fill us in. 'Luxor is on the site of the ancient Greek city of Thebes which was described in Homer's Iliad as the 'City of a hundred gates'.'

'We were told,' I said, 'to stay on the east bank and visit the Karnak Temple.'

'Quite right,' he replied, 'I will take you there. It is three kms north of Luxor.'

The Karnak Temple complex covers 25 hectares and is the largest Pharonic monument in Egypt after the Giza Pyramids. Just inside the gate that we entered was the Mut Temple; it was mostly in ruins but was being rebuilt. The Avenue of the Sphinxes led to the heart of the complex where we found the Temple of Amun, the Temple of Khonau, the Shrine of Ramses III and the Shrine of Seti II; all were open and had displays of ancient artifacts.

'Look at that!' Ginger pointed to a Pylon that was 130 metres wide with two towers that were 43 metres high. We gaped. There were ten such Pylons around the site, each one added to by a different Dynasty.

The Hypostele Hall had 134 giant columns topped with sandstone slabs.

There were several large Obelisks in various states of repair.

The afternoon passed quickly as we explored and reacted to one of us saying: 'Look at this . . . look at that!'

A sign told us that the 'See, Sound and Light' performance for the evening had been cancelled. Too bad.

We took a taxi to Luxor and had dinner in a hotel overlooking the Nile. We were tired but happy: it had been another great day!

'Just follow the Nile River for a while,' I said to Harry as we took-off from Luxor for Shallufa on the following morning.

'All right,' he agreed.

'I'll give you an ETA when I find out what our ground speed is,' I added.

The Nile River was cultivated by irrigation ditches on both sides to a mile or so. Beyond that, on both sides, was desert. We could see people working in the fields, their broad hats protecting them from the fierce sun that would produce a temperature of 41°C.

Our destination, the RAF base at Shallufa, was due east of Cairo near the Suez Canal. I gave Harry an ETA for Cairo, saying: 'Let's have a look at Cairo from the air.'

'Okay,' he agreed.

As we approached Cairo, Harry shouted over the intercom: 'Look at the Pyramids on the port side! Ginger, come up front!' (Ginger had no view from his seat).

Harry let down to 2,000 feet so that we could have a good look. Although we didn't know it at the time, these were the complexes of Dahshur, Saggara, Abu Sir, Zawiyat and Giza. We could see the Sphinx, with the body of a lion and the head of a man, at Giza. It was a thrilling sight to four young men who had rarely even been outside of their own country. (The only 'foreign' country that I had been to was the United States).

'Eh, by Goom,' said Ginger, in awe.

From the air, the city of Cairo was circled with radiating avenues and dull brown buildings enlivened with stunning Mosques. The Nile River was wide with two large islands - Gezira and Roda.

Our sightseeing came to an abrupt end as the VHF crackled into life. 'Aircraft circling Cairo, this is Heliopolis Control. Who are you and what are your intentions?'

Harry replied. 'Heliopolis . . . this is RAF Beaufort DW-862. We are en route to Shallufa.'

'Beaufort 862 . . . get on your way.' The voice was brisk, not to say angry. 'It is forbidden to fly low over the city as you are doing.'

'Wilco,' Harry said, banking the aircraft.

'Steer 078 degrees,' I said to Harry.

It was only a few minutes before the Suez Canal came into sight and then Shallufa.

'Shallufa Control,' Harry called, 'this is Beaufort DW-862 . . . how do you read?'

'Five square, 862. Welcome to Egypt . . . we have been expecting you. Land on runway 27 . . . there is no other traffic.'

'Wilco,' Harry replied.

He landed smoothly and taxied towards a hangar, following a ground crewman's instructions. Harry shut down the engines. We all climbed out and gave the aircraft a pat on the flank. The sturdy Beaufort had flown 4,000 miles and, except for the wiring fault at Kano, without a hitch. The steady Bristol engines had never missed a beat, in spite of an ingestion of sand now and again.

Chapter 5

Egypt

Shallufa was a permanent RAF base with paved runways and buildings of wood and stone. There were only two Beauforts on the tarmac and the place looked very quiet. We were greeted by F/O Quinn, an experienced pilot, who was to be in charge of us. 'Welcome to Egypt,' he said, shaking hands with each of us. 'Good trip?'

'Fine,' Harry responded. 'Where is 39 Squadron?'

'Gone to Malta,' Quinn replied, 'where you'll join them after a couple of weeks training and acclimatization.'

'Oh, great!' I mumbled, sarcastically, 'just what we need . . . more training!' I was wrong. Everything that we learned in Shallufa was important.

No. 39 Squadron had been formed in 1916 and saw action in W.W. I flying Bristol fighters. One of its pilots, Lt. Robinson, won a Victoria Cross for shooting down the Schutte-Lanz airship, the first ever shot down over England. In the late 1920s the squadron was sent to India, on the North-West Frontier, and remained an overseas squadron from then on. In 1940, flying Blenheims, it moved to reinforce Middle East Command where it supported General Wavell's offensive in the desert. Towards the end of 1941 the squadron converted to Beauforts.

Our working day was from 0600 to 1300 hours, after that it was too hot to work. Normally, we would fly for two or three hours, have a break, then be in the classroom for a couple more hours. In the afternoon we would have a siesta. In the evening we would read, played cards or snooker and some times went into Suez or Ismalia for a meal and a look around.

'You will make dummy attacks,' Quinn said, 'against a target in

Aboukir Bay and we will try to get a Royal Navy minesweeper for a moving target. (This didn't happen). 'You must get the attack sequence down to rote so that on ops, when all hell is breaking loose, you do it right. The approach is at ultra low level, 20 or 30 feet. Climb to 60 feet and drop the torp at 13-1500 yards. Then go down again to 20 or 30 feet and fly right over, or just behind, the target with the navigator using his twin machine guns to keep the ship's gunners heads down. Then slip and jink until you are out of range of the ship's guns.'

'Can I fire at this dummy target we are to use?' I asked.

'Yes,' Quinn replied. 'It is full of holes.'

'Good.' I knew that I needed practice with the machine guns.

So we dropped dummy torpedoes by day with both Harry and I shouting 'Now' when we estimated the range to be correct. I got used to the clammer of my two guns as they threw me around in the nose. At night we made practice runs with another aircraft dropping flares to illuminate the target. We practiced mock combat with a Hurricane fighter, Taffy giving Harry orders on which way to turn, side slip or skid.

Harry called us together one evening and said: 'I want each of us to learn as much as possible about another person's job so that if someone is injured in flight, another can take over if need be. Lee - you and I will understudy. Ginger - you and Taffy learn to change positions.'

'I've had gunnery training,' I remarked, 'and could take over for Taffy.'

'We'll keep that in reserve,' Harry replied.

So I gave Harry some rudimentary lessons in navigation and he gave me some flying instruction. On our way home from an exercise, I would take the controls, with Harry sitting in the jump seat to coach me right up to the landing phase but not actually making the landing. As Harry remarked, dryly: 'You don't need to take off . . . just land.'

Ginger had a go with Taffy's guns but Taffy would not learn Morse Code. 'Just show me how to talk into that radio,' he said.

On the ground, each of us was paired with our opposite number in Quinn's crew. His navigator was a Sgt. Blair and we spent some time together on ship recognition, first aid, photography and the use of intelligence. Since Blair had not seen the ASV before, he came along on a couple of flights.

We all got wet during dinghy training in the Suez Canal. Harry and I were to put it to great use in later days.

We had a lecture from an Arabic fellow on Muslim customs and the Arabic language. Without going into too much detail, some most useful words were:

Aywa-Yes

La-No

Inshalla-God willing (used frequently by Arabs)

Bitkallam Ingleezi-Do you speak English?

Baksheesh-The ubiquitous plea for money by beggars and street urchins.

Imshi-Go away!

Yallah-Hurry Up!

Bint-girl

Mallaish-Never mind

We were shown a 'Goolie Chit'. This was a square of silk on which was written a promise in Arabic (we changed this to Italian) that the British would pay a reward to anyone who helped a flyer in distress.

This may be a good time to explain about our Escape Kits. Everyone had their own idea of what should be contained. Most of us wore a leather belt with pouches. Mine held:

-Italian lira

-Topo map of the area of that day's operations.

-Goolie Chit

-Compass

-Boy Scout knife

-Small mirror

-Aspirin and Benzedrine tablets.

We were close to the end of our time in Shallufa when the accident happened. It was my habit to come out of the nose when landing and fold down the jump seat next to Harry. It was a flimsy affair and, although it had a seat belt, would not take any punishment. On this day, for some reason, instead of pulling down the jump seat, I perched on a cross-spar that was lower down.

The landing was routine and a green light indicated that the under-carriage was down and locked. Suddenly, about half-way down the runway, the gear collapsed. I shot forward like an arrow, ducking my head to go under the instrument panel, and ended up face down in the nose. Beneath my face about one half-inch of metal separated my visage from a grinding mass of sparks and macadam as the Beaufort ground to a halt.

There was an eerie silence as if both men and machine were silently calculating what damage had been done to them. None of my three Brits had been hurt; they were all safely strapped in their seats. As I climbed shakily out of the aircraft, Taffy said: 'How come your face is so white?'

I shot him a dirty look. I didn't trust myself to speak right then.

I never gave the accident much thought at the time. It was over and quickly forgotten. Tender years and philosophy do not travel together. But now I wonder what inspired me to sit on the spar that day. Had I been in my usual position in the jump seat I would not have been able to duck below the instrument panel and would likely have smashed into it head first.

'It will take us about two weeks to repair your aircraft,' F/O Quinn told us, 'so you might as well go on leave. You'll go to Cairo, of course, so have a few words with our Chief Steward, Saad Mazari, and he'll fill you in on places to go.'

This we did and Saad was full of information.

Shepheards Hotel was a large, lugubrious hostelry that had been virtually taken over by the military, so we checked in there. There were British, Australians, South Africans, New Zealanders, Indians, Ghurkas and even a few Canadians. Since the clientele was mostly military there were M.P.s to keep order.

One story making the rounds was about an Army Captain who was caught chasing a girl down a corridor, both sans clothes. He was charged with 'Conduct Unbecoming . . . ' but he was acquitted because his crafty lawyer had found a sentence in Kings Regulations that read: 'An Officer must be suitably attired for the sport in which he is engaged.'

Cairo is the largest city in Africa, the fulcrum of the Arab world, and the antiquities to the south of the city are priceless treasures.

But one's overwhelming impression is heat, crowds of people, immobile traffic, dust, dirt, the smell of dung and musk, voracious street peddlers, the constant cry for 'Baksheesh' and the offers of the street urchins: 'You like my sister (or brother)?'

We found the Sukh (Market) to be depressing with deformed beggars covered with flies, ragged coolies and merchants who grabbed us by the arm, saying: 'No need to buy . . . just look!'

I visited Cairo several times during my years in the Middle East and never found any reason to change my poor opinion of the place.

We had been told by Saad to see the Citadel with the Mohammed Ali Mosque atop. We walked from the hotel. The street buildings were all a dull brown as if to blend with the impinging desert. It was a long walk. When we arrived the Citadel was closed for repairs but it was still very impressive from the outside. Afterwards, we found a cafe with outdoor tables and thankfully sat down.

'What's Arabic for beer?' Taffy asked, as a waiter approached.

'I don't think we need worry,' Ginger replied. He held up four fingers and said: 'Beer'.

'Ah . . . Stella . . . Stella.' The waiter hurried away and returned with four green bottles of Stella Beer, a light lager.

'Very tasty,' Harry remarked.

We all agreed and ordered four more. Then our taste buds were awakened by an enticing smell from inside the cafe. Suddenly, we were all hungry and went inside to have a look. An elderly man was placing chunks of spicy meat on a skewer over a charcoal fire. Small piles of vegetables were nearby. He gave a wide, toothless smile and said: 'Shish Kebab . . . Shish Kebab.'

'Aywa,' I said, in my fluent Arabic and held up four fingers. It was delicious. We later learned that the meat was lamb seasoned in a marinade of onion, parsley, majoram and lemon juice.

'I wonder how many Mosques there are in Cairo,' Harry remarked as we strolled back towards the city centre. 'There's one everywhere you turn.'

'Why don't you count them?' Taffy said.

'All right.' But Harry gave up when he got to sixteen.

The bar in Shepheards was about a mile long and always crowded. There we were introduced to Lebanese brandy, poor local wine and the anisette-flavoured Zibib which turns a milky colour when water is added. Popular throughout the Middle East, this drink is known as Arak in Lebanon, Raki in Turkey and Ouzo in Greece. We preferred the Stella beer.

The bar also produced some tasty snacks. Batarikh, Egyptian caviar; Baba-ghanouf, baked egg plant mixed with sesame paste; Mish, cheese made into a paste; Waraq anab, rolled grape leaves stuffed with rice and meat.

Saad had told us which bus to take to go to the pyramids. We spend six alternate days at Giza, Al-Aryan, Abu Sir, Saggara, Memphis and Dahshur.

Giza was the most impressive. Dominating the site are the pyramid complexes of Khufu (Cheops), Khafra (Chephran), and Menkaure (Mycerinus). Each featured a difference in both design and scale. Cheops held the body of a long-dead Pharoah but the adjacent Museum was closed.

Best of all was the Sphinx, 190 feet long and 66 feet high, it was carved in situ from natural rock. The body of a recumbent lion with the head of a man. The lion is a symbol of kingship and the man intelligence. It's head gear is called a 'Klaft', a striped hood with two flaps placed behind the ears and brought forward to rest on the shoulders.

We spent so long looking at the Sphinx that Taffy grumbled: 'Is this all we're going to do today - look at a lion?'

I will not go into detail about the various sites. Suffice it to say that we were thrilled and amazed. Please remember that it was 1942, before television and guided tours, and that these antiquities were not known as well as they are today. Indeed, some that are great attractions today had not yet been discovered.

At the Blue Mosque we removed our shoes and tip-toed inside. The lovely columns and blue mosaic walls were awesome. There was a large paved courtyard, rubbed smooth by millions of shoeless feet. In the middle was an ornamental fountain. A veranda ran around the courtyard supported by beautiful slender columns, thousands of years old.

One morning we inspected the Mosque of Ibn Tulum with its splendid mosaic tiles, ornate stucco and minarets that rose gracefully in front. Afterwards we sat on the bank of the Nile and watched small ducks paddling around at the water's edge in papyrus - and thought of Moses. A stately felluca with a beautiful triangular sail eased by with a cargo of lumber.

Looking at our map, Harry came up with a suggestion that turned out to be brilliant. 'The British Embassy is just down the way . . . why don't we drop in?'

This we did and found ourselves talking to a Third or Fourth Secretary. He was about our age with a plummy, upper-class accent. When we asked him about things to do he said: 'What you need, chaps, is a pass to the Gezira Sporting Club. It has a pool, tennis courts, squash courts, a race track and a great restaurant. We here are all members. Just hang on . . . I'll get you some.'

'Here we are,' he said, as he returned with four passes. 'You can walk from here . . . just go over the Tahrir Bridge on to Gezira Island . . . you can't miss it.'

We thanked him and the Gezira Club became our home away from home. I even managed to get in a few sets of tennis but I lost money at the races.

Of course, we sampled the Cairo night life. It wasn't very interesting. There were plenty of bars but they were dingy and dirty, with the drinks watered and over-priced. In the cabarets there were few women, apart from singers and belly-dancers, and they were in uniform and well escorted. Muslim law forbade women to go out at night. There were brothels but we declined.

Every place was crowded with soldiers. Most were from the British Eighth Army and the Australian Ninth Division who had been fighting, and losing, the desert war. They would soon get their revenge on Rommel's Afrika Corps at the battle of El Alemein. (Assisted, I am glad to say, by No. 39 Squadron).

The Australians in particular were a rough lot, recruited from the welfare rolls and prisons (Like the Canadian First Division in the U.K.). No evening was complete without a fight and they all carried a weapon of some sort - knives preferred.

At the end of our leave we returned to Shallufa, air tested our Beaufort (Cycling the under-carriage up and down a few times) and prepared to go to Malta.

'At last,' I said to myself, 'I am going to war.' It was 30 June, 1942, and I had been in the RCAF for 20 months.

Chapter Six:

Malta

Let's have a look at this small island and its war up to July, 1942, when I arrived there.

Occupied variously by Phoenicians, Carthaginians, Romans, Arabs, Normans and Castilians, Malta had no stability until 1530 when the Knights of St. John came. For 250 years they built and transformed Malta into a viable country. Cities such as Valletta, Cospicua and Senglea rose from the dust. After a brief hiatus with Napoleon, they asked Britain to take control and this was done about 1813. The British found an island rich in fortifications, palaces and churches but woefully lacking in administration. However, since this was a forte of the Colonial Office, things were quickly put right.

With its satellite island of Gozo, Malta contains 117 square miles and, in 1939, a population of 270,000. Its strategic position in the centre of the Med, 1,000 miles from both Suez and Gibraltar, made it a milestone on the great trade route between Britain and the Far East. The Grand Harbour of Valletta is one of the finest in the world; a narrow entrance easily guarded, opens into nine miles of coves and inlets giving shelter to wharfs and drydocks. It has long been the home of the Royal Navy.

Most of the land is under cultivation and feeds about one-third of the population. Crops are potatoes, corn, wheat and fruits such as figs, peaches and oranges. Wells of immortal antiquity determine the sites of farms. To protect crops from the fierce wind that sweeps over at times of the year, each tiny field is enclosed with stone walls so that the whole island is a criss-cross of walls and narrow lanes. Motor buses supply transport but for short distances a 'Carrozzi' is used; this is a four-wheel cab drawn by little barbs, their harness splendid with brass and tassels and a pheasant tail surmounting the horse's head-dress. Between harbours a 'Dghaisa', a gondola-like boat whose rowers stand facing the bow, provides transport.

Valletta

The towns and villages, connected by roads between walls of limestone (so prevalent on Malta) are built of the same material, flat roofed, each clustered around its baroque church with shrines and effigies of saints at cross roads and street corners. In the hour before sunset the whole island takes on a soft radiance that deepens to rose, transforming it into a fairy land. The immense fortifications with their deep ditches and airy bridges, the palaces and the churches are a fabric of enchantment while the light lasts.

Before the war life was simple and static for the Maltese people. They lived for their families and trusted in God. The only two outlets from the daily routine were the Band Club and the Feast Days. The local band was supported by all, and, with the church, a pillar of the town.

Feast days were many and a festive occasion. The bands would parade the streets, hawkers would sell nougat (a sweet delicacy), church bells would ring, rockets and Roman Candles would soar into the sky. The women wore voluminous skirts and patterned blouses; the men wore bright shirts, waistcoats and uncomfortable shoes. All of these would be put away at the end of the day, untouched until the next feast day.

The economy was based on farming, fishing and the British fleet and Garrison. Wages at the dockyard were two pounds a week and on this a man raised a family, sent his children to school, staked something on the weekly Lotto, had a few glasses of wine and put a little aside for a rainy day. There was poverty but people shared with the less fortunate. Rents were low and taxation negligible.

This is how the Maltese people lived in 1940. With 60% of the population illiterate, they lived poorly. There were a few who had a lot of money and could afford a higher standard of living. Of course, there were doctors, lawyers, teachers and civil servants who formed an upper middle class. There were numerous priests and nuns who provided the help that non-existent social workers did not.

The war changed everything for the people.

The first air raid on Malta, in June, 1940, was carried out by the Italian Air Force. (The Luftwaffe was not yet in Italy). Just 15 minutes flying time from Sicily were some 360 bombers (Cants, Savoies, BR-20), and 200 fighters (CR-42, Reggiane-200, Macchi-202) - the cream of the Italian Air Force.

Mussolini boasted that he 'would be in Grand Harbour within a few weeks.' Count Ciano announced that 'it has been decided that Malta must be obliterated.'

The Air Officer Commanding Malta, Air Commodore Maynard, had little to defend the island with. In England, the Chiefs of Staff had stated that Malta could not be defended and had virtually written her off. But Winston Churchill insisted that it not fall to the enemy. His were brave words but Britain was so hard pressed at home in 1940 that little could be spared for Malta.

Maynard had one stroke of luck. He got to hear that there were some mysterious packing crates at Kalafrana. On opening them he found that they contained component parts for eight Sea Gladiators which had been overlooked by the Royal Navy. He negotiated with his opposite number, Rear Admiral Willis, to keep half of them in Malta.

The Gladiators were sturdy little machines but sadly out-dated by the Regia Aeronautica. They were single-bay bi-planes with fixed undercarriage, one-pitch props and a top speed of about 220 knots. But they were tough with their compressed-steel ribs and highly manoeuvrable. There were about a dozen pilots on Malta, none of whom had ever flown a Gladiator. They all volunteered to train on the aircraft. One plane was used for spare parts and the other three became known as 'Faith, Hope and Charity'. They were to become a legend in Malta's air war. ('Faith' is now on display in the War Museum in Valletta).

Gloster 'Gladiator'

The Gladiators did not concentrate on enemy fighters but tried to break up the bomber formations. This, together with anti-aircraft fire, caused the bombers to miss their target. Many of the Italian pilots were loathe to press home their attack in the face of enemy fire.

So the days passed with an air raid, or two, every day and the Gladiators facing odds of fifty or more to one, cheered on by the people every time they took to the air. Obviously, it couldn't last as both pilots and aircraft grew very weary.

In late June, four Hurricanes on their way to the Middle East landed in Malta to refuel. A/C Maynard promptly kept two of them for himself. On the next raid, the Italians were astonished to be faced with the Hurricanes; many bombers dropped their loads prematurely and headed for home. Later, using this same technique, Maynard added three more Hurricanes to Malta's defences.

In August, 12 Hurricanes arrived having been flown off the aircraft carrier 'Furious' out of Gibraltar. (This was to become the standard method of getting fighters to Malta). But the Italians stepped up the tempo of their attacks, added Stuka dive-bombers to their fleet, and by October only four Hurricanes and one Gladiator were left.

Now the British seemed to realize the desperate plight of Malta and assembled a large convoy at Gibraltar. The aircraft carrier 'Argus', with 14 Hurricanes aboard, was escorted by two battleships, Renown and Ark Royal, three cruisers and seven destroyers. The plan was to fly the Hurricanes off when within range of Malta, whence the ships would return smartly to Gib to avoid running into the Italian Battle Fleet. With a Met forecast of a tail wind the fighters were launched some 40 miles before their planned position, guided by a Squa aircraft. The Met forecast was wrong, a head wind developed and only five of the Hurricanes made it to Malta; the rest ran out of fuel and were lost at sea. It was not a glorious episode in the history of the Royal Navy.

Towards the end of 1940, things looked a bit brighter for the island. The armour-decked carrier 'Illustrious', with a heavy escort, roamed the Med with success. In Taranto harbour 21 of her aircraft put out of action three Italian battleships, two cruisers and two auxiliary vessels. Admiral Cunningham dared the Italian Fleet to come out and fight. They would not.

Then Mussolini called on Hitler for help. Annoyed with the failure of the Italians to subdue Malta, Hitler obliged with 350 Heinkels, Junkers-88, ME-109 and Stukas. This was Fliegerkorps X - the cream of the Luftwaffe.

Ju 87 'Stuka'

This flying armada, in Jan 41, caught an Allied convoy in the Pantelleria Narrows and inflicted severe damage. The carrier 'Illustrious' was their prime target. Wave after wave of Stukas attacked and soon the ship was burning from stem to stern. But its engines were still turning and it made for Malta, some 100 miles away. Under attack the whole way, the carrier still managed to limp into Grand Harbour where it was towed to Parlatario Wharf in French Creek. Gangways came down and hordes of people stormed aboard - firemen with hoses to put out the fires which were still burning, doctors and ambulances to attend to the wounded, seamen from other ships and surveyors with the near-impossible task of making the ship seaworthy. In an effort to finish off Illustrious the Germans, between 16-23 Jan, mounted eight large scale raids on the dockyard. They used over 500 aircraft of which 61 were lost.

Heinkel He 111

They hit the carrier once and near-missed several times. But the repair crews were not daunted. On the night of 23 Jan, escorted by the Australian cruiser 'Perth', Illustrious slipped out of Grand Harbour and arrived safely in Alex. She went to the U.S. for repair and was then back in the fight.

Now the sea between Sicily and Libya was dominated by Fliegerkorps X. Not only did these highly-skilled Luftwaffe squadrons close the Med to Allied shipping, they also escorted Rommel's Afrika Corps to Libya. As for Malta, they now unleashed an attack that made earlier ones look like pinpricks. The cities of Senglea, Cospicus and Valletta were reduced to rubble, their historic buildings shattered.

The daily life of the people was horrendous. They lived in tunnels and deep rock shelters. Old tunnels hewed by galley slaves to link the fortifications and palaces in Valletta gave shelter to thousands. The dockyard forges turned out picks by the thousands and an army of volunteers burrowed into the soft limestone of ramps and fortified ditches. It was still not enough. But the spirit of the people would not break.

For the next six months the onslaught continued with only a dozen or so Hurricanes to defend the island. Day after day, against odds of 20 to one and more, the Hurricanes fought on. When one was damaged it was patched up. When a bomb cratered a runway it was filled and patched. But the end was in sight.

Valleta,, world's safest shelters

Then in June, 1941, a miracle happened. The German aircraft disappeared from the sky! They had been withdrawn to help in the war against Russia. Once again, the air battle would be fought against the Italians, although the Germans had left some aircraft behind.

From June to December, Malta lived from convoy to convoy, all badly damaged en route, ever short of food, fuel and ammo. But an offensive force, now under Air Vice Marshal Lloyd, gradually built up to a total of 105 bombers such as Wellingtons, Blenheims and Marylands. These bombers, together with submarines also based in Malta now started to inflict losses on Rommel's supplies to the Western Desert.

Their very success was Malta's undoing. For in Nov, 1941, Hitler, balked of a quick victory in Russia, turned his attention again to the Middle East. He stated again that 'Malta must be obliterated.'

The task was given to General Kesselring, who had directed the Luftwaffe in the Battle of Britain. Fliegerkorps X returned - and not alone - they brought with them squadron after squadron of battle-tested veterans from France and Belgium until they totalled 400 bombers and 400 fighters, all within 15 minutes flying time to Malta. Kesselring could hardly fail to give this stubborn little island the 'coup de grace'.

Kesselring's plans were simple. Obtain air supremacy by destroying the airfields and the remaining Hurricanes. Pulverize the ground defences. Amass a fleet of gliders and para-troops on Sicily and escort them to Malta. 'Eight weeks,' he told the German General Stag, 'should be enough.'

On 3 Jan, 1942, the blitz began. In that month there were 107 air raids, some lasting eight hours. The three airfields of Luqa, Hal Far and Takali took 800 hits and were pitted with craters. Over 50 aircraft were destroyed on the ground and by 1 Feb only 28 Hurricanes remained.

A brief respite came from 1-14 Feb when there was low cloud and rain. The bad weather didn't of course stop the air raids but they were not as accurate and it gave the workers a chance to patch up their defences.

In addition to the selected bombing of cities, docks and airfields, the Germans dropped parachute mines which, played by the wind, dropped anywhere and did wide spread damage to the crowded island. In the streets and roads it was common to see nomad families in search of shelter; horse-driven carts, loaded with belongings, became the order of the day. Some where, some how, people helping people, they survived.

Parachute mine

The main problem was the airfields. They were vulnerable targets: hangars, planes and petrol bowsers all crammed together. In Jan an average of two aircraft a day had been destroyed on the ground. The answer lay in bomb-proof disposal pens built outside the airfield perimeter. Easier said than done! But Lloyd recruited from 1,500 to 3,000 soldiers and, with RAF and civilians, built pens of used five-gallon petrol tins filled with sand and earth and lashed together with wire.

To house a Wellington required three walls, each 90 feet long, 14 feet high, consisting of 12 tins at the bottom and tapering to two at the top - 60,000 tins and two miles of wire. Each pen required 30,000 man-hours to build. Through Feb and Mar, an average of 40 pens a week were built until by Apr there were 350 large, strongly-built, linked and dispersed pens. It was a Herculean effort - clerks, photographers, storemen, radio operators, officers, - anyone who had an hour or so to spare went to work on the pens.

Even though the bombs rained down, somehow the runways were patched by the soldiers and the Hurricanes rose for battle every day. But by 23 March there were only 11 Hurricanes left. How long they could have held out if Kesselring had continued his assault is problematical - maybe two weeks or so. But he didn't!

Kesselring made the same mistake that Herr Goering had made in the Battle of Britain. He switched his attacks from the airfields to the dockyards when a few more weeks of assault on the airfields would have finished off Malta's air defences. There was a reason for the change; a large convoy was approaching Malta and it was a tempting target - many of the ships were sunk but a few vital ones got through.

On 15 Apr, King George awarded the George Cross to Malta. It was carried to the island by Lord Gort when he took over as Governor. While it was a nice gesture, and the people surely deserved it, it did nothing to alleviate their distress.

Far more important was the arrival of part of a convoy, and 46 Spitfires flown off the carrier Wasp out of Gibraltar with another 63 to follow in May.

Now Kesselring had other problems. On 22 June he flew to Libya to congratulate General Rommel on his great success in capturing Tobruk with a vast bounty of ammo, fuel and arms. Kesselring also wanted Rommel to return some fighter squadrons to assist in subduing Malta but Rommel, his eyes fixed on Egypt, refused to do so. The diversion of the two generals was referred to Hitler and Mussolini. A decision came quickly, obviously because it had been burning in the minds of the two dictators.

Hitler had very serious doubts about the success of the invasion of Malta. He felt that the Italian Navy would fail to back the invasion force in the face of the Royal Navy. In addition, the fact that the invasion force included a seaborne landing of Italian forces, the success of which he doubted, there was the question of supplies and reinforcements; Hitler felt that his para-troops would be left without support.

Mussolini was relieved by the possibility of a safer and more glorifying operation than the invasion of Malta, which had been terrifying him. Rommel's alternative of pressing on to occupy Egypt weighed more heavily in appeasing his vanity. On 24 June he sent Rommel the message: 'Duce approves Panzerarmee intention to pursue the enemy into Egypt.'

A few days later Mussolini flew into Derna with all his dress uniforms, a White Charger following in another aircraft, for his triumphant entry into Cairo.

When Rommel met fierce resistance by the Eighth Army at El Alemein, Kesselring had to give him forces which had been earmarked for the invasion of Malta. This, and the arrival of the Spitfires, put an end to 'Operation Hercules' - the invasion of Malta.

During the second three months of 1942 two major convoys failed to get to Malta. One through incompetence - it was given a 180 degree change of course four times; the other through enemy action. Thus by the end of June the island was desperately short of food, fuel, ammo and other supplies.

Almost none of this was known to the neophyte crew that filed into the office of the C.O. of 39 Squadron, Wing Commander Pat Gibbs, on 3 July, 1942.

'Sit down, chaps,' he said, 'tell me your names and where you are from.' He seemed older than his 25 years with sharp features, receding black hair and restless eyes.

We identified ourselves.

Gibbs picked up a piece of paper from his desk but his hands shook so much that he put it down again. 'I'm expecting good things from you. F/O Quinn says that you are the best crew to come through Shallufa. Deacon - you have more flying hours than most of my pilots. Heide - you have the only radar on the squadron, although we will shortly be getting Mk II Beauforts that have the ASV.'

Harry said: 'We hear that fuel is very scarce and that ops are limited.'

'Yes,' Gibbs replied. 'We can't take off without a confirmed sighting by a recce aircraft, a sub or some other source. Of course, if the Italian Battle Fleet sails . . . ' His voice trailed off and his eyes seemed unfocused. There was a strained silence.

Then Gibbs pulled himself together. 'We have some mines to lay in Tunis. This will be a good way for you to break in and with your radar you'll be able to get them in the right place.' He looked at me.

Gibbs stood up. 'That's all for now, chaps.'

Outside, I said to Harry: 'I wonder why he's so nervous?'

We soon found out. Gibbs was a sensitive, highly-strung individual and a strong advocate of torpedo bombing. He had completed a tour with 22 Squadron in the U.K. during which a bad crash had resulted in a broken arm and head injuries. He came to 39 Squadron without a proper rest and had had one encounter with the Italian Fleet (with which he had a fixation) and another crash. He was living on his nerves.

The crew gathered around as I made out our flight plan for planting mines in Tunis harbour.

'How long a flight?' Harry asked.

'About two hours,' I replied. 'It should show up nicely on the radar.'

'What about shore defenses?' Ginger asked.

'I doubt if they will even see us.'

'What about night fighters?' Taffy asked.

Harry replied. 'The I.O. says that there aren't any but I only half-believe him so keep your eyes open.'

'Radio silence, I presume,' Ginger said.

'Yes. We have another aircraft with us,' Harry said. 'I'll go and get them.'

Although we were all a bit nervous at first, we soon settled down and the mission was routine. There was a bright moon and the other Beaufort had no trouble staying with us. Tunis harbour showed up well on the radar and we dropped our mines in the right position. There was some desultory flak from the shore defences but it was nowhere near us. No enemy night fighters appeared.

Joining 39 Squadron at the same time as ourselves was a tall, handsome South African named Captain Don Tilley. He was to become one of the outstanding torpedo pilots of the war in the Med.

Now came our baptism of fire! A convoy consisting of the tanker 'Pozarica' of 8,000 tons and a small merchant ship named 'Dora', escorted by two destroyers and two flak ships, had been spotted leaving Messina for Benghazi.

Led by W/C Gibbs, 12 Beauforts took off and formed up west of Malta. Here we were joined by 10 Beaufighters from 227 Squadron as top cover and flak suppression. Light signals were used (to keep radio silence) to pass instructions such as set course, take over lead, fighters seen, prepare to attack and top cover rise. Having formed up, the Beauforts flew in VICs of three at sea level with the Beaufighters weaving on the wings. We were 'Tail-end-Charlie' in the last VIC.

John Creswell, Gibb's navigator, found the convoy and we got in position to attack. The Beauforts split to attack from two sides; the low cover Beaufighters climbed to 500 feet for flak suppression while the top cover looked for enemy fighters.

The flak from the defensive ships was intense in spite of the fact that, there being no enemy fighters, all 10 Beaufighters attacked them. I could see one destroyer on fire. The 'Pozarica' took violent evasive action. On our run in we could see that the tanker had not been hit and was still turning hard to port. Harry carried out a text-book attack. Low at 30 feet on the approach, climb to 75 feet for the drop (we both shouted 'Now' at the same time) and then down to sea level again. One of the flak ships had moved closely behind the tanker and Harry flew between them. We were so close to the flak ship that I could see the gunners turning to fire at us as I opened fire with my two machine guns, forcing them to duck for cover. Even so, we took some hits in the tail plane.

Ahead of us a Beaufort slammed into the sea, skipped and sank. I was glad to be busy with my machine guns because it gave me something to do and stopped me from being too scared. (Perhaps 'terrified' is a better word).

'We didn't get it,' Taffy said from the rear turret, 'the ship is still turning.'

'Shit!' Harry swore. We learned later that the tanker was not as low in the water as was anticipated and hence the depth setting on the torpedoes was too great and they all passed under the ship.

The Beaufort that I had seen crash was flown by a Canadian pilot named Roper. Another was also shot down, flown by an Australian named Condon. All eight men survived and were taken POW. In addition, one Beaufighter was lost. So three aircraft and crews were sacrificed to no avail.

W/C Gibbs was nothing if not determined. On the next day he led nine Beauforts to the same target escorted by eight anti-flak Beaufighters and five more with bombs. Again, we were 'Tail-end Charlie' in the last VIC. This time, Gibbs and his wingman both hit the 'Pozarica' with their torps. When we made our run the tanker was dead in the water. I saw our torp running true before I had to turn my attention to fire at a flak ship.

Suddenly, the air was full of shouting - no longer was radio silence needed. 'We got her!' Taffy shouted.

Photos taken later showed the 'Pozarica' stationary with oil flowing from both sides; she was towed to Italy but so badly damaged that she took no further part in the war.

In spite of our flak suppressors the enemy fire was ferocious. A Beaufighter was shot down as was a Beaufort with a South African pilot named Wolfe; the crew became POW.

So it cost the loss of three Beauforts and two Beaufighters, and their crews, to cripple one tanker and damage one destroyer.

In the evening we got together in the Mess for a watery beer. 'Well,' Harry opened, 'what did you think of those two operations?'

'The first one was a fiasco,' I replied, 'because of the wrong settings on the torps.'

'Yeah,' Taffy agreed. 'The Intelligence Officer should be court-martialled . . . we lost two crews for nothing.'

There was a silence. 'How about the second strike?' Harry asked.

'Well, we got the ship,' I replied.

'Aye,' Ginger added. 'It was summat to see.'

'Two things need fixing,' Harry remarked. 'We need better flak suppression and we need to get the target ships slowed down somehow; perhaps some of the Beaufighters could attack with bombs before we go in.'

'Some of the Beaufighters carried bombs,' Taffy said, 'but they only used them on the escorts.' (Shortly after this 227 Beaufighter Squadron was assigned to join us as an attack force).

Harry glanced at the three of us. 'Were you scared?'

'Out of my wits!' Taffy said.

'By Gaw!' Ginger exclaimed. 'Ah had a mind to be somewhere else.'

'I changed my shorts when we got home,' I said.

'I threw mine away!' Harry laughed.

The Adjutant, the lanky Scot with the baggy eyes, called me into his office. 'Have a seat.'

'I sat.

'I have here a signal from RCAF HQs in London,' he picked up a paper from his cluttered desk, 'saying that you are promoted to Pilot Officer. It is effective several months ago . . . looks as if they have been chasing you around the world. I don't know how this came about . . . we didn't recommend you . . . you just got here.'

I knew but I kept quiet.

'So move your stuff to the Majestic Hotel in Sliema. They have a room for you.'

'All right.' I had mixed feelings. I would enjoy the perks of being an officer but I would be separated from my crew who would remain in barracks in Luqa. (In the event we still spent most of our time together).

'We give a uniform allowance of 100 pounds to those who are newly commissioned,' he continued, 'you might as well have it . . . see the Paymaster.'

'Thanks,' I said. Since all we ever wore was shirts and shorts, I bought a pair of shoulder tabs and a hat and blew the rest on a big party at Maxime's Club in Valletta.

I sent Mary a telegram.

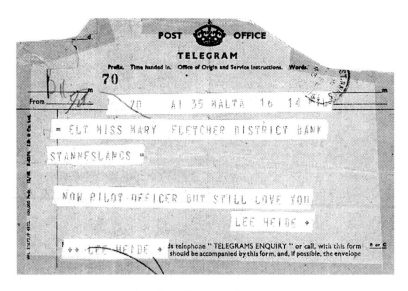

'Now Pilot Officer but still love you!'

Of course we followed the fortunes of the British in North Africa closely. On 4 Aug 1942, we were startled to hear that Winston Churchill had relieved General Auckinleck of command and replaced him with General Alexander. Command of the 8th Army was given to General Gott but, before he could take over, he was killed in a plane crash. General Montgomery replaced him.

There was an air raid or two every day. If we were on stand-by at Luqa (we spent a lot of time on stand-by) we would go to the air raid shelter. If I was off duty at the Majestic Hotel in Sliema I would dash across the road, dive into the sea from the rocks, swim out a few hundred yards, roll over on my back and watch the air battle.

The Spitfires would take on the top cover of ME-109s while the Hurricanes went after the bombers. The ME-109 was armed with two 20-mm canon and two machine guns while the Spitfire had two machine guns and one Hispano 20-mm canon that frequently jammed. The ME-109 was faster and had a better ceiling but the Spitfire was more maneouverable and could win the inside-out chase. The Hurricanes had a field day with the bombers but had to be careful not to fly into the heavy flak thrown up by Malta's anti-aircraft gunners.

Since there wasn't enough avgas for us to go on Rovers, we had to have firm info on an enemy convoy before taking off. This came from a variety of sources, one of which we knew nothing about - the Code and Cipher School at Bletchley Park in Buckinghamshire, England. Using a captured German 'Enigma' coding machine, they were regularly decrypting messages to and from Rommel's forces to Germany and Italy. They knew the sailing routes and dates of almost all the Axis convoys together with the names of the vessels and their cargo. (We thought that this info came from spies in Italy). At midnight on 28 October, 1942, Bletchley Park picked up an urgent signal from Rommel to Kesselring demanding immediate dispatch of fuel for his forces. It is said that this was the point at which Rommel knew that the battle of El Alamein was lost.

We were very dependent on No. 69 Squadron for photo recce. They had a mixed bag of Baltimores, Marylands, Spitfires and one P-38, called a Lightning, an American twin-engine, twin-boomed fighter which, stripped down, could make 450 knots at 35,000 feet. The Germans called it the 'Forked-Tail Devil.' This machine was

Adrian Warburton: leading British photographic ace.

*Warburton had to crash-land this aircraft, but twenty
minutes later he was taking off in another plane.*

flown by the C.O., Squadron Leader Adrian Warburton, who became a legend in photo recce circles for always getting his pictures no matter how fierce the opposition.

Watching him land was to see an aerial display. He would scream down from on high, roll his P-38 over Valletta, pull up in a stall turn, flip down his flaps and undercart and land at Luqa. Warburton was killed on operations over Europe in 1944, then a Wing Commander with a DSO and Bar, DFC and two Bars and an American DFC.

Another legend in Malta at this time was the Canadian ace, George Frederick 'Screwball' Beurling. He was a loner and not popular on his Spitfire squadron where he treated his wingmen like hired lackeys. Beurling refused a commission for some time, remaining an NCO, because he didn't want any responsibility.

Harry told us the story of Beurling being called to the phone in the Sgt.'s Mess. Harry overheard the following:

'Beurling here.'

'Yeah . . . who?'

'When . . . today?'

'Tell him I can't make it today . . . it's my day off and I'm going fishing.'

The phone call was from the office of the AOC, Malta- Air Vice Marshal Sir Keith Park.

Beurling was killed in a crash at Rome in bad weather, in 1946, while flying supplies to Israel. His uniform and decorations are on display at the War Museum in Valletta.

A few days after the 'Pozarica' strike we were off again. A convoy of one tanker, 'Giorgia', of 5,000 tons, escorted by two torpedo boats, was found en route from Taranto to Tobruk. Six Beauforts, led by Fl/Lt Wally Alsopp, were accompanied by eight Beaufighters, three of which carried bombs. We attacked in VICs of three, with us leading the second VIC. The violent evasive action by the tanker resulted in no hits. A Beaufighter claimed damage but the 'Georgia' got through to Tobruk. I didn't hit anything with my machine guns - the torpedo boats were far too agile.

A Beaufort flown by Larry Dewhurst was shot down and all the crew were killed.

After a strike each crew was debriefed by the Station Intelligence

Officer. We all reported no torpedo hits on the 'Giorgia' but the navigator on one crew, a Canadian named Fraser with a wacky sense of humour, remarked casually: 'Oh, by the way, I killed the Captain.'

'You what?!' shouted the I.O.

'I strafed the bridge . . . he was standing there . . . I could tell he was the Captain by the gold braid on his hat.'

'How do you know you killed him?'

'I saw him go down . . . full of bullet holes.'

There was not a trace of expression on Fraser's face and the I.O. didn't know whether to believe him or not.

Neither did I.

Tribute must be paid to the RAF ground crew who kept our kites flying under the most difficult of circumstances. The Axis blockade had a strangulation effect on the supply of spare parts for both airframes and engines.

It was usual, for instance, to see a fuselage patch bearing the logo of the supplier of petrol tins. The Maintenance Wing at Kalafrana collected every piece of a crashed aircraft from anywhere on the island. Engines, air frames, radios, armament - all were put to use again.

Even toilet paper was used! The 20-mm Hispano canon on the Spitfire was having stoppages due to dust and sand being sucked into the breech while the aircraft was taxiing. The solution was to glue thin paper over the opening which would tear away on the first round being fired. Ordinarily toilet paper issued to the rank and file was too thick and tough. But a softer brand for the delicate asses of 'HQ and Civil Servants Only' was ideal. The Armament Officer rode triumphantly back to base on his bike with his handlebar basket piled high with his stolen cargo. The stoppage rate of the Hispano 20-mm canon declined considerably!

We wanted to explore the island. It quickly became apparent that it would have to be by bicycle. We bought four, second-hand. We needed the exercise with spending so much time on stand-by. However, we found that we tired quickly and had to have a frequent rest. This, I put down to our meagre diet:

Breakfast: a slice of bread, one sausage and tea.

Lunch: cabbage soup and a hardtack biscuit.

Dinner: bully beef and perhaps a vegetable.

To counteract the lack of fresh fruit we took ascorbic tablets for Vitamin 'C'. Still, we remained healthy and quite fit even if thin.

The capital, Valletta, was in shambles. Its charm of bastions, ramparts with loopholes projecting at odd angles overhead, airy bridges and fabulous buildings was mostly destroyed. The Grand Master's Palace, the great cathedral of St. John's and the Opera House were all hit by bombs. The narrow streets were choked with masonry and there was always the danger of more falling from above.

Opera House, Valletta

The original capital of Malta was the walled city of Medina. Although it had no military significance, it was bombed by the Italians. This was the seat of the Roman Governor, Publius, who received St. Paul with such hospitality when he visited Malta. Surrounded by a moat, it has 26 towers and two bridges for entrance. Its fabulous buildings include a Magisterial Palace with French baroque influence, the Santa Sophia Palace, a domed Cathedral, a Seminary and a Nunnery which still adheres to strict rules and allows no men to enter except for the doctor and the white-washer. We spent a whole day in Medina.

In the small town of Mosta we found a wonderful church which has the third largest dome in the world. The interior of blue tile and gold is fantastic. Only one bomb hit the church during the war; it fell through the middle of the dome into the nave but did not explode.

The island of Gozo was lush and green when Malta was brown, bleached by the sun. Throughout history, Gozo has been a land apart and its people even look different - short and stocky. This is 'Calypso' island, where the sirens lured Odysseus by their beauty. We saw the nymph's cavern, high above the sandy bay of Ramla. The capital city of Rabat still has a medieval quality with its narrow, twisting streets. Gozo is famous for its lace-making and we watched three ladies on the street working at their craft.

Everywhere we went on Malta the people smiled and waved. Farmers stopped work in their fields to shout a blessing. An old lady, enchanted by Ginger's red hair, bent over to kiss his hand.

The daily air raid was over. It was afternoon on a hot, humid day. Ginger and Taffy were off somewhere else; Harry and I sat in the Barrakka Gardens in Valletta over-looking Grand Harbour. 'How do they do it?' I asked. 'How do the people survive? They aren't living . . . they are just barely existing. There's no food . . . no fuel oil for them to cook with . . . no clothes . . . nothing but the constant air raids.'

'Well,' Harry replied, 'they have one good thing. All the buildings are made of limestone. There's no wood at all, so there are no fires. And the stone is easy to work into air raid shelters.'

'They sure are brave. You remember that old man in Medina? We asked him what he did when there was an air raid. He answered: 'Go on the roof and spit at the Italians.''

'Yes. They hate the Italians. Maybe that helps to keep them going.'

'A lot of people have been evacuated from the cities to the country. We saw a lot on Gozo from Malta. They must miss their homes, though.'

'I think Gozo has more food than Malta,' Harry said.

'Speaking of food,' I replied, 'if I have to eat any more corned beef - you guys call it 'Bully Beef' - I'll throw up. Two or three times a day - raw, cooked, baked, sautéed - when this is over I'll never eat corned beef again as long as I live!' (and I haven't).

Harry laughed. 'But you had your egg!'

'Oh, great,' I scoffed. On one of our excursions into the country-side I bought a single egg from a farmer. It cost five shillings ($1.25 Can). I carried it safely home, took it into the kitchen the following morning and stood by while the chef fried it (over easy).

We didn't know just how bad the situation was in that August of 1942. Malta was literally starving. If a convoy didn't get through soon, the island would have to surrender.

A few days later recce aircraft found a 5,000 ton tanker named 'San Andrea' near the toe of Italy. This particular tanker was critical to Rommel's fight in the Western Desert because he was very short of fuel. The tanker had an escort of one destroyer with an air umbrella of seven Macchi fighters, one JU-88 and a Cant. In an effort to avoid torpedo attack the tanker was hugging the coast with its destroyer to seaward.

W/C Gibbs led nine Beauforts in three VICs. We were in the second VIC, led by 'Hank' Sherman. For top cover we had nine Beaufighters from 227 Squadron. Gibbs elected to attack from landward and drop at close range to reduce the likelihood of the torpedoes fowling in shallow water. The Beaufighters went after the enemy fighters and the battle was joined.

Gibbs' VIC dropped at only 500 yards and got a hit. When Harry dropped, behind Sherman, the whole world in front of us exploded like a volcano. Flames spurted up from the tanker and then great, billowing waves of smoke as it blew up. Our aircraft shuddered as it was hit on the starboard wing by debris from the ship. Harry fought for control as Taffy shouted: 'Whoopee . . . look at her go up!' The air was full of shouts and cheers. One Beaufighter was lost.

We limped back to Malta, Ginger informing them of our trouble. I never knew whether it was reassuring or depressing to see the crash tender and an ambulance at the side of the runway when we landed but Harry set the kite down nicely.

Three days later 'Hank' Sherman led the squadron (our aircraft was being repaired) against a big and heavily defended target of four merchant ships escorted by eleven destroyers. Sherman and one other crew were shot down and all were killed. One merchant ship was damaged.

We found W/C Gibbs a difficult man to live with. He was always positive that he was right. Anyone who disagreed, no matter what their rank or their counter-argument, was wrong. Extremely sensitive, he would brook no criticism. The climax came when Gibbs

called us together for a briefing on the Italian Fleet, which was still
a danger. He described the various ships in detail, their armament
and their capabilities. Then he concluded: ' . . . and if I am hit on
the way in I'll crash on the deck of the leading battleship and I
expect everyone else to do the same.'

'He's crazy!' I whispered to Harry.

It was a prophetic statement. Only a few days later Gibbs had a
complete nervous breakdown. He was flown back to England where
he entered a psychiatric hospital. His treatment was slow, painful
and incomplete. He was invalided out of the RAF in 1944.

We come now to the convoy that saved Malta, known as the
'Santa Maria' or simply the 'August Convoy.' Winston Churchill
knew the dire situation and, on his orders, the largest convoy of the
war in the Med was assembled in Scotland. The epic battle of this
convoy is not as widely known as it should be. For details, I am
indebted to Ian Cameron and his book: 'Red Duster, White Ensign'.

Under the command of Vice-Admiral Syfret, the convoy
consisted of 14 merchantmen, two battleships, three aircraft carriers,
seven cruisers, 24 destroyers, seven motor vessels and eight
submarines. With Axis spies in Gibraltar and southern Spain, there
was no way to keep such a large force a secret as it entered the Med.
The Germans and the Italians knew all about it.

The Axis attack was not long in coming. A day plus out of
Gibraltar U-Boat - 73, under Lieutenant Rosenbraun, slipped
through the destroyer screen and put four torpedoes into the carrier
Eagle. She sank in eight minutes but most of her company was
picked up.

Admiral Syfret knew that the next vicious attack would come
when the convoy was within range of aircraft from Sardinia. So it
was. The first attack was made by 24 Junker-88s but was not pressed
home and little damage was done. Next came a synchronized attack
in five waves of 70 bombers, 60 long-range fighters and 42 Savoia
torpedo bombers. The convoy's sea Hurricanes rose to give battle.
The merchantman Deucalion was badly hit, pulled out of the convoy
and was later sunk. Other ships were damaged but not badly.

So far, the convoy had lost one carrier and one merchant ship.
The enemy had lost 26 aircraft and two subs sunk by the destroyers.
But soon the convoy would come within range of aircraft based in

Sicily, where U-Boats and E-Boats were gathering.

On the following afternoon a force of 42 Junker-88s, a squadron of ME-109s and 40 Savoia concentrated their attack on the carriers. Illustrious took three direct hits; her flight deck was buckled and twisted and she was of no further use. Her fighters landed on Victorious which was also badly hit but still in operation. The destroyer Foresight was sunk. But the 13 merchants ships, including the only tanker - the Ohio, of 15,000 tons - were still sailing.

Now came a decision the wisdom of which will be debated by war historians, probably forever. Within 36 hours of Malta, in the most dangerous part of the Med, Admiral Syfret turned back for Gibraltar taking with him two battleships, two carriers (one of which was useless), two cruisers and 11 destroyers. (Presumably this was in fear of the Italian fleet). The convoy was left with four cruisers and 12 destroyers - and no fighter protection.

The first attack came at dawn by a pack of five submarines. They concentrated on the cruisers. Cairo was sunk, Nigeria so badly damaged that she started back for Gibraltar, Kenya was badly hit. With three of the four cruisers out of action the convoy was in confusion and open to attack. It came in the form of 30 Ju-88s and 11 Heinkel-111 torpedo bombers. The merchantmen Empire Hope, Glenorsky and Clan Ferguson were sunk. The tanker Ohio was dead in the water. The Brisbane Star, badly hit, left the convoy and headed for the Tunisian coast.

At dusk came the E-boats. The cruiser Manchester was sunk, as were the merchantmen Santa Eliza, Wairingi and Admiral Lykes.

Dawn showed only the merchantmen Melbourne Star, the Rochester Castle and Port Chambers in vague convoy position. Ohio, the only tanker, was far behind and Brisbane Star was missing. Another Ju-88 attack had sunk the Wainarama. But now the convoy remnants were close enough to Malta to receive Beaufighter and Spitfire protection.

The word spread like wildfire around Malta that convoy ships were seen only a few miles away. All the people around Valletta and Grand Harbour ran to get a position on the bastions. Men, women and children; soldiers, sailors and airmen; priests and nuns; they were all there to witness the ships' arrival which would decide the fate of Malta.

Lord Gort, the Governor of Malta, was there with a word and a smile for everyone. Suddenly the Melbourne Star arrived with two tugs assisting her. The crowd cheered and sang Rule Britannia. Then came the Rochester Castle, her deck shattered but her head still up. Now came Port Chambers, badly damaged but holds still intact. The cheering was now choked by tears and everyone was moved with emotion at seeing these three brave ships which spelled salvation.

Late that evening the Brisbane Star limped into harbour after a series of adventures with French forces in Tunisia that reads like fiction.

But where was the only tanker, Ohio, whose cargo of oil and gas was so desperately needed? The saga of the Ohio is one of the most stirring naval tales of W.W. II, and deserves to be told in some detail.

Ohio was an American-built tanker, owned by Texas Oil Company, on loan to Britain. Built in 1940, she was a modern ship with strength and grace. Captain D.W. Mason, a soft-spoken Englishman of 39 years, had an all-British crew of 59, all of whom had been hand-picked because of her vital cargo. For anti-aircraft defense the Ohio had one five-inch gun, one Bofors, six Oerlikons and four PCA rockets - all manned by 24 Royal Navy gunners, whose skill would be sorely needed.

After Admiral Syfert had left the convoy to its own devices, Ohio was hit amidships by a U-Boat torpedo and ground to a halt. The pump room became a shambles and laid open to the sea. The main steering gear telemotor pipes, electric cables and steam pipes were carried away and she was soon on fire with flames rising to mast height.

One thing helped Ohio. The torpedo had blasted a hole 24 feet wide by 27 feet long through which water came pouring in to help the crew, with the aid of formite, to put out the fire. The ship got under way but could only proceed in lurching circles because of the damage to her steering gear. Captain Mason requested a guide ship and the destroyer Ledbury came to her assistance.

At 0830 hours the following morning the Axis dive bombers appeared. A 500-lb bomb burst flush under Ohio's bow, buckling the forward plating and flooding the forepeak tanks. The RN gunners shot down an attacking JU-88 but it hit the water about

50 feet from the ship, bounced off a wave crest and landed flush on the tanker's foredeck. Fortunately, it had already dropped its bombs. Ohio struggled on.

At 1000 hours the tanker was hit again. Two sticks of 500-lb bombs fell amidships on either side. Ohio was lifted clear out of the water. She shook, vibrated and quivered but still kept on.

A few minutes later a JU-87, damaged by the Oerlikons, hit the sea, bounced into the air and landed on the poop. Wreathed in smoke, cordite fumes and fire the Ohio reeled and staggered, listing to five degrees, the wreckage of two enemy planes on her decks. At 1030 hours the Ohio came to a halt.

Captain Mason requested help from the convoy Commander. At 1130 hours the destroyer Penn came alongside. She passed a ten-inch manila line and tried to take her in tow, but Ohio now weighed some 30,000 tons, drew 37 feet of water and her list was pulling her off course. The Penn could only move Ohio slowly and in circles. At last the Penn gave up and Ohio drifted helplessly.

Captain Mason, now in his third day without sleep, gave his crew the option of abandoning ship or staying with him to fight on. To a man, they volunteered to fight on.

In the late afternoon the Penn returned with the minesweeper Rye and they again took Ohio in tow. She was now lower in the water, had no light, no power and her steering was damaged beyond repair. At 1840 hours the Axis bombers again appeared, determined to sink this stubborn tanker. Ohio was hit on the bow deck and a fire started. Tow lines were cast off. Twelve bombs landed within 20 yards of Rye which did some damage. When the bombers left, the tow lines were reconnected. Hour after hour Ohio struggled on until, at dawn, she was only 75 miles from Malta.

At 0830 hours the JU-88s began their final assault to finish off Ohio. But this time they were met by Spitfires; only three JU-88s got through and of these only one pressed home his attack. But it was almost enough to give Ohio the 'coup de grace'. A 100-lb bomb landed flush in the tanker's wake. The ship was flung violently forward, her stern twisting out of alignment and water gushing in through a large hole.

Captain Mason reported to the convoy Commander: 'There is a strong possibility of our breaking in half but even if this happens I estimate that our forward portion which contains 75 per cent of our oil fuel could still be saved.'

The defenders of Malta were not about to give up on the gallant Ohio. Spitfires circled continuously overhead. There was still danger from U-Boats. Ledbury, Penn and Rye kept Ohio moving and were joined by the destroyer Pilditch and three tugs. Aircraft scouted the sea for submarines. Finally, her decks awash and barely afloat the Ohio limped into Grand Harbour to cheering crowds on the bastions. Captain Mason was awarded the George Cross.

The damaged tanker 'Ohio' reaches the Grand Harbour

Of the 14 merchantmen that had left the Clyde only five, all of them damaged, made it to Malta. But they unloaded 60,000 tons of supplies and the vital gas and oil. The siege of Malta was lifted. A convoy from Alexandria in November was virtually unopposed. The Axis powers had other things to worry about now, in particular the victory of the Eighth Army over the Afrika Corps at El Alemein.

Our new C.O. was Wing Commander Larry Gaine. A regular officer, he had been in the Middle East in 1938 when he set a record from Egypt to Australia in a Wellesly. He was 31 years old, a careful and precise pilot who had been an instructor at Abbotsinch. He took command of 39 Squadron on the 9th of September, 1942. He had an air of detachment and seemed very aloof but, while he was never 'one of the boys', he became well liked.

We walked towards our Beaufort to take it up for a flight test after its repairs, kidding Taffy for 'acquiring' an orange. The air-raid siren sounded and, simultaneously, a pair of low-flying Me-109s streaked across the airfield, all guns blazing.

'Run for the pen!' I shouted. This we did and huddled against a wall as the Me-109s wheeled around for another pass. Our pens were made of five-gallon patrol tins filled with sand lashed together with wire, and stacked to a height of 14 feet. They gave protection to anything but a direct hit and a good place for people to take shelter.

After two mine laying missions to Taranto, we joined W/C Gaine as he led his first strike with the squadron. A convoy left Brindisi for Tobruk; it consisted of the 'Zara,' loaded with fuel, the 'Brioni,' loaded with ammunition, and an escort flak ship named 'San Martino.' Their cargo was vital to Rommel's army.

We caught the convoy about 50 miles from Tobruk. There were six Beauforts escorted by seven Beaufighters. The convoy had an air cover of two ME-110s, two JU-88s and two MC-202s. While the Beaufighters engaged the enemy fighters, we lined up to attack. In the lead, Gaine flew like it was a training exercise at Abbotsinch - in copybook style, no evasive action, straight at his target, ignoring the flak. Our first three aircraft dropped their torpedoes at the Brioni but she was fast and maneouverable and there were no hits. The second VIC, of which we were one, hit the Zara amidships; there was a great column of smoke and she started to sink. After our drop Harry flew right at a flak ship. We were so close that I could hear the 'POM-POM-POM' of the deadly German gun that we called a 'Chicago Piano'. I prayed and returned fire with my machine guns but saw no hits. We took several hits in our aft fuselage but none were serious.

We lost two aircraft. One flown by one of our Flight Commanders, Sqn/Ldr Ken Grant, whose crew became POW. The other, with Oscar Hedly as pilot, were all killed.

By the end of October, 1942, we had been with 39 Squadron for four months. In that time we had lost nine aircraft. The normal complement was 18 aircraft and crews. Statistically, then, the entire squadron would be wiped out in eight months. This made us very cautious in forming friendships; crews came and went before you got to know them. It also led to a firm belief in 'Fatalism'. The only attitude to take was: 'It can't happen to me . . . it's not my time.'

A furious blitz by the enemy took place in mid-October. A formation of bombers, with a large escort of fighters, was surprised by a new British tactic - they were met by Spitfires several miles from Malta and took heavy losses. Air Sea Rescue launches were on hand to pick up downed Allied pilots, one of who was Beurling. He had shot down one bomber and four fighters before being shot down himself - he was not injured.

Then the Germans tried a new tactic of splitting their bomber formation and attacking from East, North and South at nightfall. It was not a success as Air Vice Marshal Park now had a squadron of Beaufighter night-fighters. Also, for the first time in the Med, 'Chaff' was used. This was metallic strips of paper, sent up by the anti-aircraft gunners which interfered with the enemy radar.

In one week the enemy flew 1,400 sorties, during which he lost 114 planes and 200 of his best aircrew. British losses were 25 Spitfires but 14 pilots were rescued. It was one more blow to Kesselring's dying plan to invade Malta.

There was a sprinkling of Canadians and Australians on our squadron. One of our favourites was an Aussie named 'Moose' Marshall. He was a great bear of a man, well over six feet with a powerful, jutting jaw. I never knew whether his nickname came from his gigantic frame or the fact that he had been trained in Moose Jaw, Canada. He had no inhibitions and a wonderful capacity for enjoyment which, of course, frequently got him into trouble. His navigator was another Aussie named Paterson who was so slap-happy that he soon got the nickname of 'Slap'. They both had buoyant, independent spirits but were incapable of malice. Moose was an outstanding pilot who rose from an NCO to a Squadron Leader, DFC, in eight months. When they were killed in March, 1943, a dark pall settled over the squadron for several days; we simply could not believe that they were gone.

It was difficult to keep the squadron up to strength. Replacements trickled in, some by the trans-African route that we had taken. They arrived with Mark II Beauforts which had the ASV radar, a new dihedral tail which gave added stability and new Pratt and Whitney 'Wasp' engines of 1,200 HP. At first, however, the squadron had no technicians trained on these engines and maintenance was a problem.

One Saturday night in November, with no flying the next day, we were in a party mood. It started at the Union Club in Valletta which had five hot tubs; we took four of them. The charge was nine pence - three for the attendant and six for the gas burner that measured heat into a metal cylinder at the foot of the tub. A waiter brought glasses of local wine and beer and our bathroom singing was soon lusty, if off key:

'I don't want to join the Air Force,
I don't want to go to war,
I'd rather hang around
Picadilly Underground
Living on the earnings of a high-born lady . . . '

We decided to eat at Maxime's. As usual, it was crowded. The owner, Tony, a fat little man barely five feet tall, found us a table and produced a very tasty stew. We refrained from asking what was in it. There were very few dogs and cats in Malta.

Afterwards, we wandered down the 'Gut'. This side street ran steeply down hill towards the docks. It was the lowlife area of Valletta, a solid row of saloons, brothels and dance halls. 'Exhibition!' an old crone cried, 'only one shilling.' We declined.

Taffy said, 'Let's go to the Rainbow.' It was a bar and dance hall favoured by the Other Ranks where officers seldom went. But we were all a bit high - so what! It was jammed with soldiers, sailors and airmen. There were some Maltese girls and Ginger, whose height and red hair always seemed to attract them, was soon dancing. The wine was terrible but we drank it anyhow.

Then a drunken Army corporal, looking for a fight, lurched over to our table and sneered at me: 'What are you doin' here? Officers ain't allowed.'

'Bugger off!' Harry said.

'Oh, yeah.' The man snapped open a switch-blade knife.

I tensed in my seat and grabbed a wine bottle by the neck but before the soldier could act Ginger's big arm circled his neck in a choke hold and he ran the man into a wall - head first.

The place grew quiet. There was an angry murmur as some soldiers started to rise from their seats. Taffy stood up and said: 'I think we should leave about now.'

Which we did - in a hurry.

We then went to Monica's bar which, while busy, was much more civilized. There was only one loose girl in the place and, before we even realised it, Ginger had scooped her up. After that things got a bit hazy but, as I recall, Ginger was not with us as we went home.

On 20 Nov, 227 Squadron found a merchant vessel near Pantelleria, a small Italian-held island between Malta and Africa. It was the 'Lago Tana' of 785 tons with military supplies bound for Tripoli. Their Beaufighters left the vessel on fire but not sinking. At 1455 hours, W/C Gaine led three Beauforts to the scene with F/O Cartwright as Number Two and ourselves as Number Three. We had no trouble finding the ship, which was still smoking. All of our torps hit and she burst into towering flames and began to sink. We could see the crew taking to the life boats.

This was a routine attack and we thought little of the consequences to the 'Lago Tana'. After the war I came across an Italian report which detailed the horrors of our action. In part it said: 'The Lago Tana had a crew of 90 and carried 127 Italian soldiers. Many were killed in the enemy attack and those who made the life boats found them full of holes and they sank quickly. Apart from two survivors, all on board lost their lives.'

I felt very sad when I read this account.

In early December Rommel was made aware of some unpalatable facts. Fourteen of the 22 supply ships sent from Italy to North Africa during November had been sunk, taking with them 62% of his supplies. Short of fuel, spares and ammunition, he fell back under the attack of the Eighth Army. Rommel formed a new line about 30 miles west of Tobruk. The eight-month siege of that port was over. On 13 December Montgomery attacked these new defensive positions forcing the Afrika Corps even further west.

The constant harassment of Rommel's supply lines by submarines and torpedo bombers was a major factor in winning the desert war.

For us, December was a quiet month. We did some mine laying (we called in 'gardening') at Bizerta, Tunis and Palermo. Two crews were lost. It was impossible to tell what befell them - a prowling enemy night fighter JU-88 or an aircraft malfunction.

There was now sufficient Avgas for us to do some Rover patrols but generally they were not productive. A convoy of two merchant ships, escorted by two destroyers, en route from Naples to Tunis was found by F/O Hewetson's crew on a moonlit night. He turned to attack, keeping the ships silhouetted in the moon's path. But somehow he misjudged his height and flew the Beaufort straight into the sea. Three members of his crew, Sgt.s Coles, Bryce and Bradford survived and were picked up by one of the Italian destroyers to be made POW. There was no sign of Hewetson who had gone down with the aircraft.

In mid-December some reorganization took place in the squadron and we were given two weeks leave in Egypt. We spent it in Alexandria - probably the nicest city in the Middle East.

I was tipped off that the manager of the Cecil Hotel, the largest and finest in the city, was a Canadian and could always find room for a fellow countryman. And so it was. Just one room for the four of us but it was large and had its own bathroom. The hotel also had a casino and a night club. It was expensive but we got a cut rate.

Alexandria was of course the home of the Royal Navy at this end of the Med and the harbour was full of their ships and merchantmen. The oval harbour was guarded by Fort Qaytbay on the east and by Fort Silsilah on the west. A promenade circled the front.

The city was founded by Alexander the Great in 332 B.C., it became a great cultural centre and attracted the most famous scientists, scholars, poets and artists of the time. But, unlike Rome or Athens, there is little remaining of the ancient city. It is not possible to see Alexander's tomb or the place where Anthony and Cleopatra committed suicide. The great Lighthouse, one of the Seven Wonders of the ancient world, stood 120 metres high inside a colonnaded court with a statue of Poseidon, but it was destroyed by an earthquake in 1100 A.D.

However, there was still plenty for us to see. The Mosques of Ibrahim and Abu Et-Abbas were splendid as was the Palace of Ras et-Tim. The Roman baths were in ruin but the Catacombs of Kam el-Shuqafa were traditionally spooky. We enjoyed the Royal Jewelry Museum with all its glittering gems set in tiaras and necklaces.

After lunching in the dusky splendour of the Pastroudis Cafe (mostly large prawns and steins of beer) we decided to see an American movie in a theatre down the street. In front of the cafe was an elderly Egyptian man in ragged but clean clothes who had a rug for sale. It was not large and consisted of three squares, each about two feet, joined together by heavy woollen threads some six inches long. I was interested. The workmanship looked good and it could be folded into a package two feet square and about one foot deep.

'Aday?' I asked.

'For you, good Sir,' he smiled, showing some gaps, 'only 300 piastres.'

'One hundred,' I countered.

'Ayi!' he cried. 'Feel . . . how good . . . how thick.' His English was good but accented. 'A bargain at 275 piastres . . . a bargain!'

'One hundred and twenty-five.'

'But Sir . . . I cannot . . . '

We started to walk away but he followed behind. 'Sir', he called, 'I could sell for 250 piastres.'

'One hundred and fifty,' I said.

He gave an anguished cry.

By this time we had reached the theatre; we bought our tickets and went inside. The movie took about an hour and a half. We came out, blinking in the bright sunlight.

The old man got up from where he had been sitting on the curb. 'I give to you, Sir, for only 240 piastres.'

'One seventy-five,' I offered.

'Ayi!' he cried. 'I have six children to feed and can not make any profit . . . 225.'

'Two hundred and it's a deal,' I said.

'Sold!' he shouted. We parted on good terms.

We were sitting in the bar of the Cecil Hotel on our fourth night in Alex when Ginger said: 'I wonder where all the girls are in this city? We've seen hardly any.'

'Don't ask me,' I replied.

There were some Navy junior officers at the end of the bar. Ginger stood up. 'I'm going to talk to them.'

He came back in a few minutes with a piece of paper in his hand. 'The thing to do is to call the Wrenery.'

'What's a Rennerry?' I asked.

'W-R-E-N,' Ginger spelled it out. 'Navy girls.' He looked at us.

'How many do we want?'

'Not for me,' Harry said.

'I'll pass,' Taffy said. 'I'll keep Harry company and I fancy a look at the Casino.'

'I'm game,' I said.

'Right . . . two girls.' Ginger went to find a telephone. I admired his confidence; it was as if he was going to the corner store for two cartons of milk. He returned shortly. 'Okay . . . Susan and Betty . . . six o'clock . . . I promised 'em dinner and dancing.'

I shook my head in amazement; such initiative would not have occurred to me. At the WREN hostel we told the girl who answered the door who we were after. She left and a moment later two girls, in civvies, came down the hall.

'Mine is pretty,' I whispered to Ginger, 'your's has personality.'

They knew a delightful French restaurant on Nabi Danval that we would never have found by ourselves. Over wine we got acquainted. When Ginger was in top form (as he was this evening) he could charm a butterfly into his hand; he soon had the girls relaxed and laughing. As it turned out, I hit it off best with the 'not-as-pretty-one' whose name was Susan Lazenbury and who came (I gathered) from a prominent Sussex family. She was petite with her dark hair in a Dutch bob, brown eyes, a lovely complexion and a sparkling, witty intelligence.

After dinner we danced to a smooth band in the Windsor Hotel. The girls made our remaining time in Alex very pleasant and I was to see more of Susan in other times.

After our leave we went to Shallufa to collect a new Mk II Beaufort and then returned to Malta. It was the start of a new year, 1943, and we found that we had all been promoted: Taffy and Ginger to Flight Sgt., Harry to Warrant Officer and myself to Flying Officer. Air raids were still going on but life was much better with another convoy arriving from Gibraltar in December with little opposition.

In the Western Desert the Afrika Corps was still fighting a retreating battle. Rommel informed Hitler that North Africa would be lost if supplies did not arrive, especially petrol. Of course, this situation was apparent to the Allies and all intelligence sources were ordered to look for enemy ships, especially tankers.

First blood for 1943 went to F/O Cartwright on the 14 January.

On a Rover he sighted an Axis submarine ahead of a British convoy skirting the shore near Tobruk. He dropped four depth charges, blowing the bow into the air. Then came along F/Sgt. Gillies whose depth charges finished off the Italian submarine 'Narvado'.

A few days later Sqn Ldr Les Wordsell and F/O Hugh Wadlington, on a Rover, found a convoy bound from Palermo to Tunis consisting of three merchantmen: 'Campania', 'Jacques' and 'Garda Tofz'. They were escorted by three E-Boats. The convoy had a charmed life. Both Beauforts dropped torpedoes but no hits were seen. Wadlington's aircraft was badly hit but he managed to nurse it back to Malta. Another attack in the evening by four Wellingtons and two more Beauforts also failed to get a hit.

On the night of 23 Jan, '43 we saw some action. A convoy of two merchant ships, 'Varona' and 'Pistonia', escorted by a flak ship and a destroyer, was found en route from Naples to Bizerta. The Italians expected a night attack and as soon as aircraft engines were heard they turned up-moon thus making smaller targets while the escorts made smoke. Don Tilley dropped his torpedo but didn't get a hit. F/O Cartwight dropped four 250-lb bombs but no hit was seen. We were carrying four 250-lb bombs and on our run in the destroyer was right in our line so we dropped the bombs on it; we saw a hit but the ship did not appear to be disabled. But the last Beaufort to attack hit 'Varona' with a torpedo and she began to list. Then Wellingtons from 221 and 458 squadrons finished off the two merchant ships the next day.

Spending so much time on stand-by did two things. It improved my bridge game and gave me time to write letters to Mary. She was a good correspondent. Her air mail cards arrived regularly and were a boost to my morale. Our romance was now a long-distance one but it didn't appear to be flagging.

Please inform your correspondent that he MUST head his letters with his :- Number, rank, name and the Postal address of his Unit. Failure to do so will cause delay in your mail.

BASE CENSOR
ROYAL AIR FORCE.

On 21 Feb we dealt a smashing blow to Rommel's fortunes. A 10,000-ton tanker, 'Thorsheimer', disguised as a merchant vessel, was found by some USAF Mitchells and slightly damaged. She was off the coast of Sicily, escorted by three E-Boats. The word was quickly flashed to Malta and we dispatched six Beauforts led by Captain Tilley. When we found the tanker it was moving slowly with the E-Boats and a tug circling around. Tilley's torpedo hit amidships with a flash and a column of water. Then F/S Gillies dropped and hit the stern. Then our torpedo hit and set off a tremendous explosion and a raging fire that engulfed the whole ship. There was no need for another torpedo. Three million gallons of fuel had been denied the Afrika Corps.

'Thorsheimer'

'Yipee!' Taffy gave a cowboy yell from the rear turret.

Ginger came forward to look out. 'They'll not be usin' that ship again, anyroad.'

'We've earned our pay today,' Harry said with satisfaction, as he wheeled the aircraft around for a better look at the towering flames.

'You bet!' I agreed. I fished out the bulky air force camera that I had never used and took some pictures. A Canadian reporter put the sinking on the wire services and I was a one-day hero in Vancouver.

We hoisted a few glasses that evening.

In March the air raids stopped. Food was now adequate although still rationed. Better times lay ahead. But the war had taken a heavy toll in Malta. The disease of scabies, which had made its appearance months back, was still rife and no amount of sulphur would placate it. Everywhere one looked people were scratching some part of their body. And now, when the siege was finally lifted, came the dread Poliomyelitis and most of its victims were young. Cinemas and other places that were open through the blitz were now closed to prevent crowds from gathering.

All this suffering the Maltese people took with courage and forbearance. Their simplicity and faith in God,which had enabled them to survive the loss of their homes and buildings, 1600 people killed, 1800 wounded and 2000 lightly injured would not waver in their determination that they would survive and create a new life. Victory was theirs.

Our squadron had many brave and determined pilots but there was something charismatic about Flight Lieutenant Stan Muller-Rowland. He loved combat and seemed indifferent to danger. Quietly spoken, slightly built, he had a ready smile and liked horseplay. He and his two brothers, born in Woking and educated at Uppingham, all joined the RAF. His older brother, Eric, a pilot on Beauforts with 42 Squadron, was killed in action over Pantellaria - a small island south of Malta. His twin brother, John, survived the war (with a DSO and a DFC) but was killed in 1950 flying an experimental 'Swallow', a flying wing, out of Farnborough. Stan survived his tour with 39 Squadron but was killed in 1944 while flying Beaufighters with 236 Squadron in England. Stan and I had an incident which I will describe later.

Thus all three brothers of the remarkable Muller-Rowland family lost their lives flying for their country.

In late March, W/C Gaine led nine Beauforts, escorted by nine Beaufighters, to attack a convoy off the toe of Italy. We led the third VIC. The convoy consisted of two merchant vessels, 'Marco Foscarini' (6,000 Tons) and the 'Nicolo Tammaseo' (5,000 tons), escorted by a destroyer and two torpedo boats. The convoy was en route from Taranto to Bizerta. It had an air cover of two JU-88s and ten ME-109s. The flak was intense. W/C Gaine, F/Sgt. Twiname, F/L Muller-Rowland and us all claimed hits on the two merchantmen; none were sunk but the convoy had to put into Messina for repairs. A Beaufort flown by an Australian pilot named Fraser was shot down by an ME-109 but the crew managed to ditch and were picked up by one of the torpedo boats to be POW.

Then on the night of 11/12 April, 1943, came the catastrophe for our crew.

FO. LEE HEIDE.

City Flyers In Action Over Sicily

Four Vancouver flyers are mentioned in despatches from North Africa as having taken part in large-scaled raids on Messina and Axis shipping in the Sicilian campaign.

Destruction of a 5000-ton Axis tanker, bombing of a 1000-ton tanker which was left sinking, and direct hits on a 9000-ton supply-ship was part of the day's work for the Canadian airmen.

FO. Lee Heide, son of Mr. and Mrs. A. J. Heide, 1317 East Fourteenth, navigator, said a torpedo from his aircraft scored one of two hits on the supply ship. He said the 5000-ton tanker was blown "sky-high."

STAGED AIR CIRCUS.

"That tanker went up 1500 feet," said FO. Heide after returning flyers had staged an air circus over their home field to celebrate the successful outing.

We were briefed on a convoy of five merchant ships escorted by three Italian destroyers and a flak ship en route from Sicily to Tunis. Four Beauforts and three torpedo-carrying Wellingtons took off. It was a foul night. We were in cloud immediately at 5,000 feet and had no idea where the other aircraft were. Our Met forecasts were generally of little use. More by luck than good management I found the convoy on the radar.

'I've got them,' I said on the intercom. 'Harry, turn 20 degrees Port . . . range is 18 miles . . . looks like ten ships.'

'I'll start to let down,' Harry put the aircraft into a shallow descent. At 1,000 feet we were still in cloud and Harry was reluctant to go any lower. Then we glimpsed a ship as we passed directly over the convoy. The ASV was of little use low down as targets got mixed up with the sea returns.

Harry made a wide turn, let down to 500 feet but we were still in low cloud and fog. 'It's no use . . . I can't make an attack . . . I can't see a damn thing.'

Harry pulled up. Then all hell broke lose. We were right over the convoy; every gun in the escorts seemed to open fire at once. We had been told that the Italian Navy did not have radar-controlled guns but I reckon that information was false. There was an almighty crash as we took hits in the mid-section. The Beaufort staggered and rose in the air as if a giant hand had lifted it. Shrapnel careened around and cordite stained the air.

'Crew . . . report in,' Harry's voice was hollow.

'I'm all right,' I said.

'I'm hit,' Taffy said, 'but it's not serious.'

There was no reply from Ginger.

'Lee,' Harry had his voice back under control. 'Give me a course for Malta and see what's happened to Ginger.'

'Steer due east,' I made a note of the time in my log. 'How are the engines?'

THE MALTA FRONT :

3,000,000 Gallons Of Axis Petrol Goes Up In Flames

ENEMY TANKER TORPEDOED OFF SICILY

The following communique, issued by the Information Office at 5 p.m., covers the period of 24 hours ending 4 p.m., February 22 :

OUR torpedo-bombers struck a heavy blow at the Axis last night when they sank a very large enemy tanker off Sicily. The tanker had been found by our reconnaissance aircraft and had been previously attacked. Yesterday she was again sighted, this time stationary off the coast of Western Sicily, which suggested that she had been damaged in the first attack.

Malta-based torpedo-bombers went out again, and the tanker made a good target in the light of the full moon. A salvo of torpedoes struck her amidships. A tremendous explosion followed immediately and the entire ship was enveloped in flames. She burned furiously, with continuous explosions punctuating the fires, and sending up mushrooms of smoke. An hour later the tanker was still afloat, so another of our aircraft put a further torpedo into her. The vessel then began to settle in the water and by midnight had broken up. At two o'clock this morning — only six hours after the attack — her only remains were some pieces of frame work floating in a large patch of burning oil.

Many of our aircraft brought back their torpedoes from this attack, as to aim them at the burning ship would have been a needless waste. From the fury of the fires aboard this tanker it would appear that she was laden with petrol. A tanker of this size would hold about 3,000,000 gallons of petrol.

RCAF Son Of News-Herald Employee Escapes Death When Plane Shot Up

'Okay.' Harry replied.

The radio compartment was a shambles and only the armour plate in front of it had saved Harry from injury. It appeared that a shell had exploded right in front of Ginger. He was semi-conscious, slumped across his table, moaning. I undid his Mae West. His whole upper body was covered in blood. I lowered him to the deck and shouted for Taffy to come and help.

He came forward and saw Ginger. 'Good Christ!'

'Where are you hit?' I asked.

'In the ass . . . but I'm okay.'

'Get the medical kit while I try to get his upper clothes off.' The shrapnel had made a mess of his chest and stomach. Some of the wounds were shallow but others were deep and bleeding freely. I gave him a shot of morphine and we bandaged the wounds as best we could. He lost consciousness. 'Oh, Ginger,' I pleaded, 'don't die!'

We took off our Mae Wests and sweaters and tried to keep him warm.

'Let's have a look at you,' I said to Taffy, 'pull your trousers down.'

He did so. A glancing piece of shrapnel had made a shallow groove across one cheek. I put some mercurochrome on it and it stopped bleeding.

Taffy winced. 'Don't tell anyone where I got hit, will you?'

'Why not?'

'Well, it's embarrassing . . . people will think I was running away from something.'

'Not likely. Your turret is armour plated . . . how did you get hit?'

'When the shit started to fly I lowered my seat to get right behind the armour plate but I forgot that the flak was coming up from below.'

'Tough luck. Look after Ginger while I tell Harry what's going on.'

I filled Harry in, adding that he was lucky that a piece of armour plate separated him from the radio compartment. 'How are things here?'

'The engines were not hit, thank God, so we are still flying but the tail plane took some damage judging by the feel of the rudder. I can't jettison the torpedo; a shell must have damaged the mechanism.' We later discovered that our lives had been saved by the torpedo taking several hits. Fortunately, it was not armed and so didn't explode.

'I'll try to find out where we are,' I started for the nose.

'No need,' Harry said. 'I've got the Malta radio beacon. Go and tend to Ginger.'

Ginger did not regain consciousness. Harry reported our situation to base and an ambulance was waiting our arrival. His wounds were too severe to be treated in Malta and he was taken to Cairo by air ambulance on the next day. Ginger recovered but it was slow and painful. We never saw him again but he did write us a letter.

The loss of Ginger was devastating. The life and spirit seemed to go out of us without his cheerfulness and vivacity. Harry and I would try a joke but it would fall flat. Taffy would sink into one of his Welsh funks and go a whole day barely saying a word. We worried about Ginger but Cairo was so far away that we got no reports on his condition.

Oh, we did our job. We acquired a new WOP named Neil Adams but he was a taciturn Scot who was just trying to finish his tour and never said much. Fortunately, April was a quiet month. We did some 'gardening' and a few Rovers but no convoy attacks.

Then in May the RAF saved Harry and me. The squadron stood down. The aircrew were to convert to Beaufighters! The ground crew and admin staff were to go to an airfield near Tunis which would be our new home. Taffy and Neil were posted to a Wellington squadron.

It was exactly what we needed! A new aircraft, a new mission and away from Malta! We were overjoyed! To add to our delight Harry was promoted to Pilot Officer and we would now be together.

Chapter Seven:

Tunisia

For some reason not known to us Wing Commander Gaine left the squadron; his place was taken by Sqn Ldr Harvey, O.C. of 'A' Flight, who was promoted. Stan Muller-Rowland received his Sqn Ldr and took over 'A' Flight. Of the 18 crews who had been on the squadron when we arrived, none had completed a tour and only three remained: Muller-Rowland; Major Don Tilley (a South African) and Paddy Garland (a Canadian). How many other crews had come and gone, I don't know.

On the first of June, 1943, we left Malta for our new base at Protville, near Tunis. Just Harry and I. We found a bare airfield. Our ground crews had not arrived and nobody was expecting us. We ended up sleeping under our aircraft and scrounging some food.

After a couple of unpleasant days we left our old Beauforts there and hitched a ride to Egypt in a Wellington. We would convert to Beaufighters at Shallufa while our ground forces established a camp at Protville.

Harry's conversion started with 'dual' instruction by an experienced pilot. This consisted of being shown what to do and then doing it while the instructor stood nervously behind the seat watching every move and trying not to interfere. This was followed by formation flying and, when I joined Harry, torpedo and bombing runs and flak suppression exercises.

Part of my conversion consisted of learning about the radio transceiver and sending and receiving morse code at 20 words a minute; practice flights were done in a Beaufort with the same transceiver. Another task was to study the electrical system of the Beaufighter since the panels were in my position and my responsibility; they were somewhat complex and took time to master. (I had now been trained as a navigator, a radio operator, an engineer, a bomb aimer, a gunner and a cruise-and-landing pilot).

'Making - do'

Our new Mk 'X' Beaufighters had two 1,770 HP Hercules XVII engines giving a top speed of 300 mph at 1,500 feet. The aircraft were rated for sea level and the engines did not have superchargers. Armament was four Hispano 20-mm canon in the nose, six 303 Browning machine guns in the wings and one Browning in the rear cupola. However, we replaced the wing machine guns with fuel tanks for better range and, since I had a choice, the rear machine gun was taken out of our aircraft. The aircraft could carry one 2,000 lb torpedo or four 250-lb bombs over a range of about 1,500 miles. It could fly on one engine provided that the other prop was 'feathered' - blades stopped and turned into wind. The engine noise seemed to flow out behind the aircraft and it was difficult to hear a Beaufighter coming. The Germans called it 'Whispering Death'.

The crew layout consisted of a pilot's cockpit in the nose with a fabulous view and a navigator Wop cockpit in the rear with a good view aft. Entrance to both positions was via a ladder/hatch which closed flush with the fuselage. The space between the crew was occupied by the four 20-mm canons and their magazines which held 250 rounds per gun. There was an armoured door aft of the pilot which, when closed, prevented the crew from seeing each other.

The front cockpit was not easy to enter. The pilot would climb up his ladder. His seat would collapse and buckle forward; he would then grab two bars on the side of the perspex hatch and swing himself into position. A crewman would assist to pull the seat upright and help with the shoulder straps. (We did not carry parachutes since we seldom flew high enough to use them). Once in place, the cockpit was roomy and the controls and instruments well placed. The upper hatch was used as an emergency exit.

The rear cockpit was entered by the ladder/hatch which a crewman would close. There was a swivel seat behind a table which could be folded up against the fuselage. To the right, slightly aft, was the radio transceiver and morse key along with read-outs of height, airspeed etc. The cupola was hinged on the starboard side for exit. It was also the navigator's job to clear any jam in the canons which happened occasionally in level flight and always in negative 'G'.

The Beaufighter had great power, speed and rugged good looks. It could take a lot of punishment and still stay in the air. Photos of returning aircraft with trees in their wings, missing wing tips, large

'Beaufighter'

holes in the fuselage and battered engines are legion.

We inspected our new kite, named 'J' for Johnny with a pair of baby boots painted on the nose, prior to our first flight together. 'How do you like the Beau?' I asked.

'Great!' Harry enthused. 'It's only poor feature is a tendency to swing on take-off. When you open the taps it really responds. How about you?'

'Lovely! Everything I need is right handy. The canopy is a bit close to my head but I can live with it.'

'I see you had your machine gun taken out?'

'Yeah . . . I'd rather have the space and the visibility to give you directions if there is anyone on our tail. Do you mind?'

Harry shrugged. 'It's up to you.'

After our conversion we got a week's leave. Harry stayed at the Gezira Club, informing me that he couldn't get into trouble in Cairo because W/C Harvey's father was the Chief of Police! He dropped me in Alex. My romance with Susan had not diminished and we had great fun; my friend at the Cecil Hotel obliged with a nice room. Looking back, I am amazed at the freedom we had with our aircraft. They were ours and we could go wherever we liked. For instance, Stan wanted to see the Holy Land so he and his navigator flew to Tel Aviv. We carried vouchers for gas and oil in case there was no RAF base there.

On the 18 June we set out again for Protville with a refuelling stop at Benghazi. There were two airfields at Protville, a mile or so apart, each with a 6,000 foot runway of silty clay loam rolled hard. At Protville II, our base, the previous tenants had left a reminder in

FW 190

the form of an almost intact FW-190.

Our ground crews had arrived and set up a camp of sorts - all under canvas. (More on living under canvas later). In Malta we had centralized maintenance and hence did not get to know the aircraftsmen who worked on our machines very well. This now changed and we had our own Fitter (engines) and Rigger (airframe). They would work only on our Beaufighter. The Fitter was named Alan and the Rigger was Victor. We would become fast friends because our lives were in their hands. Both were Corporals.

The main evacuation of the Germans and Italians from Tunisia took place at Cape Bon, a few miles north-east of Tunis. We heard that they had departed in such a hurry that much of their equipment had been left behind. So five of us set off one day in a 1,500 - weight, with Stan Muller-Roland driving, to have a look. From a low hill overlooking the beach the sight was astonishing; more than a mile was littered with vehicles of all kinds.

Most of it was immobilized. The field guns had been spiked. The interiors of tanks were a mess, probably from a grenade or two being tossed inside. Most of the cars and trucks had been machine-gunned. However, checking closely for booby traps, we found two vehicles that would still operate. One was a small Volks, a 'Peoples Car', that didn't need a key; we just pushed the starter button and it fired. The other was a big Mercedes-Benz staff car with armour-plated sides, no roof and damaged inside. It had no key but one of our guys (with a misspent youth?) hot wired it and we got it going.

Stan and I drove the staff car home. We had only gone a very short way when we sniffed the air and recognized the 'burble-burble'. 'Diesel!' we said, simultaneously.

'What will we do for fuel,' I asked, knowing that the squadron didn't have any.

'Don't know,' Stan replied. 'Maybe we can find some in Tunis.'

But we couldn't find diesel fuel anywhere so we put in 100-Octane laced with a little oil. It was great fun to drive! We often went from 'A' to 'B' in a straight line, ignoring hedges, ditches, fields or whatever. But it didn't last long; the engine ran so hot that the block cracked and that was the end of it. But it was great while it lasted!

Two other camps were set up at Protville and we were joined by 47 and 144 Squadrons, both flying Beaufighters, giving us a three-squadron Wing. Six new aircraft arrived from England for us, bringing 39 Squadron strength to sixteen.

Now came a flurry of activity.

On 11 July, 1943, photo recce found a convoy of one 4,000-ton MV escorted by two destroyers and a flak ship going south down the Italian coast. Stan Muller-Rowland led eight Beaus, four with torpedoes and four anti-flak. We did not fly this day. The MV was hit in the bows and crippled and a destoyer was also damaged by a torpedo. Returning to base our Beaus were jumped by ME-109s. A fierce fight followed. F/L McIntyre was shot down; he was killed but his navigator, Sgt. Fletcher, survived to become a POW. Stan's aircraft was so badly damaged that he had to crash land at Protville.

On 12 July we got word of two large troopships of 12,000 and 8,000 tons in the Bonificio Strait between Sardinia and Corsica, escorted by two flak ships. W/C Harvey led eight Beaus, four with torpedoes of which we were one, and four anti-flak. On the outbound leg two of the anti-flak aircraft peeled off to strafe a train ferry and then rejoined the formation. We led the second pair with torpedoes. Getting ready to attack we could see the W/C Harvey or his wingman had hit the larger ship so we went after the other one. Both ours and our wingman's torpedoes hit and the ship simply blew up in a blazing inferno - it must have been carrying ammunition.

'Way to go!' I shouted.

But we were sad to see a Beau ditch with its port engine in flames. The pilot, F/O Dodd, got out of the aircraft and was made POW but his navigator, Sgt. Fox, was killed.

Living under canvas left a lot to be desired. Harry and I shared a tent. It had a table with two drawers on which rested a kerosene lamp. There were two chairs. A metal rod on two stands was used for hanging clothes. The beds had a metal rod running length-wise overhead from which mosquito netting was hung. There were a variety of biting bugs at night and we always 'cleared' our netting before going to bed. In one location (from which we moved smartly) there were so many ants that we placed all legs in tins of water. I never saw a scorpion but I shook out my shoes each morning as I had been told to do. Considering how hot it was during the day, it was amazing how chilly it got at night; we usually slept with two blankets underneath and one on top.

Worst of all were the flies. The Mess tent was sprayed continuously but the little demons got in anyway. It was standard practice to eat only with the right hand, leaving the left to ward off flies. One day a fly settled on my left hand. I waved it off. It made a small circuit and returned to the same spot. I waved it off a total of 19 times; on the 20th I killed it. I could catch a fly in flight.

There must be zillions and zillions of flies in the desert. Where do they all come from? And what do they live on when there are no people about?

Privy

On 14 July we found a convoy off the coast of Sicily. It consisted of two tankers, one called the 'Captaine de Diabat' of 3,000 tons and a smaller one of 1,500 tons. Their escort was two flak ships with a cover of six Macchi-202s. Stan led our force of 8 Beaus with torpedoes and 8 for anti-flak. He led us to the larger MV while the anti-flak Beaus went after the flak ships and the Macchis. It seemed that both Stan and his wingman had hit the ship when we came in; our torpedo was the culmination and the MV sank in towering flames.

I winced as I saw one of the anti-flak Beaus crash into the sea and explode; both the pilot, F/L Cartwright, and his navigator, Sgt. Colley, were killed.

Harry put the nose down and we passed between the burning ship and a flak ship. When out of range of the flak ships, Harry climbed to look at the carnage below. That's when a Macchi got on our tail. My head was on a swivel and I picked him up as he was closing in. It was up to me to tell Harry which way to turn to avoid the attack. Too soon, and the fighter would just turn with us. Too late, and we would be full of bullet holes.

I gave Harry the warning: 'Macchi on our tail'. When I thought the range was right, I said: 'Turn Port . . . Port . . . GO!' On the word 'GO' Harry threw the Beau into a vicious turn and headed for the deck at full speed. I was a bit late with my command and a row of bullet holes stitched across our tail plane. The Macchi turned, rolled and came in again. 'Get ready,' I said, 'here he comes again.'

Just as the Macchi was lining us up a Beaufighter crept up behind him. The four 20-mm canons literally blew the Macchi out of the sky; it just disintegrated in front of my eyes. I gave our friend a thumbs-up and told Harry what had happened.

Thus, in three days, we had sunk three MVs, damaged several escorts and shot down one Macchi. But it cost us three crews and four aircraft.

A few days later Harry was promoted to Flying Officer.

On the following morning I walked to the flight line. Alan had the port engine cowling off and was doing his D.I. (Daily Inspection). Victor was patching the holes in the tail. It was a blistering hot day, 95°F and only 0900 hours, and they wore only shorts and a slouch hat.

'Good Morning,' I said to Victor.

'Mornin', Sir.'

'How's it going?'

'Almost finished. Try not to bring it back with holes in it,' he grumbled. After all, it was HIS airframe!

'We'll try,' I replied, dryly. 'Where are you from, Victor?' He was 21 years old, about 5'9" tall, sandy hair and blue eyes.

'South London.'

'Did you know anything about aeroplanes before you joined the RAF?'

'No. There was an airfield near our house and I always liked to watch the aeroplanes.'

We chatted for a few more minutes and then Victor asked: 'Could you loan me 50 Bob (about $12) until payday, Sir?'

'I guess so.' I knew there was a running poker game in the NCOs Mess and that Victor liked to gamble. 'Cards not going well?'

'No . . . but they'll change.'

Harry and I borrowed the small Volks and went to Tunis. Once there, we disabled the car by removing the rotor arm. It was an Islamic city of about one million people, crowded and somewhat dirty. The oldest building was the Great Mosque, built in the 8th Century. It was very hot so we spent some time in the cool interior of the Dar Ben Abdallah Museum. The area around Lake Tunis was pleasant with many fine homes. We inquired about Carthage, about 10 kms north of Tunis, but were told that the Romans did such a goof job of destruction in 146 B.C. that there was very little to see.

There were a lot of Americans in Tunis from, we discovered, a Supply Depot and a major hospital. Over drinks in the late afternoon we chatted with a doctor from the hospital. 'Why don't you come to the hospital tonight . . . Bob Hope is giving an open-air concert . . . it's free and everyone is welcome.'

'Thanks!' we replied, and got directions.

The show was good, Bob Hope having his usual entourage with Skinny Ennis and Francis Langford. There were about 200 spectators, who showed their appreciation with cheers and whistles. After the performance we went to the Officer's Club. Hope appeared and, after a few drinks, was persuaded to sit at the piano and tell jokes. His stories were foul. They were sexually explicit and biased. I could see some nurses frowning.

I looked at Harry and he nodded; we went to the bar in the next room. Neither of us could stand such filth. Several people joined us.

Our next strike was on 21 July. Stan led six aircraft against a convoy of two MVs escorted by four destroyers and four flak ships. Harry and I did not fly this day. The flak was fierce and no hits were seen on either of the MVs. P/O Hunter, a New Zealander, and his navigator, Sgt. Booth, were shot down but became POW.

Through the next couple of weeks we flew some Rovers but there was no action.

Then, on 12 August, Sqn Ldr Petch, Commander of 'B' Flight, led eight Beaus on a Rover south of Naples. Harry and I did not fly this day. They made no sightings but had the bad luck to get jumped by four ME-109s and two FW-190s. In the battle that followed Flight Sgt. Spackman, a Canadian, and his navigator, Sgt. Lawson, were shot down but survived to become POW. A Beau flown by W/O Patterson returned to Protville badly shot up with the navigator, Sgt. Cole, dead in the back seat.

On 16 August, Stan led eight aircraft in our standard mix of four with torpedoes and four anti-flak. We led the second pair with torpedoes. We found the convoy north of Naples with two MVs of 3,000 tons each, escorted by three destroyers. This was one of our most successful strikes. Stan and his wingman attacked one MV and both torps hit. Harry held off until he saw the results of Stan's drop and then went for the second MV; both ours and our wingman's torps hit. Both vessels sank. The anti-flak Beaus left one destroyer on fire. No aircraft were lost.

One day in September Stan Muller-Rowland said to me: 'Lee, I want to practice some dog-fighting against Paddy Garland. My navigator, Gary, is sick. Will you fly with me?'

'Sure,' I replied. I felt sorry for Stan. He was near the end of his tour and his nerves were fragile. He had the tent next to ours and I could hear him screaming with nightmares. Also, I knew that he felt badly about his brother getting killed.

Today's flight was not to help his composure.

We took off and flew over the water, climbing to 7,000 feet. Since we could not win a dog fight with a FW-190 or an ME-109, our nemesis in the air because of their superior speed and turning power, our usual tactic was to head for the sea at full throttle with the navigator facing backwards to give evasive instructions. It was difficult for the enemy fighter to attack at very low level and more than one had hit the sea trying to do so. Another tactic was to pull the throttles back and slam down full flap; the Beau rose like an elevator and the enemy fighter would over-shoot.

Stan made some attacks on Paddy and then it was his turn to attack us. I gave Stan some mild jinks and turns and then when Paddy got into firing position I called: 'Buster (full speed) . . . turn Port . . . turn Port . . . GO!'

Stan rammed the throttles forward and threw the Beau into a high 'G' turn. Then there was an almighty 'Bang' as the port engine seized; the prop tore off and spun over my canopy a bare five feet over my head.

Stan jammed on rudder and fought the controls as we went into a spiral dive. He finally got control at about 1,500 feet.

'What the hell caused that?' I asked, shakily.

'Don't know . . . my instruments didn't show anything . . . looks like a complete loss of oil.' His voice was strained.

We were now in a gentle descent. The aircraft would not maintain height even with the other engine at full power.

'Can you make the shore?' I asked. 'I hate getting wet.'

'I think so . . . I'll try to put her down on the beach.'

'Okay.' I thought about my canopy. There were stories of it jamming in a crash landing and the navigator being unable to get out which could be very awkward if there was a fire. If I released the catches and gave it a sharp push upwards, the slipstream should tear it away. But it might hit the tail and give Stan another problem when he had enough already. I decided to leave it in place.

'Lee, there's a plowed field just back of the shore. It looks like a better place to put down. I'll leave the gear up . . . get ready.'

'All right,' I stuffed my navigation articles in their bag, stowed the table against the fuselage, turned my seat around so that it was facing the rear and slumped down a little so that my head was resting against the seat back. 'Oh shit!' I mumbled. 'Here we go!'.

It was a rough landing as the Beau hit the ground, bounced once and then careened across the field coming to a stop just short of a deep drainage ditch. Again came that complete, eerie silence broken only by the ticking of the hot starboard engine, its propeller blades folded back like a half-peeled banana. There was no fire and my canopy opened as did Stan's escape hatch. Aside from a sore back, I was not injured but Stan had a nasty bump on his forehead from striking the gun sight.

Paddy had given a running commentary to base as he circled above us, waving as we both climbed out of the aircraft. A local farmer appeared, bemused at the sight of the interloper in his field. A car came to pick us up and a crane and crash tender retrieved the Beau a few days later.

On 8 Sep, 1943, Italy surrendered. This made little difference to our operations as the Germans fought on even harder. The Italian Fleet, based in Taranto, which had never left harbour to fight, now sailed in surrender to Malta. By 10 Sep there were 28 warships of all types laying at anchor off the island. After a week the number grew to 65 and the brave people of Malta knew that their war was finally over. Admiral Sir Andrew Cunningham sent the following signal to London:

"PLEASE TO INFORM THEIR LORDSHIPS THAT THE
ITALIAN BATTLE FLEET NOW LIES AT ANCHOR
UNDER THE GUNS OF THE FORTRESS OF MALTA."

On 15 Sep Stan led eleven Beaus against a tanker, escorted by four flak ships, off the Italian coast. The flak was intense and the tanker took prompt evasive action. No hits were seen. Two aircraft were shot down. F/O Howard and his navigator, Sgt. Goldie, were taken POW. But F/Os Yorke and Matthias had an adventure. They were picked up out of the water by Italian sailors and taken to the island of Gapraia. Here they persuaded some Italians to defect and sailed to the island of Ponza, off Naples, which had been taken by the Allies. From there they went by U.S. launch to Capri; thence by the Royal Navy to Malta where we sent an aircraft to pick them up.

This was Stan's last mission with 39 Squadron. He was posted to Shallufa as an instructor. He had a DFC and Bar.

We shoe-horned six people in the small Volks and went into Tunis for his farewell party. The Restaurant de Bleuet, on Rue Marsailles, was a night club that stayed open to all hours and had music and belly dancers. We drank too much of course and serenaded Stan with our squadron song:

'When you hear the news that a ship has been sunk,
That another Jerry cruiser is just a heap of junk,
Then you know that the boys are going to get drunk.
That's good old 39
Torping shipping.
Everybody thinks it's awfully ripping.
Look out for that mast!
Or it may be your last!'

When we came out of the club in the wee hours of the morning our Volks was gone. 'Damn!' I swore, 'Some rotten sod had a spare rotor arm!' We finally had to roust a taxi driver out of bed to get back to the airfield.

A couple of days later, coming in to land after an air test, I spotted a Volks in front of 47 Squadron on the other side of the airfield.

'Hey,' I said to Harry, 'that looks like our Volks.'

So we sneaked across the airfield late at night and stole it back again. I believe it changed hands several times; it had an adventurous life - that Volks!

Intelligence reported that the Germans had withdrawn from Sardinia to Corsica in good order with all their arms and equipment. All their ferries and transport aircraft went to Bastia, on the north coast of Corsica. From there they withdrew to Leghorn, in Italy, mostly by JU-52, a three-engine transport.

Both 47 and 39 Squadrons were sent out after these transports. On 23 Sep two Beaus from each squadron attacked and shot down two JU-52s. Later on the same day two Beaus from our squadron shot down two more JU-52s but neither of our aircraft returned. F/L McCurdy and his navigator, Sgt. Burton, became POW. F/O Cox whose navigator, Sgt. Speary, was badly wounded, managed to get to Italy where Speary was taken to a U.S. hospital.

On the morning of the next day Sqn Ldr Petch, one of our Flight Commanders, led four Beaus against a stream of JU-52s escorted by ME-109s. One transport was shot down but so was Petch. He and his navigator, F/O Williams, became POW.

Later that same day, 24 Sep, F/L Butler led five Beaus with Harry as his Number Two. Butler had engine trouble and had to return to base so we took over the lead of the remaining four aircraft. We found eight JU-52 in the strait between Corsica and Elba, escorted by three ME-109s. Harry gave the order for two Beaus to attack from the port side while we and our wingman attacked from the starboard. I saw one JU-52 break formation and head for the sea when raked by our canon fire. Unfortunately, I also saw F/O Twiname, a Canadian pilot, and his navigator, Sgt. McCleod, peel off and go down - both were killed.

Harry rolled out and came in again for another attack. In the confusing melee of the fight it was difficult to see exactly what was going on. Our wingman was not with us anymore; the JU-52s had dispersed and we could not spot the ME-109s. Going after a stray JU-52, neither Harry nor I saw the ME-109 that got us; it may have come up from below. Canon shells thudded into the port engine as the Beau shook, vibrated and headed for the sea in a steep dive. The port propeller slowed down and then speeded up as it began to windmill.

Harry got control at about 2,000 feet. For some reason, for which we were thankful, the ME-109 didn't follow us down.

'Are you hit?' Harry's voice was shaky.

'No . . . are you?' My voice was equally shaky.

'No . . . but I can't get proper control. There's no oil pressure left in the port engine so I can't feather the prop; it's windmilling in fine pitch and creating max drag.'

'Can you hold height?'

'I don't think so.'

Harry managed to slow down the rate of descent but we were still sinking and the aircraft was vibrating badly. At 500 feet Harry said: 'I can't hold it, Lee. We'll have to ditch.'

'Okay'. For some reason I was quite calm. I sent out three SOS, knowing that we were too far away from base and too low, for them to be received and screwed the key down.

'Brace yourself,' Harry said, 'the sea is rough.'

'Right.' I stuffed my navigation articles in their bag, stowed the table against the fuselage, turned my seat around so that it was facing the rear and slumped down a little so that my head was resting against the seat back. 'Oh, shit!' I mumbled, 'here we go again!'

Chapter Eight

Elba

Harry did his best with the ditching but the sea was rough and the laws of physics are immutable - water does not compress. The aircraft slammed into the sea like running your car into a brick wall at 50 mph. My seat tore loose from its mounts and I tumbled backwards into the ammunition cans; I was bruised but not hurt. I looked forward to see Harry opening his emergency hatch - Good! - he was not hurt.

I threw off my straps, opened my cupola, inflated my Mae West and jumped into the water. The dinghy had popped out of the wing and self-inflated as it was supposed to do on contact with the water with its immersion switches.

Let me now describe this dinghy, which was to be our abode for the next five days and four nights. It was circular, about six feet in diameter with an oval brim about two feet high, and was made of a thick, heavy polyethylene material. It came equipped with two paddles, a drogue anchor, a hand bellows for re-inflation, a canvas bucket for bailing, two cans of drinking water (one large and one small), a Very Pistol with six flares, two packages of yellow florescent dye, small rations of hardtack and Horlick's tablets, two collapsible poles about five feet long, three grooved wooden cones for repairing leaks and a knife.

As I swam towards the dinghy Harry emerged from his hatch, walked across the wing and stepped into the dinghy. He didn't even get wet - that would come later! 'Are you hurt?' he shouted.

'Just some bruises,' I yelled. 'How about you?'

'Sore head,' He pointed to a swelling on his forehead, 'where I hit the gun sight.'

Now I could see that the dinghy was only partially inflated. 'What's the matter with the dinghy?'

'Must have a hole.'

At this point the Beaufighter sank with loud gurgles. It had floated for only 30 seconds. The dinghy was tethered to the aircraft by a cord so that it wouldn't float away and there was a quick-release catch to set it free as the aircraft sank.

'Where's the hole?' I asked.

'I dunno.' He looked around the inside as I swam around the outside.

'I found it,' I said. It was low on the outside of the brim and quite large; it had likely snagged on some sharp metal while coming out of the wing.

'Get me the biggest cone,' I said.

Harry handed it to me. It was about a foot long, six inches wide at the bottom tapering to two inches at the top. It had grooves and was meant to be screwed in but the hole was larger than the cone. 'Damn!' I swore. 'Get me some cord . . . maybe I can bind it up.'

By this time the dinghy was so low in the water that the waves were breaking over it and filling it with water. The larger can of drinking water had floated away. I was having trouble staying up in the water because my desert boots were now water-logged and pulling me down. So I took them off and tossed them into the dinghy. In the confusion, they floated away which was to have dire effects.

Harry cut the tethering cord and handed it to me. I bunched up the material around the cone and wrapped the cord around and around; it was the best I could do but it always had a slow leak and the dinghy had to be topped up frequently.

I clambered into the dinghy. 'Which do you want to do,' I asked, 'bail or top-up?'

'I'll start with the bellows,' Harry replied. 'We can trade later.'

'Okay,' I started bailing.

In about half an hour the dinghy was inflated with a half-inch of water on the bottom.

We took off our Mae Wests and our clothes and tried to get dry. I hadn't been able to get the water from the bottom of the dinghy with the canvas bailer so we used our shirts as sponges to remove most of the water. The dinghy was pitching up and down through waves and troughs about three feet high.

'I hope you're not sea sick,' I said.

'Not usually . . . how about you?'

'I'm okay. How's your head?'

'I've got a head ache.' The bruise on his forehead was turning purple. 'But I've got some codeine.' He fished a small bottle from one of his pouches. (We were both wearing our escape belts). He washed the pills down with a swallow from the small water container.

'Where's the big water container?' I asked.

'It got washed overboard, along with your boots.'

'Too bad . . . we'll have to ration the water.'

'Yes. I wonder how long we'll be in this dinghy and where we'll wash ashore?'

'I've got a map,' I replied, 'but we don't need it. You can see both Corsica and Elba from here.' I pointed. 'This strait is about 40 miles wide. We seem to be a bit closer to Elba . . . about 15 miles or so.'

'Can you tell which way we are drifting?'

'South, I think. I'll take a bearing and let you know shortly.'

After about two hours the dinghy needed to be topped up again and Harry did this. Resting afterwards, he said: 'You know what?'

'No, what?'

'Our families will get a telegram saying that we are 'Missing in Action'.'

'Oh, hell!' I responded. 'I never thought of that. Still, it should be only for a few days; either we'll evade capture and get to the Allied lines or we'll be taken POW in which case the Red Cross will notify them.'

'I guess so.' Harry was sad.

We were silent for a while, each with our own thoughts. Then, about 1600 hours, we spotted a formation of six Beaufighters flying south. I got out the Very Pistol and fired a red flare. One of the Beaus saw it and circled us for a few minutes. It dropped something in the water but it landed too far away to be retrieved.

'Do you think they were from our squadron?' I asked.

'Don't know. Can you tell now which way we are drifting?'

I lined up my markers. 'South . . . no doubt about it.'

'X marks the ditching spot!'

'I guess we're at the mercy of the wind and the currents. These little paddles,' Harry held one up, 'are no good in a sea like this.'

'You're right.'

We got dressed but our clothes were still damp. After a little dry food and a sip of water, we prepared for the night. But it was impossible to sleep in the damp and cold with the dinghy pitching worse as the night went on and having to be topped up every two hours or so.

By dawn the wind velocity had increased to 30-35 mph and waves were close to breaking over the dinghy. We were both quite miserable. In the afternoon the enemy found us. Three Arado - 190s (an Italian single-engine float plane) swept down the strait, about a mile apart, obviously looking for us. When one spotted us the other two came over and they circled around.

Then one Arado made an attempt to land. He came in slow, flaps down, but as he neared the water he decided that the waves were too high and pulled up.

'Do you think that they'll fire at us,' I asked, 'since they can't pick us up?'

'I don't think so. The Arado has no forward-firing guns and I don't see anybody at a window with a machine gun.'

'I hope they're Italians and not Germans!'

'Me, too.'

The Arados hung around for about 20 minutes and then flew away. We both breathed a sigh of relief.

'We're drifting south-east now,' I remarked. 'You can see Elba fading.'

'Yeah.' Harry was despondent.

We were bored. We invented some word games to pass the time. One was to name all of the countries in a continent and their capital cities; this showed how weak our geography was after Europe and North America. Another was to go through the Greek alphabet but we only identified 16 out of 24 and these not in the right order. I made a mental note to add a deck of cards to my escape kit.

By evening the wind was so strong that some waves were breaking over the dinghy. The night was spent topping and bailing.

When dawn broke on day three we could see that we had drifted to a position about two miles south of the small island, Pianoso, just south of Elba, which we had not been able to see before as it was flat and low-lying.

'What's the name of that island?' Harry asked, as we bailed and topped.

'Pianoso.'

'Are there any Germans there?'

'I don't know. I wouldn't think so.'

'Do you think we could paddle to it?'

'It's worth a try.'

So we each took a paddle and rowed for about an hour but it was of no use. The sea was too rough and the wind and current pushed us away to the east.

At noon we had some dry food and a sip of water. Neither of us had an appetite.

In the afternoon our friendly Arado came to look us over. Since the sea was rougher than it had been yesterday, there was no chance of him landing. He obviously wanted to check our progress and see where we finally ended up.

'I wonder why they don't send a patrol boat to pick us up,' Harry speculated, 'since the Arado can't land.'

'Good question. I'll bet he's Italian . . . not German.'

After about 15 minutes the aircraft flew away.

Sitting in the dinghy, Harry was facing north, upwind and I was facing south. As the sun set, Harry said: 'look at that.'

'What?'

'The weather to the north of us.'

I turned around. Black, ominous clouds filled the northern sky. 'Oh, hell!' I exclaimed. 'We're in for a rough night.'

And so we were. The rain lashed into us as waves broke over the dinghy and we had to bail frantically. The cone plug loosened and we had to top-up every hour. It was a miserable night and we were close to exhaustion by the end of it.

Dawn on the fourth day found us drifted to a position about three miles due east of the southern tip of Pianoso. Now the wind and the current changed and we began to travel north towards Elba.

'I wish we had a sail,' I remarked.

'What are those two collapsible poles for?' Harry asked.

We fished them out. They were thin aluminum and extended to

five feet. There seemed to be no place to anchor them for a sail and we had no material that could be used for a sail. That plan came to a dead end.

In the late morning our Arado appeared but didn't linger long as a heavy storm gave thunder and lightening but little rain. Heavy seas arose and the dinghy had to be topped-up every half hour. We both realized that the cone plug was weakening and in danger of slipping out, in which case the dinghy would sink.

By late afternoon we were midway up Pianoso, still going north, and it appeared certain that we were going to land on Elba the next day.

'What do you know about Elba?' Harry asked.

'Napoleon was exiled there,' I replied, brightly.

'I'm sure that knowledge will be a great help to us,' Harry said, drily.

'Wait.' I fished in a pouch and extracted a map of the area that I had folded into three inches square and wrapped in plastic so that it wouldn't get wet. I had written some notes on the map. 'German occupied but mainly around the Capital city of Portoferraio which is on the north side of the island.'

'That may be a help since we are going to wash up on the south side.'

'Yeah. Sixteen miles long, three miles wide and very mountainous.'

'What else do you know?'

'Nothing.'

Here the conversation was interrupted for a spell of topping and bailing. To pass the time I suggested: 'Let's see if we can figure out when Napoleon was here.'

'Well,' Harry ventured, 'it was before Waterloo and that was in 1815.'

'Yeah . . . but how far before?'

'He was brought here in a British frigate,' Harry said, not answering the question.

'Really?'

'Yes.'

'How did he get back to France?'

'In a French boat, I guess.'

'How long was he on Elba?'

'I don't know. About two years, I think.'

'So what's your guess as to when he was on Elba?'

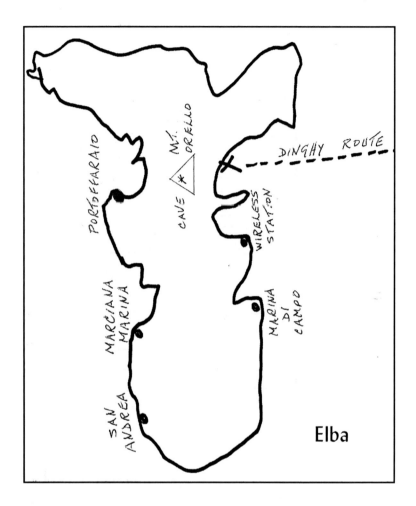

'From 1813 to 1814.'

'I bow to your superior knowledge of British history.'

We were wrong by a year.

It was getting dark now so we topped and bailed and got ready for another miserable night. The sea was as rough as ever but our spirits had improved with a landing on Elba in sight.

At dawn on the fifth day we were about two miles from the south coast of Elba. The sea was still running strong and the wind and current were favourable. By 1100 hours we were 200 yards off a rocky shore and faced the problem of being bashed on the rocks. Then we saw half a dozen people, who had noticed our plight, waving at us from on top of the rocks. On our first attempt to land we bashed against the rocks and then the undertow swept us out to sea again. Our second attempt was no better.

Then we saw that the people were pointing to a small, sandy beach to our left. Getting out the paddles we pushed the dinghy in that direction and made it on the fourth try. The Italians helped us ashore. We shouted 'Inglese' but it wasn't necessary - they knew we were.

We were not in good condition. The constant salt spray had chapped our lips and caked our faces and hair. Our eyes, already red from lack of sleep, were inflamed and sore. The swelling on Harry's forehead had gone down but it was still red. Our legs were so rubbery from five days of non-use that we staggered around like newly-born calves, each supported by an Italian. It took us a while to get our 'Land-Legs'.

Two men with machetes cut the dinghy into four pieces which they hid in the rocks. I had the impression that they had a use in mind for the polyethelene and would retrieve it later.

As we were led over a rocky trail from the beach I was immediately in trouble with just my stocking feet. I gestured to my guide about having no shoes but it made no impression. Nobody spoke English.

We were taken to a house where a buxom Italian lady fussed over us, made a meal and put us to bed. We realised that we were usurping someone's bed but were too exhausted to protest.

In the morning we rested and in the afternoon were sent off with a guide. He was about 25 years old, with dark eyes and a wild mop of hair that seemed to start in the middle of his forehead. He led us to a deserted Wireless Station on the coast where he removed bread, fruit and water from his back pack and indicated, by placing both hands on the side of his head, that we were to spend the night there. Then he left.

'Well, here we are,' Harry said, as we sat on the bare floor.

'Yeah. I wonder what's next?'

Who knows.'

I stood up and went into the small room which had a table and shelving and looked as if it had held the radio equipment. 'Eureka!' I shouted.

'What is it?'

I held up a dog-eared Italian/English dictionary. 'Now we can communicate.'

'Gimme.' Harry snatched it away and began to study.

Then I made another find. This was an old pair of running shoes which I adapted to my sore feet. The right one was intact but I had to use my Boy Scout knife to cut a hole in the toe because it was too small. The left shoe was in tatters but I found some rags and bound them around with the shoe lace. It was make-shift at best.

We spent the remaining daylight hours eating and having an Italian quiz. The bare floor was uncomfortable but we were still tired.

At mid-morning our guide rushed in and was quite startled when Harry greeted him in Italian: 'Buon giorno. Come sta?'

'Bene, grazie,' he smiled, revealing poor teeth.

'Come si chiama?'

'Tomas.'

Harry pointed to himself. 'Harry.' And then to me: 'Lee'.

Tomas nodded and then suddenly became very agitated as he remembered why he had rushed in. 'Ger-mans . . . pronto . . . pronto!' He waved at us to follow as he raced out of the building.

We crossed the road and ran up a hillside which was a vineyard with rows of vines; while the season was over there was still plenty of foliage and some grapes left on the vines. We had only gone up six rows when we heard the 'Tromp-Tromp' of boots. Tomas whispered; 'quieto . . . quieto' and gestured to us to lay down.

The German patrol passed about 25 feet below us - four soldiers led by a Corporal. We hardly dared to breathe. We found out later that they had looked in the Wireless Station and then continued to the small town of Marina Di Campo where they did a house-to-house search. Obviously, the Arado that had followed us at sea had told them where we would land.

Tomas then took us on a route march. Down the hill to the road, about two miles east and then up Mount Orello, about 3,000 feet, whose side was covered with grape vines and vegetable gardens. Just below the summit was a cave whose entrance was hidden by a large rock; it was about 30 feet deep, 15 feet wide and dry.

Here Tomas left us indicating that he would return soon, saying: 'Aspettare.'

'I guess this is home for a while,' I said, as I unwrapped the rags from my left foot which was cut and sore.

'We'll have to come up with a plan,' Harry said. 'We can't live in a cave for God knows how long.'

'I agree.'

A few hours later Tomas returned with blankets, water, bread and a kerosene lamp. He showed us where to dig up potatoes but indicated that we couldn't have a fire because the smoke would give our position away.

He also showed us the Italian method for eating grapes. This was done by holding up the stalk right beside his mouth, eating a row vertically, turning the stalk and then eating another row. We were amazed at how quickly the grapes disappeared.

Tomas then left, saying that he would return tomorrow: 'Domani . . . Domani.'

We found some ferns to make a bed and passed a reasonably comfortable night.

Our cave was below the summit of Mount Orello and thus our view was to the south where we overlooked two bays and the small town of Lido Beach. Eating breakfast (grapes and raw potatoes) we saw a German patrol boat in one of the bays.

'They are still looking for us,' Harry said.

'They will never find us up here,' I replied.

'Let's hike to the top of this mountain and see what we can see.'

'Okay . . . but I come from British Columbia, and this is just a hill, not a mountain.'

The peak was about 500 feet above us. Here we found that we could look down at the Capital - Portoferraio - but too far away to see much detail. When Tomas appeared in the afternoon I asked him to bring us some binoculars - 'Binocolo' - easy to pantomime.

This he did the next morning and we hiked again to our vantage point and examined the small city. We could see the gun emplacements around the harbour so I got out my map and sketched them in along with the docks and the ships at anchor. Further details, such as the German HQs, were added by men who had worked there. I gave the map to the French army in Corsica.

'Obviously,' Harry remarked, 'the only way to get off this island is by boat.'

'True,' I acknowledged. It was our fifth day on the mountain and we were bored.

'The trouble is,' he continued,' that I know nothing about sailing. Do you?'

'No . . . but I'm an expert on dinghies.'

'Great.' Harry raised his eyebrows. 'If we got a boat it would be no use sailing down the Italian coast; we'd just get picked up by a German patrol boat . . . probably the one that we saw in the bay.'

'So?'

'So we would have to go Corsica . . . the Germans should be gone by now.' We had seen the JU-52s tail off.

'Maybe we could buy a boat with a motor,' I said.

'How many Italian Lira do you have?'

'Two thousand,' he replied. (About $120 Canadian).

'Me, too. That doesn't seem like enough to buy a boat.'

'No. Let's ask Tomas when he arrives.'

But we couldn't seem to get through to Tomas. We showed him our money and said: 'Motore barca'. He just shook his head and said: 'No barca . . . no barca.'

Our diet consisted of grapes and whatever vegetable we could find in the garden plots. - usually potatoes and carrots. Eating one day I said to Harry: 'How would you like a nice steak, cooked rare, with mushrooms and a baked potato with butter and . . . '

'Stop . . . stop!' he moaned. 'You're killing me!'

Then help arrived from a completely unexpected source a couple of days later. Tomas arrived with two Italian Army Lieutenants in tow. Introductions were made; their names were Pietro and Giovanni. They had deserted from the Army and were being sought by the Italian forces on Elba.

They were both in civilian clothes. Giovanni was the younger; about 25 years old, 5'7" tall, light complexion and in good condition. Pietro was about 35 years old, swarthy looks with the start of a beard, 5'9" tall, with a beer belly and out of shape. He was the spokesman and started off in rapid Italian until Harry held up his hand and said: 'Non Parlo Italiano.'

Pietro then startled us by saying: 'Parlez-vous Francais?'

Simultaneously we replied: 'Oui . . . un peu.'

So we spoke to Pietro in French, with recourse to our Italian dictionary if we didn't know the French word. He translated to Giovanni in Italian. We showed them our Lira and suggested that they buy, beg, borrow or steal a boat and sail to Corsica with us. On arrival there, we would explain to the authorities how they had helped us escape and thus they would be well treated.

Pietro was cautious and only semi-agreed to our plan. On the next day they left to do a recce. In the evening they returned with the following information: the nearest town of any size, Marina Di Campo, had only a few fishing boats which the owners would not part with. We would have to go to the west end of Elba where there were two larger towns - San Andrea and Marciana Marina - and some hope of finding a boat.

We decided to go on the following day. We thanked Tomas for his help and gave him a few Lira. I asked again about shoes but he only shrugged and pointed at his own threadbare boots.

Civilians on Nazi-held Elba Assist Escape of City Flyer

A four-day trip in a rubber dinghy to German-held Elba and a rough crossing to Corsica, 45 miles away, after being shot down over the Mediterranean, were among experiences related today by FL. Cecil L. Heide, D.F.C., of Vancouver, who is back home for administrative duty after having completed two tours of operations.

He and his English bride were met at the C.N.R. station this morning by his family. His wife, whom he married in February in Lytham, Lancashire, accompanied him.

FL. Heide, an R.C.A.F. observer, took to the emergency dinghy when his aircraft was shot down while leading an attack on eight Junkers transports over the Mediterranean.

The dinghy was circled daily by British and German aircraft on the trip to Elba.

It was a two-hour walk to San Andrea. Nobody took any notice of us. Harry and I had not shaved or had a decent wash for two weeks. The clothes we had been given on our arrival, shirts and trousers, were well used and were now grubby. We looked like two itinerant Italian workers. If anyone noticed my left foot bound in rags, and my limp, they gave a smile of sympathy, probably assuming that it was a war wound. Pietro and Giovanni were not in uniform but also wore shirts and trousers - cleaner than ours!

San Andrea was a quiet fishing town with a main street fronting the harbour and side streets leading up an incline. The marina held

30 or 40 boats of varying size and shape. We gave Pietro our Lira and sat on a bench facing the water while he and Giovanni left to scout around.

They returned after a couple of hours and Pietro said: 'Voila! We have a small boat with a sail. But we must wait until dark before we leave.'

I thought about asking him how much it cost but decided that he could keep any change for helping us out. Instead, I said: 'How about some food . . . I'm starving!'

'We better not go to a restaurant,' Pietro said. 'Wait here and I'll get some.'

He brought thick sandwiches of meat, cheese and lettuce and cold beers. Delicious! He also brought some food and water for the boat trip.

When it was dusk we set out. The 15-foot rowing boat had a sail made of sack-cloth and a pair of oars. It was a little over-laden with the four of us. There was no wind while we were in the lee of Elba so Pietro and Giovanni manned the oars. Outside the harbour a breeze sprang up but it was hardly enough to keep the sail full so the rowing continued. The sea was calm and the sky clear. I was able to steer in a westerly direction by keeping Polaris where it should be. I had the rudder.

As the night went on the rowers were getting tired so I fed them Benezdrine tablets from my escape kit. After midnight a wind sprang up and we could set sail and give the Italians a rest. Dawn found us about three miles from Corsica, its mountains clearly visible, but with no idea of exactly where we were on the coast. I knew that the island was very sparsely populated on this coast and that there were no large towns between Bastia on the north end of the island and Porto Vecchio on the south.

As we neared the coast we saw a small village with a few houses. We grounded on the beach and Pietro left to ask directions. On his return he said: 'The natives say to go south for two miles and we will come to the Tavignano River. Follow that to Corte, in the middle of the island, from there is a railway to Ajaccio, the Capital. But they don't know if the train is running.'

'Good stuff!' Harry clapped.

So we got back in the boat and rowed until we came to the river entrance. Here we abandoned the boat, collected our supplies and started to follow the river alongside which was a dirt road running gradually uphill. It was a nice day for walking - the sun was warm and the river chortled and sparkled.

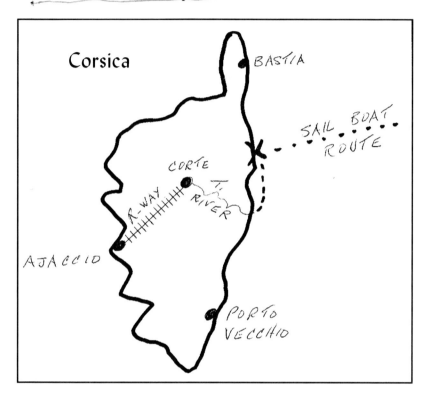

As nightfall we came to a farm where we got permission to sleep in the barn. Communication was difficult; the farmer didn't speak the same dialect as our two Italians. However, in the morning the farmer's wife cooked us a breakfast of eggs and sausages. Noting my plight, the farmer gave me a cane.

At mid-morning we came to deep gully, where a major stream entered the river, to find that the Germans had destroyed the bridge. So we had to clamber down one side, wade across the stream and climb up the other side. It was hard on Pietro and me; me because of my feet and him because he was so badly out of condition and short of breath.

But shortly after that we got a lift in a farm truck taking produce to Corte. 'Hooray!' I shouted, as we settled amongst the vegetables, 'no more walking!'

Corte is a scenic town, nestled amid the mountains with the Tavignano River almost circling it. The first thing we saw were French soldiers - lots of them. Then we saw the French tri-colour above the Citadel, obviously HQs, and went inside. The major who listened to our story didn't seem to be very impressed. He called two guards to take Pietro and Giovanni away, barely giving us time to say goodbye. I hoped that they would be all right; at least they were out of the war now.

The major informed us that we would take the train to Ajaccio at 0800 hours the following morning and report to the British Liaison Office there. He would give us tickets. Meanwhile, we were free to use the Officer's Mess and the Steward would find us a room. We asked for transport to the station in the morning because of my feet and he reluctantly agreed.

By now it was dinner time. Food in the Mess was buffet style. We filled our plates but then found we could only eat about half of it. I pushed my plate aside. 'Rather cavalier treatment, eh? We weren't offered any clothes or shoes or even any shaving gear.'

'Yes,' Harry agreed. 'The French are a queer bunch. It looks as if they drove the Germans out of Corsica.'

'It appears so.'

'How long is that train ride tomorrow?'

'Looks like about three hours.'

'Good. Let's find our room . . . I'm tired.'

The Steward took us to a room with two beds and not much more. We talked for a while and then turned in but we both had trouble sleeping on a soft mattress.

The train ride was spectacular! Hugging the mountain sides looking down into deep chasms with a river below as if we would fall over at any time. Arriving in Ajaccio we were lost; the French had not given us an address nor any directions. We tried to ask our way in the station but nobody spoke English.

'What'll we do now?' I asked.

'Let's walk down the street and see if we can spot anyone who looks as if they might speak English.'

'Okay.'

In a matter of minutes we saw approaching us a Royal Navy

Commander with a row of ribbons. 'Excuse me, Sir,' Harry stepped in front of him.

The Commander was nonplussed by being greeted in perfect English by such a pair of ruffians. We had not had a bath or a shave in over two weeks. Our second-hand, misfit clothes were filthy. I was leaning on my cane. We both had to laugh at the expression on his face.

'Pardon me, Sir.' Harry got his face composed. 'We are RAF Officers who were shot down near Elba. We made our way to Corsica and just got off the train from Corte. We are looking for the British Liaison Office.'

'Well, I'm damned.' He shook his head. 'Yes, I know where the British HQs is but it is too far to walk.' He looked at me. 'What happened to your feet?'

'I lost my shoes and couldn't find another pair.'

'You're not English?'

'Canadian, Sir.'

'For Heaven's sake,' he said, 'stop calling me 'Sir'. My name is Ian Spencer.'

We introduced ourselves.

'Look, I've got a Minesweeper just down the way. Come along with me and have a drink and a sandwich. I want to hear your story and then I'll get you on your way.'

It was not far to his ship. A Petty Officer on the deck looked at his Captain as if he was mad in bringing two such specimens aboard. In the wardroom, he said: 'Sit down . . . gin and tonic all right?'

'Fine,' we both said.

He mixed the drinks and sat down. 'Now, tell me what happened to you two.'

This we did, alternating with the narration.

The Commander interrupted us only to refresh our drinks and order some sandwiches. When we finished he said: 'You've had quite a time. You'll be glad to get back to your squadron.'

'Yes,' I said. 'What are you doing here, Sir? Are there mines around?'

'Yes. The Jerries left quite a few around the harbour entrance . . . we've been clearing them out.'

He went to the door and shouted at the Petty Officer: 'Danny, get these boys a taxi.'

'Yes, Sir,'

We waited a few minutes and then the P.O., still not sure who we were, said that the taxi was there.

'We haven't any money,' Harry said.

'That's all right,' Spencer replied, 'I'll pay.' Which he did and gave the driver instructions in Italian to get to British HQs.

We thanked him as we drove away. 'He's a nice chap,' Harry said.

'Sure is,' I agreed. 'A hell of a lot different from those French in Corte.'

Ajaccio seemed like a pleasant city. The bay that we were now leaving was as spectacular as many that are much more famous. The city is framed by the mass of Monte d'Oro, one of the island's highest peaks, and sweetened by the Prunelli River which cascades down from Monte Renoso.

We were surprised by the number of palm trees, more prolific here than in Italy, which lined the streets and squares. The buildings were mostly white and crowned with the universal red of Provencal tiles. We did not have time to investigate Napoleon's habitat.

At the British HQs we were treated like royalty. It was a large mansion of ornate design with two pillars in front. There appeared to be 40 or 50 people, mostly officers, looking after British interests in Corisca, headed by General Peak. We were taken directly to his office. He was a large, imposing man, about sixty years of age, with three rows of W.W.I. ribbons.

He listened to our story with rapt attention, interjecting 'Wonderful' now and again. He particularly liked our story of feeding Benzedrine to the two Italian soldiers so that they could keep on rowing.

When we finished he said: 'I want you to have dinner with me tonight. I'll ask General Martin, head of the French forces, to join us.'

We were given new clothes, a hot bath and shaving gear. A doctor was called to look at my feet. He cleaned them up, dressed them with an ointment, bandaged the left one and found a large pair of bedroom slippers for me to wear. As he left, he said: 'Stay off your left foot for a week or ten days and you'll be all right. Get a pair of crutches when you get home.' I thanked him.

FO. C. R. HEIDE
... reported missing

✦✦✦ ✦✦✦ ✦✦✦

Vancouver Flier Posted Missing

FO. Cecil Roy Heide is reported missing after air operations, according to word received by his parents, Mr. and Mrs. A. J. Heide. Mr. Heide is a member of the advertising department of The News-Herald.

A navigator who participated in the destruction of a 5000-ton Axis tanker, bombing of a 1000-ton tanker and direct hits scored on a 9000-ton supply ship, FO. Heide enlisted in the R.C.A.F. in May, 1941. He took basic training in Brandon, Man., and received his wings in April, 1942.

After two trips to Labrador with Clyde Panghorn, he was given a ship which he flew to Scotland and while there escaped from a crash without injury.

On the North Sea convoy route for a time, FO. Heide went to Suez and moved along with Gen. Montgomery as far as Bizerte. Transferred to Malta for seven months, he was then posted to British Northwest Africa from which point last word from him was received.

PAIR RESCUED FROM CORSICA

FO. Cecil Leroy Heide, son of Mr. and Mrs. J. A. Heide, 1317 East Fourteenth, and an English pilot are back with their R.A.F. Beaufighter squadron again after a series of thrilling escapades that began when they were forced to abandon their aircraft in the Mediterranean near Elba.

After four days in a dinghy the two men reached the island and from their hiding place in the mountains watched the Germans evacuating troops, tanks, and transport from Corsica while Nazi patrols searched the surrounding country for them.

Then, aided by Italians, the pair escaped to Corsica, late rejoining their squadron. Elb is between Corsica and Italy in the Tyrrhenian Sea.

BAG ENEMY CRAFT.

Details of their adventure were learned in London when the air ministry said Heide and the pilot were forced to abandon the aircraft after shooting down a Nazi JU-52 troop carrier and damaging another. The airmen rigged up a sail from the dinghy cover to travel 25 miles across the water to Elba. They feared capture several times after German planes circled low.

Heide said, "after we had been in Elba two days we made friends with some Italians who wanted to get to Corsica to escape from the Germans."

"We found a fisherman prepared to make the crossing. There were seven in the party, including two R.A.F. men.

IMPROVISE SAIL.

"We made the 45-mile trip in 14½ hours in a small rowboat, with a rough and ready sail made of sacking. We arrived undetected on a barren stretch of coast. For the next couple of days we travelled by foot and donkey into central Corsica. Our clothes were falling off and we were suffering from hunger and exposure but we were in the best of spirits."

Then the weary wanderers met a Frenchman who obtained fresh clothes for them and arranged preliminary negotiations leading towards reunion with their squadron.

We had a splendid dinner with Generals Peak and Martin and discussed our exploits once again. To our surprise, General Martin thanked us for the map of Portoferraio harbour which we had given to his staff in Corte and said that it would be useful because Elba was his next target.

VETERAN FLIER AWARDED DFC

FO. C. L. HEIDE

Has been awarded the DFC for participation in many and varied types of operational sorties. "His devotion to duty and fine fighting spirit has played no small part in the successes attained by his crew," his citation says. On one occasion he was forced down on enemy waters but reached safety after three days in a dinghy.

FO. Heide is the son of Mr. and Mrs. A. J. Heide, 1317 East Fourteenth. He served in North Africa during Montgomery's advance and in October, 1942, went to Malta. In July, 1943, he was navigator of an aircraft that blew a 5000-ton Axis tanker "sky-high."

FO. Cecil Lee Heide

AWARD D.F.C. TO CITY FLYER

The Disinguished Flying Cross has been awarded to Flying Officer Cecil Lee Heide, son of Mr. and Mrs. A. J. Heide, 1317 East Fourteenth.

Veteran operational flyer, FO. Heide's Malta-based plane sank a tanker off the coast of Italy a year ago. He is an observer.

His citation reads:

"FO. Heide has participated in many varied types of operational sorties and by his devotion to duty and fine fighting spirit has played no small part in the successes attained by his crew. On one occasion his pilot was forced to bring the aircraft down on to enemy waters but reached safety after three days in the dinghy."

More Disinformation!

We had asked that our squadron be notified at once of our safety. Reading the signal on our return to Protville, we decided that it had been sent by the French. It read:

'FLIGHT OFFICERS HEIDE AND DEACON WHO IN THE SEA ON 24TH ARE SAFE IN AJACCIO'

Anyhow, on the next day 'Chalky' White arrived in a Beaufighter to take us home.

Our first priority was to ensure that our families were notified since they had received a 'Missing in Action' telegram. Since Mary was not on my family list, she knew nothing about my adventures until later.

Awarded a DFC for our escape, we were now close to the end of our time with 39 Squadron. Officially, a tour of operations was 10 torpedo drops or 100 hours, whichever came first. We had done 11 drops and 147 hours. Early in the new year of 1944 the squadron moved to Sardinia and we left - Harry to return to the U.K. and myself to a Beaufighter OTU in Cyprus.

We said our good-byes. I made copies of all my notes and photos for Harry to take home to his son. Harry did some more ops from England. He survived the war and later became a pilot for British Airways.

DO/HPL
                                            Headquarters,
                                Mediterranean Allied Coastal Air Force.

                                    16. April, 1944.

Dear Heide.

            I was very pleased to hear that you had been awarded
the Distinguished Flying Cross in connection with your excellent
work with 39 Squadron. Please accept my heartiest congratulations.

            I do not know to what O.T.U. in the Middle East
you were finally posted on the conclusion of your tour with 39
Squadron, but I hope that you are finding it very interesting and
instructive.
            Again with my congratulations and best wishes for
the future,

                            Yours sincerely,

                                  H.P. Lloyd

Flying Officer C.L.R. HEIDE, D.F.C. (J.16650)
c/o Headquarters,
ROYAL AIR FORCE,
MIDDLE EAST.

OFFICE OF THE

HIGH COMMISSIONER FOR CANADA,

CANADA HOUSE,

LONDON, S.W.I.

14th April, 1944.

Dear Mr. Heide,

    May I congratulate you very warmly indeed on
the decoration which you have just received.
Canadians everywhere will, I know, be happy that
such fine service as you have given has been thus
recognised.

    With warmest good wishes in which Mrs. Massey
joins,

               Yours sincerely,

               Vincent Massey

Flying Officer C.L.Heide, D.F.C.,
    J.16650,
      No.39 Squadron, R.C.A.F.

HEADQUARTERS OF THE
AIR OFFICER COMMANDING-IN-CHIEF
R.C.A.F. OVERSEAS

20 Lincoln's Inn Fields,
LONDON   ..   W.C.2.

15th April 1944.

Dear Heide,

It is very gratifying to me to
learn that you have been awarded the
Distinguished Flying Cross by His Majesty.
I congratulate you most warmly and wish
you continued success.

Yours sincerely,

(N.R. Anderson)
Air Vice-Marshal

Flying Officer Cecil Leroy Heide, D.F.C.

Chapter 9

Some Other Escapes

It might be of interest to you if I digress from my own affairs to describe some other escapes. The chances of surviving a tour on strike operations was very low. With so many crews shot down it was inevitable that they would have some interesting and exciting escapades. Here are a few.

Sqn Ldr Derek Frecker was O/C of 'B' Flight on No. 252, a Beaufighter Squadron. His navigator was P/O Tom Armstrong. Their mission on this day was to strafe enemy trucks and tanks on the coast road near Sirte. Frecker had long been badgered by his fitter, Sgt. 'Paddy' Clark, to go along on a mission. (There was room to stand behind the pilot). Finally, Frecker gave in but Clark picked a bad day.

Attacking the enemy airfield at Tamet, the Beaufighter was hard hit by flak; the starboard engine was smashed along with the air cooler. Frecker crash landed in the desert. The three men were unharmed but they were a long way from home and had only a few cans of bully beef, salmon and sardines for rations. They took a can of water and began to walk towards the Allied lines, hiding when enemy transport appeared and huddling together for warmth during the cold nights. At one stage, they watched Italian troops mining the coast road. On the seventh day they fell in with some Senussi Arabs who gave them food, water and shelter. Fifteen days after their crash they were rescued by an armoured car of the First King's Dragoon Guards and the Arabs were suitably rewarded.

Hit badly by flak while attacking a convoy, F/Lt Strever of 39

Squadron ditched the Beaufort off the Italian coast. The crew got safely into the dinghy. They were F/O Dunsmere, navigator; Sgt.s Williamson and Brown, WOP and AG. They were sighted by a Macchi and shortly afterwards picked up by a Cant seaplane. After a mild interrogation at the seaplane base, they were told they were to be taken to Taranto the next day to 'Discuss their future.'

The Cant was crowded on the following morning with the four Cant crew, the four prisoners and their guard. Waiting for the right moment, about half-way to Taranto, the prisoners acted. Williamson knocked out the radio officer and Brown seized the gun from the lax guard. Strever took the gun and secured the cooperation of the pilot. Soon all the Italians were over-powered and tied up. Strever took over the controls and headed for Malta.

CRDA Cant. Z. 506B

Dunsmere worked out a course but he wasn't sure of their position. They decided to make straight for Malta with the proviso that they would turn and make a land-fall in Italy if nothing was seen in 30 minutes. This they had to do. After a rough pinpoint they turned again for Malta; the Italian engineer indicated that they had fuel for about one more hour. There was jubilation as Malta came into sight but it was short-lived as Spitfires appeared. One sprayed a wing on the Cant to 'persuade' it to land. Strever set the Cant down smartly on the water and they all waved anything white they could find, mostly clothing, to show they were not hostile. An Air Sea Rescue launch quickly picked them up and there was a jubilant reunion with their mates on the squadron.

A large convoy of four merchant ships, escorted by five destroyers and two flak ships, was spotted near Sicily en route to Benghazi, by a recce aircraft. This was a prime target in spite of the fact that it was within range of enemy fighters. Eight Beauforts attacked with five Beaufighters as top cover. It was carnage. In addition to the heavy flak from the ships they were jumped by a force of 18 ME-109s, six ME-110s and several JU-88s. Of the eight Beauforts, four were lost.

Returning to Malta, a Beaufort flown by P/O Seddon with P/O McGregor and Sgts Miller and Keegan in his crew, was literally blown out of the sky by a ME-109. Seddons managed to ditch about six miles from Malta. The dinghy was shredded and of no use; all were injured, Keegan seriously. McGregor, a Canadian, was a powerful man and a strong swimmer. He decided to swim to Malta and was joined by Sgt. Miller. They left Seddon and Keegan in the sinking Beaufort.

McGregor soon left Miller behind. McGregor was wearing only a pair of khaki shorts and a bush shirt but they began to irritate him and he slid them off. But before he did so he remembered that he had an Egyptian pound note in his hip pocket. He was not a canny Scots-Canadian for nothing; he removed the note and held it in his hand. He swam for two hours, three hours, four hours, and still Malta was tantalizingly out of reach. His left arm was numb and he had shrapnel wounds in his back. Only will power kept him going for the fifth hour when he reached a rocky shore. A Maltese farmer had seen him swimming and helped him ashore. He still had the pound note. Seddon, Keegan and Miller were never seen again.

A Beaufighter of 272 Squadron with P/O Crawford as pilot and Sgt. Taylor as navigator was badly hit while strafing tanks and trucks of the Afrika Corps near Benghazi. They crash landed and were quickly taken prisoner by Germans who were in a convoy. The two airmen were separated. On the next morning while it was still dark, Crawford was taken to one of the trucks where the Germans were preparing for the day's trek. For a few moments he was left unguarded and bolted towards the nearest skyline which he managed to reach before he was missed.

Crawford had nothing to aid his foolhardy escape - no compass, no map, no food or water and no protection from the blazing desert sun. Completely lost, hungry and dehydrated, he was close to the end when he was found by a wandering party of Bedouins. They treated him well and, although it was 36 hours before he could be moved, took him back to the British lines where they were well rewarded. Crawford returned to operations a month later.

I could not find a written account of the Beaufighter crew who stole a submarine. I know it to be true because they were on my squadron and told us the story when they returned. Both were officers. The pilot, John Elliot, was an Englishman of slim build with sandy hair and freckles who was 24 years old and looked nineteen. The navigator, Leo Marcus, was a Canadian who had been born in Italy; his parents had emigrated to Canada when he was 16 years old and he had been back to Italy several times. He spoke Italian like the native that he was. He was 30 years old with a stocky build, brown eyes, black hair and a swarthy complexion.

It was August, 1943. The Allies had taken Sicily and fighting was now at the Strait of Messina. John and his wingman were on a Rover south of Naples when they were jumped by the nemesis of all Beaufighter crews, a pair of ME-109s. His wingman flew out to sea at low level and was never heard from again. John stayed close to land and they put up a good fight with Leo calling the turns. John jettisoned his eight rockets and did his best to bring the power of his four 20-mm canon to bear but it was no use. Finally, with both engines hit and losing power the Beau was doomed. John ditched it nicely about 200 yards off shore. Luckily, neither he nor Leo were injured.

The dinghy popped out of the wing on impact. The ME-109 pilot flew overhead and gave them a wave as they climbed out of the aircraft. They decided not to use the dinghy since they were close to shore and both could swim.

They took off their Mae Wests and tossed them in the dinghy which was still tethered to the aircraft and Leo cut a large hole in the dinghy so that it would sink with the aircraft. Then they swam to shore.

'The first thing we have to do,' Leo said, 'is to get as far away from here as possible because the 109 will report where we went down.'

'Do you know where we are?' John asked.

Leo looked at him scathingly. 'Exactly. Now let's take off our shoulder tabs and turn our shirts inside out . . . they'll dry in no time.' Neither of them had hats. Leo left his shirt tail out because he was wearing a wide escape belt and a holster. 'Come on . . . if we meet anyone let me do the talking . . . all you say is 'Buon Giorno.'

'Okay.'

'Say it.'

'Bawn Gorno,' John said.

'Oh, God! Not 'Bawn' . . . 'Buon'. And not 'Gurno' . . . 'Giorno'. Try it again.'

After a few more attempts, Leo was semi-satisfied. 'And if anyone says anything further, you say: 'Non Parlo Italiano'. We'll have to get you some clothes and a hat . . . you look too much like a damned Englishman.'

They struck off straight inland and walked until it was dark. They didn't meet anyone. They spent the night in a small, wooded copse. In the morning, they took stock.

'How much money do you have?' Leo asked.

'Just the 1,000 Lira that they gave us.'

'Ha!' Leo jeered as he took off his belt. The .38 revolver was barely wet. In one pouch he had 9,000 Lira; in another was aspirin, benzedrine and other medications; in another was a folded topo map of the area. Leo believed in being prepared.

'Here's where we are,' he pointed out to John, 'not far from the town of Piscotta, on the coast. We need a boat. It's no use trying to go over land because we'd get caught at the Italian lines and probably get shot as spies. Besides, there's the Strait of Messina. First though . . . clothes and food.'

'How do we do that?'

'We walk to Piscotta. You wait outside the town while I go in and get us some clothes. It's better to buy them rather than steal them because that's a give-away that there are escapees in the area.'

'They'll know that anyway,' John said, 'because the 109 saw us get out of the aircraft.'

'Yes . . . but they won't know which way we went.'

So Leo went into the town, found a second-hand clothing store, and bought clothes for them both with an outsize shirt for himself to cover his belt and holster.

Properly dressed, they went into a cafe and had a meal. They were both hungry. 'Remember,' Leo cautioned, 'only open your mouth to put food in and keep your cap on.'

After the meal they walked to the small harbour. There was one fishing boat being repaired and a few small craft that didn't look very sea-worthy. 'This place is hopeless,' Leo said, 'we'll have to go to a bigger port.' He unfolded his topo map. 'Salerno should be good.'

'How far is that?' John asked.

'About 35 miles . . . we could get there easily on a bicycle.'

'We don't have bikes.'

'That's okay . . . we'll steal some.'

'I thought you said that it wasn't wise to steal things because it gives our position away.'

'Oh, that doesn't apply to bikes,' Leo said, airily, 'everybody in Italy steals bikes. Let's try the Public Library.'

Which they did, stole two bikes, and headed off for Salerno. The going was slow as the highway was crowded with military vehicles to and from the front lines. Several times they had to scramble off the road and hide. They slept rough that night and got to Salerno the next morning.

Before they got to the town they came to a small Italian Navy base, with some buildings and a wooden pier. The place looked deserted. Tied up to the pier was a submarine.

'Well, look at that!' Leo remarked.

'A submarine?' John said, skeptically.

'It's a boat, isn't it?'

Two men were sitting in folding chairs beside the conning tower. The younger one wore dirty cover-alls and had his arm in a sling. The older one wore part of an Italian Navy uniform; his cap had a peak and some gold. His right leg was bandaged.

'I'll go and have a talk with them,' Leo said. 'You stay here.'

'Buon Giorno,' Leo greeted, as he stepped aboard.

'Buon Giorno,' replied the officer. He was about 45 years old with a heavy growth of black whiskers.

'Buon Giorno,' added the seaman. He was a young man in his twenties and very nervous.

Speaking Italian, Leo asked the Navy man: 'How did you get hurt?'

'In an action against a convoy by the British.' He paused. 'I am the Third Mate. I was on the bridge. Alfonso, here, was in the engine room and had a bad fall . . . broke his arm.'

'Will the sub not go now?' Leo asked.

'It can't submerge and the engine is very rough.' He was getting suspicious of all the questions. 'Where are you from?'

'Near Milano.' Leo knew that his northern accent would place him from around there.

'What are you doing around here?'

Leo didn't answer. 'What are you supposed to be doing with the sub?'

'Guarding it until it can get to Naples for repair, but with the war so close now . . . ' His voice trailed off.

Leo gestured towards the deserted buildings on the shore. 'Where is everybody?'

'Taken away by the Germans to fight at the front. Damn Boche!' The officer spat on the deck. He gestured at John, still sitting on the pier. 'Why doesn't your friend come up?'

'I'll go and get him,' Leo replied. He walked to where John was and filled him in on the situation. ' . . . and I think we can talk them into deserting with the sub. It won't submerge. We would have to travel at night. But I don't know the condition of the engine or the fuel state.'

'Neither of them is an engineer?'

'No . . . the guy with the broken arm works in the engine room.'

'I'm quite good with engines,' John said, casually.

'You are?'

'I think I told you that I joined the RAF from Sheffield University?' Leo nodded. 'Well, I was taking mechanical Engineering. I've taken engines apart and put them back together for years.'

'But not an Italian sub engine?'

John shrugged. 'An engine is an engine.'

Leo stood up. 'C'mon . . . let's give it a try.'

It took a couple of hours of persuasion to get the two submariners to defect. The Mate - whose name was Mario - did not seem very surprised to learn that Leo and John were an RAF crew. Alfonso shook so much that he nearly fell off his chair. They were both worried about what would happen to them when the retreating Germans arrived.

It was finally agreed that, if John said the engine would run, they would sail for Palermo where Leo would see that the two Italians were not sent to a POW camp but released to stay in Sicily until the war was over.

At one point in the negotiations Leo slid his revolver out of its holster and jammed it into Mario's ribs, saying: 'We could go without you!' But it was a futile gesture. They both knew that the sub would get nowhere without Mario.

After two hours in the engine room John appeared, grimy and oil-stained, to announce: 'There is nothing wrong with the engine but the drive shaft is out of true. I think it will hold up if we go slowly . . . maybe ten knots. And there's plenty of fuel . . . the tanks are half full.'

It was agreed that they would start that night. The only things lacking were fresh food and wine so Leo made a trip into Salerno for supplies.

Mario eased the submarine out at dusk. He was an efficient seaman and soon instructed Leo in taking the conn so that he could rest his injured leg. John and Alfonso ran the engine room with hand signals since neither spoke the other's language.

'Here's our route.' Mario had a marine chart of the coastal waters. 'Down the coast to Paola . . . two nights. Then to the Lipari Islands; they are uninhabited and will make a good place to lie up. From there to Palermo is about five hours; it's open water but we shouldn't get spotted at night.'

The first two nights were easy, although John limited their speed to eight knots because of the shaft vibration. The people in the coastal towns paid little attention to blackout so there were lights visible to aid navigation. During the day they found a sheltered cove and put tree branches over the sub.

Coming into the Lipari Islands was awkward. It was very dark, with no moon, and no lights on shore. Mario was worried about the rocky shores and held off landing until there was enough light. There was no cover for the sub and they all worried that they would be discovered during the day. Leo thought that it would be the height of irony if the sub was shot up by a Beaufighter from his own squadron! They heard aircraft but none came near them.

It was a five-hour sail to Palermo and Mario set off so that they would arrive at first light. He sacrificed one of his white dress shirts for a flag that was tied to the low mast.

The Italian port authorities could hardly believe their eyes as the submarine entered harbour and tied up at a dock. And they certainly couldn't believe their ears when Leo greeted them in English. It was agreed that Mario and Alfonso would be released after interrogation. A signal was sent to the RAF and a squadron Beaufighter collected John and Leo on the following day.

The two couples parted with hugs and back-pats and Leo promised to look Mario up after the war. I wonder if he did?

Chapter 10

Cyprus

I knew little about this beautiful island when I arrived in Jan 44. For some reason (no doubt sexual) I remembered that Aphrodite, called Venus by the Romans, was given sanctuary in Cyprus. She was born of white sea foam produced by the severed genitals of Uranus when he was castrated by the Titans. In Cyprus she was disarmed by the Greeks and reduced to the erotic functions associated with her and her lover, Adonis. The name of her son, Eros, was the abstract noun for sexual desire.

At this time, nobody had yet told the Greeks and Turks that they hated each other so all was quiet and peaceful and there was no racial disharmony between the two groups. In Jan 43 Winston Churchill visited Cyprus and wrote:

' . . . both the Turkish and Greek elements on the island were very thankful that the Allies were winning and not at all inclined to object to British rule.'

No. 79 OTU, to which I was posted as a navigation instructor, was based at Nicosia, the capital city. The base had a long, paved runway and ample quarters for both students and instructors. There were two courses running with 30 students in each - 15 pilots and 15 navigators. Most of them were recent graduates from South Africa which was a partner in the Commonwealth Training Plan. About one half were British (sent from the U.K.) with the rest from New Zealand, Australia, and South Africa. They were left to get acquainted and form their own crews by week six, half-way through the course.

My students needed little instruction on navigation. Flying at sea level the water streaks could be easily lined up in the driftmeter; in fact, with experience one could estimate the aircraft drift by simply looking at the sea. Also, at low level the Indicated and True airspeeds were close together and winds usually light. Ground speed required a pin-point but the weather was mostly good.

No - they didn't need much navigation instruction. What they needed was to learn about the Beaufighter, the geography of the Med, how to fight and what to do if they were damaged or shot down. Probably their hardest task was to learn how to send and receive Morse Code at 20 words a minute; but that wasn't my responsibility.

My work load was not heavy - two or three hours a day in the classroom and perhaps an hour at the aircraft. I spent quite a lot of time with the Chief Flying Instructor, Sqn Ldr Hubbard, planning routes for training flights. He was a lean, cadaverous fellow with the red-veined face of a heavy drinker. He would march into the Officer's Mess on the dot of noon and go straight to the bar, looking at nobody. He would order a pink gin which he drank in two gulps while the bartender mixed the next one. Then he would look around to see who was there and give a greeting or two.

Hubbard was sent away in disgrace when, probably half-drunk, he rolled a Beau at low level over his girlfriend's house. Too bad that her house was in the centre of Nicosia and right next to the Archbishop's Palace.

I was sipping a beer in the Mess one evening when I was approached by one of the flying instructors, Flt Lt Tommy Deck, whom I knew slightly. He was about 30 years old, stocky, red hair, hazel eyes and freckles. He had done a tour on Beaufighters with 252 Squadron and wore a DFC. We were later to have some adventures together. 'Hi, Lee,' he said, 'want the other half?'

'Sure . . . thanks,'

Tommy ordered two beers. 'I've just been elected bar officer.'

'I know . . . I was at the Mess Meeting.'

'So I have to go to Beirut for some grog. Will you come with me?'

'Yes.'

'Good . . . when can you get a day off?'

'I could manage tomorrow.'

'So can I. Okay, let's leave about 0900 hours. I'll get the ground crew to strip an aircraft.'

'Strip how?' I enquired.

'Take out the ammunition canisters for the canon. That will leave room for several cases of brandy.'

'Is brandy all you're after?'

'Mainly. That Lebanese brandy is the most popular drink in the Mess. But I'll see what else they have.'

'You know where to go?'

'Yes . . . the outgoing bar officer filled me in.'

'Okay.' I agreed. 'See you tomorrow morning.'

It was just a short flight and the weather was clear as usual. I was impressed with Tommy's flying; his climbs and turns were so smooth that we could have been riding on a magic carpet. 'Climb to about 10,000 feet,' I suggested, 'and let's have a look at Lebanon.'

'All right,' he agreed, and poured power to the twin Hercules engines.

From that altitude we could see nearly all of the small country. Two mountain ranges ran north-south with the Bekaa Valley between. The city of Beirut was on a promontory jutting out into the Med about the centre of the country's shoreline. I was anxious to see this city, known for its sophistication, and called the 'Paris of the East.'

At the airport we hired a taxi and made our plans for the day. I wanted to visit the university so the driver dropped me there. Tommy's liquor vendor was in the city centre, not far away.

'Why don't we meet for lunch?' I asked. 'I hear that the Hotel St. Georges is good.'

'Fine,' he agreed.

'How are you going to get your cases of alcohol to the airport?'

'The supplier will provide a truck.'

'Good. Then I'll see you for lunch and we can have a look around the city in the afternoon.'

I had heard good reports of the American University of Beirut. The main building was a large Gothic structure with an imposing clock tower. A sign stated that it had been founded in 1866, then called the Syrian Protestant College. The Jafet Library had a large collection of books both in Arabic and English.

I found the Registrar, enrolled in two correspondence courses that could be used for credits and got a list of the books that I would need. Then I walked to the hotel. Tommy arrived at noon.

We found a table and ordered a stein of beer.

'How did you get on?' I asked. 'Did you get what you wanted?'

'Yes. I got ten cases of brandy, two of gin, three of rum and two of Arak. How did you make out?'

'Fine. I've got lots of spare time so I enrolled in two courses: 'English Literature' and 'History and Myths of the Med.'

'Do you like history?'

'Yes. But I must admit to a secondary motive. My girlfriend, Susan, is coming over for a couple of weeks when she can get some leave and I want to impress her with my knowledge of Cyprus.'

'Where's she coming from?'

'Alex . . . she's a Wren.'

We finished our beer and looked at the menu. It was in Lebanese and meant nothing but our waiter spoke English. We ordered a platter of beef, chicken and shrimp - followed by a variety of fruit.

The city was a bustling metropolis with no signs of war. The streets and shops were crowded. There was a cacophony of car horns and street vendors amid a background of building construction. There were many banks. It was obvious that mammon was God, not Mohammed. Instead of Mosques there were expensive jewelry stores, imported clothing shops, hair dressers and boutiques, and casinos and clubs promising every form of sexual excitement. There were many book stores and I easily found the books I wanted.

There were many banners waving in the breeze and, although they were in Arabic, they seemed to proclaim the independence of Lebanon, achieved in 1943.

Had anyone told the vital citizens of Beirut that their gorgeous city would be reduced to rubble by the Israelis some 30 years later, they would have laughed in scorn.

Our flight back to Cyprus was routine, the aircraft loaded with alcohol.

We had on the staff at this time Flight Lieutenant Peter Northwood. He was a British admin officer, about 45 years old, who had been a theatre director in peace time. He formed a drama club. Never an actor, I helped with the stage settings and other dogs-body chores. He concentrated on light comedy such as Noel Coward's 'Blithe Spirits' and 'Private Lives'; Oscar Wilde's 'The Importance of Being Earnest' and 'The Ideal Husband.'

It was great fun; all the female parts were played by men. The spectators laughed and their occasional pithy remarks only added to the enjoyment.

Our Thespians

Drury Lane is worried

Tommy stopped me one day in a school corridor and said: 'I have to do an air test . . . will you come along?'

'Sure,' I replied. I liked to fly with him.

We flew out over the sea and Tommy put the Beau through its paces: hard climbs, stalls, sharp turns, dives, engines at full bore. Then he said: 'I'll feather the engines . . . port one first . . . watch the generators.'

'Right.' A generator ran off each engine to power the electrical systems. When an engine was stopped so of course was the generator. Sometimes, when an engine was restarted a circuit breaker popped and the generator would not come back on line. Oddly, this problem never occurred on the ground - only in the air.

Tommy

He feathered the engines in turn and adjusted the rudder and throttles so smoothly that I was hardly aware of it; apart from slowing down the aircraft stayed dead level. Then Tommy said: 'Let's see how she rolls . . . hang on!'

He climbed to 9,000 feet and threw the Beau into a steep dive. I watched the ASI increase to 300 knots, 350, 400 and then Tommy levelled out and rolled to port through 360 degrees without losing a foot of height.

His handling of the Beau was masterful. He and the aircraft were one. He felt every nuance and every motion of the kite as if it was a part of himself. When we landed the wheels kissed the tarmac with a lover's touch.

After the flight I looked in my log book and found that I had
flown with eleven Beaufighter pilots including Sqn Ldr Stan Muller-
Rowland and Major Don Tilley, both renowned for their prowess.
But none were as good as Tommy Deck. He was a natural pilot that
could make a Beaufighter perform beyond its capabilities.
Furthermore, although I didn't know it at the time, he was absolutely
fearless.

Cyprus is a lovely island. There are four main topographical
regions. The Kyrenia Range of mountains to the north; the forested
Troodos massif; the hilly landscape to the east and the Mesaoria
Plain.

The Kyrenia range is largely formed of hard, compact masses of
whitish-grey limestone. Deep river valleys, swollen in the spring
with mountain torrents, lead to the coast. Walking across the height
of the range gives some magnificent views of the steep limestone
walls and fabulous rock formations.

The other mountain range, the Troodos massif, is very different.
Mount Olympus is composed of dunite and is surrounded by areas
of peridotite, gabbro and dolerite. Over the course of millions of
years the dunite gradually changed into serpentine, leading to the
mining of asbestos.

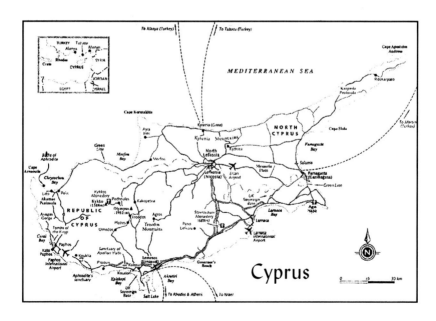

The hill country is mainly characterized by glaringly white chalk. This sun-soaked landscape is, as expected, covered by extensive vineyards.

The Mesaoria Plain lies between the Kyrenia range and the Troodos massif. It is made up of Pilocene and Quaternary strata composed of sandstone, conglomerate tufa, covered by a further layer of alluvial deposits. This rich, fertile farming area has been dubbed the 'Bread Basket of Cyprus.'

The capital city, Nicosia, is located about in the centre of the island. Legend says that it was founded in 280 B.C. by Lefcon, son of Ptolemy, as Ledra - still the name of the main shopping street. At one time the city was surrounded by a circular fortified wall with six gates that can still be identified. Over Porta del Provoditore is the inscription: 'O Mohammed, give these tidings to the Faithful; Victory is from God and triumph is very near. O opener of doors, open for us the best of doors.'

One gem in the city is the former Latin cathedral of St. Sophia, the Selemiye Mosque, consecrated in 1326 A.D. Inside it is very simple, its dignity enhanced by the white-washed walls. There is a mihrab (a niche) built into the south transept to indicate the direction of Mecca. In the same general area are samples of Ottoman architecture: the Sultan's Library, containing fine specimens of Turkish and Persian calligraphy; the Tekke (Convent) of the Dancing Dervishes; and the two Khans, the Buyuk Khan (Great Inn) and the Kourmardjilar Khan (Gambler's Inn).

In 1944 there was little sign of war in Nicosia apart from the soldiers and airmen. The produce shops were filled with fruit and vegetables and the street vendors plied their trade under the shade of wooden balconies on old houses that over-hung the street. The only shops with sparse goods were those that imported from Britain.

The most jarring note in Nicosia was the profusion and bars and strip clubs with belly dancers and prostitutes, all of whom were in the business of rooking the servicemen as much as possible. There was no black-out and, to the best of my knowledge, no Axis bombs ever fell on Cyprus.

After Nicosia, Cyprus is known for its five towns.

On the east coast is the old city of Famagusta. Once known for its wealth and extravagance, it is now largely in ruins.

Larnaca, on the south coast was, in 1944, the largest seaport in Cyprus. It was the main port of emigration of pilgrims to the Holy Land and the centre for the diplomatic corps during the Ottoman period. The town gave a home to Lazarus who became the Bishop of Larnaca. His remains were stolen from the church that bears his name in 890 A.D. and taken to Marseilles, a marble sarcophagus remains with the inscription: 'Lazarus, the friend of Christ.' Larnaca is now a popular holiday spot with a fabulous beach, marinas and restaurants.

Further along the south coast is Limassol, the second largest city in Cyprus. It is known for its large wine and beer factories.

On the west coast is Paphos, the most historical and mythological place in Cyprus.

Kyrenia, on the north coast is the most picturesque of the five towns, built around a horseshoe-shaped harbour dominated on one side by a great Byzantine castle.

I researched the history of all of the towns and gave them a brief visit. I would explore them more with Susan.

One day in mid-April I stood on the balcony of the small terminal in Nicosia and watched the Egypt Air DC-3 from Alex taxi to a halt. I spotted Susan among the deplaning passengers and went down to wait for her to clear Customs. As she came towards me I could see that her brown hair was now arranged in a flip cut which softened her sharp cheek bones. Her lipstick was a bright, glossy red. She was wearing a maroon jacket with narrow lapels over a white blouse and a gray skirt. High heels added to her height.

I gave her a hug and a kiss and said: 'You look good enough to eat!'

'Later,' she laughed, hugging me back. 'It's so great to see you!' She held me at arm's length and added: 'You're so tanned and your hair is bleached almost white by the sun. You're very handsome, you know.'

'Stop it!' I protested. 'You'll make me conceited.'

We picked up her bag and walked towards the exit. 'Where are we going?' she asked.

'I've got a car.' I had rented a small Morris - the most inexpensive one that I could find. 'And I've rented an apartment right on the beach in Larnaca. It's about a one-hour drive south of here.'

'I know where it is,' she said, tartly, 'I've looked at a map of Cyprus.'

It was very hot for April so Susan took off her jacket and we opened all the car windows. I was just wearing shorts and a T-shirt.

For the first four or five days we just lay on the beach, swan, ate, drank and made love. The small apartment was hot and stuffy so we moved a mattress out on the balcony, hoping for a breeze, and slept in the nude with only a thin sheet. One night she lay with her head on my shoulder, our legs intertwined and sighed: 'Oh, Lee . . . . I'm so much in love with you.'

'Are you?' I stroked her back. 'But you are in love with Jason and are going to marry him.' Her fiancé was serving with the British Army in Europe.

'I know. Can a girl be in love with two men at the same time?'

'I guess so.' I didn't have this problem; I liked Susan very much but I wasn't in love with her.

'I feel like a traitor,' she said.

'I don't see why you should . . . do you suppose that Jason is being celibate while you are apart?'

'No.' She rolled over on top of me. 'In that case do you suppose we could . . . Ah . . . '

We could. !

It was just a short drive from Larnaca to Famagusta along the lovely coastline. 'The name means 'Hidden in the Sand,' I explained as we drove along. 'It dates from the early Crusades.'

'Does it have any famous buildings?'

'It had but most of them have been destroyed. The wall around the town is still standing . . . so is the Latin Cathedral of Saint Nicholas built about 1300 A.D. I haven't looked inside it but we can do that today.'

'But Famagusta was once famous?'

'Yes. It is the 'Seaport in Cyprus' in Shakespeare's Othello and the Governor of the city in 1508, one Christoforo Moro, is clearly identifiable as the Moor.'

We found the old city mostly in ruins. The Latin Cathedral had been converted to a Mosque and hence had escaped damage; it was an outstanding example of original Gothic architecture. The square on which it stands, bounded on the opposite side by the palace of the Venetian Providitore, was once the largest in the western world.

We spent a day in Nicosia where I showed Susan the sights and she did some shopping. In the Algios Georgio Taverna, near the market, we had a sumptuous meal of Mousaka, made of mince, peppers, onions, courgettes, aubergines, and tomatoes.

On the following day we packed our bags and set off to drive around the coast to Kyrenia.

Our first stop was Limassol, where we stayed overnight. 'What's its history?' Susan asked.

'Well, Richard Couer de Lion landed near here when he conquered the island in 1191 during the Third Crusade. When he found the Cypriots so fierce and rebellious, he sold the place to the Knights Templar. It changed hands many times over the centuries to Romans, Greeks and Turks and finally became a British possession in 1878.'

'And it's still a British colony?'

'Yes.'

We found the city to be active and bustling, especially around the large market. The streets generally radiate outwards from the sea-front promenade. We sat in the shade of an open-air cafe, watched the scene in the harbour with both small freighters and pleasure boats, sampled the local wine and ate Shamiski - a kind of pancake served with honey that was delicious. The war was a long way away.

The drive over the winding coast road out of Limassol for Paphos on the next day was lovely, with all the car windows open to create a breeze. I looked at Susan, seated on my left. She wore a red scarf to keep her hair in place, a halter top and shorts. She was a great companion: loving, animated, witty and cheerful. I never heard a complaint or a cross word. While she wasn't very pretty, she made the best of what she had and her figure was more than adequate.

She broke my reverie by asking: 'So Paphos is where all the history is?'

'Yep.'

'How old is it?'

'About 7,000 B.C. It was the capital of Cyprus under the Romans.'

'Aphrodite lived here? She is the Goddess of Love?'

'Yes. Her cult was formed about 1200 B.C. She was called Venus by the Romans and of course is now very famous.'

'Was there ever such a real person?'

'Now you're getting into the murky dividing line between history and mythology . . . but I doubt it. She wore a magic girdle which enabled her to arouse love in men.'

Susan ran her hand up my inner thigh. 'I don't need a magic girdle, do I?'

'No,' I laughed, 'but you'll need an ambulance if you keep that up because I'll run us off the road.'

She giggled. 'What else do you know about her?'

'Well,' I replied, showing off my newly acquired knowledge, 'her cult included temple prostitution whereby young women sacrificed their virginity to whomever was passing through the temple at the time. The procedure was for the virgins to go to the temple, hang around until chosen by a man and then submit to a night of unbridled passion. In spring, the temple's Festival of Aphrodite and her lover, Adonis, drew pilgrims from all over the ancient world. When Adonis died, she changed his blood into an anemone. Since she sprang from white sea foam produced by the severed genitals of Uranus, there is a statue in Paphos of a phallus with salt.'

'My . . . my,' Susan said. 'They were a lusty lot, weren't they?'

'Yes. Botticelli's famous painting shows her rising naked from the sea, riding on a scallop shell. Where ever she stepped the ground turned green and flowers sprang up.'

'How did Adonis get the reputation of being so beautiful?'

'I don't know. He is always referred to as such so now it is applied to any handsome youth or man. I think Shakespeare wrote a poem about him and Venus.'

Arriving in Paphos (Kitme) we booked into the Apollo Hotel to ensure a bed for the night (although it wasn't crowded) had a delicious lunch of pumpkin slices fried in butter with wheatmeal pilau. Then we went exploring.

The Tomb of Kinga held no kings but just prominent people, probably Ptolemaic officials. Most of the burial places are just holes in the rock but some are in underground caverns that are really spooky.

The House of Dionysus, the Greek name for Bacchus, God of Wine, contain the famed Paphos mosaics which depict mythological themes about the exploits of Bacchus, known for drunken orgies on a grand scale. They date from about 300 A.D. and were just being excavated when we were there.

Near the Amphitheatre, mostly in ruins, is a sign saying that Apostles Paul and Barnabas arrived here as missionaries in 45 A.D. There is also a pillar to which the city's Roman Governor had St. Paul bound.

The Sanctuary of Apollo lies among pines and cypresses a little east of the Stadium. Of all the Cypriot archaeological sites it is the most beautiful and moving. It dates from about 2,000 B.C. Apollo was the God of music and poetry. In addition to the temple, the huge site contains houses, dormitories, kitchens, baths (both hot and cold), handsome colonnades with an open, paved surround, a giant cistern holding 37 metric tonnes. Much was being restored. We were awed. It was: 'Look at this . . . look at that!'

Susan grabbed my arm. 'Lee . . . look at that!'

She pointed to a volve pit. In it were hundreds of terracotta figures of people and animals. (Later almost 10,000 were excavated).

Nearby was a sign saying: 'House of Apollo Hylates, God of prophesy, archery, herds and flocks.'

'I'm confused,' Susan said. 'Were there two Apollos?'

'Yes. Apollo was worshipped until about 1600 A.D. and after that it was Apollo Hylates. Tradition says that deer sacred to the God swam to Cyprus from Asia Minor to take refuge here.'

We spent several hours at the sanctuary and returned to our hotel tired and footsore. But it had been worth it! After a rest we summoned up enough strength to have a nice meal at Theo's restaurant, fortified by some Cypriot Commandarie wine.

We found Kyrenia to be the most picturesque of the five towns. The horseshoe-shaped harbour was ringed with lovely outdoor cafes and shops. Dominating the scene is the Byzantine castle which houses the Shipwreck Museum with the world's oldest shipwreck and its cargo. The ship is believed to have sunk in a storm near Kyrenia about 3,000 B.C. The castle was built by the Byzantines as a defense against marauding Arabs.

Near Kyrenia we found the castle of St. Hilarion. It is a story book castle with ramparts and turrets surrounded by a smooth green where the Knights jousted. Small wonder that Walt Disney used it as a model for Snow White. From the summit we could see across to Turkey and the mountains of Anatolia.

Legend says that the first permanent resident was the hermit, St. Hilarion, who came from Egypt in search of solitude and a place to meditate. Settling on this isolated spot he found it occupied by devils who realized that they could not stay with such a pious companion and raised an awful din at his approach. The saint, who was known for his sense of humour, merely remarked that at least he had come to a place where he was welcomed by music. Such a reaction by the intruder was too much for the devils who had no redress and they fled leaving the saint in sole possession. In time he attracted many pilgrims and the foundation of a monastic order followed.

But soon it was time to return to Larnaca, pack our bags and say goodbye - our leave was over. As the airport, Susan hugged me and said: 'When shall we meet again, Lee?'

'I guess when we can both get leave at the same time.'

'But you will keep writing?' she pleaded.

'I promise,' I replied.

But we were destined to meet again sooner than either of us anticipated and in a very different way.

A few days later I wandered into the Mess about 2100 hours to find Tommy seated on a stool at the end of the bar. In front of him was a bottle of Lebanese brandy on which he had already made considerable inroads. I got a glass and poured myself a drink. 'Tough day?'

'They are all tough,' he replied. 'I'm fed up with these stupid students trying to kill me.'

I knew what he meant. Being an instructor pilot on Beaus was a nerve-wracking occupation. He stood behind the student telling him what to do but unable to reach the controls if the pupil fouled things up. And much of the flying was done low over the water where a mistake could be fatal. More than one Beau had not returned from a training flight.

'You had a poor one today?' I asked.

'Yes. If I'm going to be killed in this war, let it be fighting the bloody Germans.' Tommy spoke every word carefully in the manner of one who is semi-drunk and trying vainly to pretend that he is not.

He looked owlishly at me and said: 'Lee, we are good friends. Will you fly with me?'

I wasn't sure what he meant so I replied, half-jokingly: 'Tommy . . . I'll fly with you anywhere, anytime.'

'On operations?'

I was stunned by his question. 'But we're supposed to be off Ops for a year. I've only been here for four months and you for about six.'

'But would you come if I could arrange it?'

'Sure, but how . . . ?'

Tommy lurched to his feet. 'Leave it with me.'

Two weeks later we were posted as a crew to 603 Squadron, based in the desert near Tobruk.

Chapter 11

Tobruk

The C.O. of 603 Squadron was Wing Commander Christopher Foxley-Norris, a handsome and charismatic man who was to achieve some fame in the RAF (more on him later). He obviously needed us because we were both immediately promoted; Tommy to Sqn Ldr, O.C. of 'A' Flight and myself to Flight Lieutenant and Navigation Leader. It turned out that Tommy Deck and Foxley-Norris were old friends which explained our departure from Cyprus.

It was May, 1944 and the role of the Beaufighters in the Med had changed. There was no longer any enemy shipping large enough to warrant carrying a torpedo. Instead, eight rockets were fitted - four under each wing - with 60-lb explosive warheads. Our role was to interrupt supplies to the German garrisons in the Aegean Islands and to attack targets identified by intelligence and by the partisans. The Greeks never gave up their bitter campaign against the Germans and the coasts and mountains of the islands were admirable terrain for guerilla activity. We flew a mixture of Rovers and at specific targets, sometimes at night. One disadvantage was that it was a long way across the Med from Tobruk to the Aegean Islands which did not give us much time in the target area, especially for the northern islands.

The enemy defenses consisted of anti-aircraft guns on both ship and shore, flak ships as escorts and ME-109s on the larger islands. The ME-109s could out perform us but we flew below their radar coverage and interceptions were rare. There were also some Arado-196 fighters but they were slow and usually flew away when they saw a Beau.

Just prior to our arrival the squadron had carried out an attack

on an airfield being built on the island of Paros. The strip was raked
with canon and rocket fire and much damage was done. Tongue-
in-cheek, Foxley-Norris claimed: 'One diesel roller of 20/30 tons
destroyed.'

After two night patrols around Crete with no sightings, Tommy
and I flew on our first strike. The German naval command made a
major effort to stock up Crete. They formed a convoy made up of
the merchant ship Tanais (1,500 tons), the Sabine (2,250 tons) and
the Gertrund (2,000 tons). They were escorted by five destroyers,
two torpedo boats and four U-Boats. Air cover was AR-196s and
JU-88s.

The RAF were aware of the convoy and knew its route. They
assembled the largest strike force of the war in the Med. It consisted
of 12 Marauders (24 SAAF), 18 Baltimores (15 SAAF), 13 long-
range Spitfires (94 Sqn), four Mustangs (213 Sqn), ten Beaus from
252 Sqn and eight more from 603 Sqn. The Beaus were five minutes
behind the others. The first strike damaged and slowed down the
convoy; the Beaufighter attack was devastating. Both Sabine and
Gertrund were set on fire and Tanais was hit so severely that many
of the crew jumped overboard. All of the escorts were damaged and
the Spitfires and Mustangs took care of the enemy fighters.

'Sabine'

Not satisfied with just sinking ships, Tommy chased a JU-88 but couldn't catch him. We lost one aircraft, with both F/S Atkinson and Parsons being killed.

Then came a string of bad luck. On a Rover we attacked and damaged two small vessels east of Mykonos but lost one aircraft to anti-aircraft fire. Both F/S Joyce and Thomas were killed.

On 23 July we led six Beaus on a sweep in the central Aegean and met about a dozen AR-196s. In the ensuing battle Tommy shot down one Arado and I claimed another damaged. (Tommy had insisted that I not remove the machine gun from my position). However, we lost three more aircraft.

A Canadian pilot, W/O Sykes and his navigator, Sgt. Brook, ditched but were picked up later by a British submarine. In the second, F/S Rogers was killed but the pilot, F/O Jenkinson, was picked up later by a British destroyer. The crew of the third aircraft lost had a remarkable experience. The pilot was F/O Cas de Bounovialle; the navigator F/O Potter. Their aircraft was very badly damaged and had to be ditched. They were rescued from their dinghy by a Greek caique which took them to the mainland south-east of Athens. They were told to wait for partisans but after four days nobody had arrived so they began to walk. When they finally made contact, the partisans took them to the island of Euboea from where a caique carried them to Izmir in Turkey. They were accommodated in this town by an English lady, Mrs. 'Ma' Perkins who ran a hostel for RAF internees somewhat on the lines of a seaside landlady in the U.K. providing bed and breakfast. From Izmir they were taken by rail to Aleppo in Syria and then flown to Cairo, from where they were sent back to 603 Sqn.

I was not thrilled to be living under canvas again with the usual zillion flies, stifling heat and hellish when the 'Khamsin', the drying wind, blew. We had Italian POWs to do the work around the camp; they quickly picked up many English words and were always on the scrounge for something or another. Since we were not far from Cairo we often got a performance from a British touring group called ENSA (Entertainment National Service Association). The airmen dubbed them 'Every Night Something Awful'.

In peace time 603 Sqn was an Auxiliary Squadron in Scotland - the City of Edinburgh Squadron - and was greatly supported by the residents of that city. It was formed in 1925, flying DH-9A fighters. Its motto is 'Gin Ye Daur' (If you Dare) and its crest bears the Edinburgh Coat of Arms. The squadron took part in the Battle of Britain flying Spitfires. It was then sent to Malta and later to the Western Desert where it re-equipped with Beaufighters.

Officer's Mess

A large proportion of our ground crew were pre-war squadron members. Some of them even founder members with 20 years of unbroken service. The value of the cohesive spirit of these tough, loyal Edinburgh men was immeasurable. They had been through some very rough times in the Battle of Britain and in Malta and they were quite happy to go on doing so just as long as they were needed. Their senior man was a great fellow named Warrant Officer Prentice, who was a mine of both history and legend of 603 Squadron. He admitted to an age of 'just about fifty' but since his son was an NCO with the squadron this was a little difficult to credit.

The kind ladies of Edinburgh sent us heavy, knitted sweaters, balaclavas, mittens and thick, woollen socks. It was 105° F in the shade in the desert.

My best friend on the squadron, after Tommy, was another Canadian named Douglas Bridger, also from Vancouver. He was an Admin Officer who was our Adjutant. We paired up in a regular bridge game against Foxley-Norris and his partner and won enough money to pay our bar bills. We both returned to Vancouver after the war and are still friends after more than 50 years.

Our airfield did not have runways but was a 3,000 - yard square
of packed sand and loam. A van at one side provided traffic control.
We just checked the wind-sock on the top of the van and landed in
that direction. One day when we were on the approach the van, for
some reason, fired a red flare at us.

'Was that Red or Green?' Tommy asked.

'Red!' I replied. 'Hold clear until we get a Green.'

Tommy circled until a Green flare was fired.

'That was Green,' I said, 'go ahead and land. And I want to talk
to you!'

As usual, Tommy greased the kite down. After debriefing and a
change of clothes we went into the Mess tent for a coffee.

'All right,' I asked, 'how the hell did you get into aircrew if you are colour blind?'

'I'm not completely colour blind . . . it's just that some shades are hard for me.'

'Yeah!' I scoffed. 'Like Red and Green. C'mon . . . give . . . how did you do it?'

'You know those books that they use with the numbers surrounded by different colours?'

'Yeah'. The numbers from One to Nine were immersed in various colours and shades and thus very hard to distinguish.

'Well, a friend got one of those books and listed the number on each page against the page number. Then I memorized the list. I scored 100 percent.'

'Oh, you cheater!' I laughed. But I was full of admiration for this feisty guy who wanted to fly so badly that he went to such extremes. 'How about the lights in the cockpit?'

'Oh, that's easy. There's two lights for everything and I know which is which. Like for the under-cart . . . the top light is Green and the bottom one is Red and I can tell which one is glowing.'

I put an arm around his shoulder. 'Ask me anytime, pal . . . I'll help you out.'

It was sometimes hard to fill in the days when we were not flying. The nearest town of any size, Tobruk, had changed hands several times in the desert war and was now in ruins. We never knew what day of the week it was and only vaguely the date. After about 10 weeks on the squadron, I said to Tommy: 'Let's get out of here for a few days . . . go to Alex . . . it's only a short flight.'

'All right,' he agreed. 'I suppose you want to see your girlfriend?'

'Yes.'

Susan was thrilled when I phoned her from the Cecil Hotel to say that I was in the city for a couple of days. She had just been promoted to Chief Petty Officer so we had another reason for a small celebration.

Shortly after our return from Alex we went on a daylight rover. Just off Naxos we spotted a German E-Boat alone, in transit. Tommy yelled 'Tallyho!' and threw the Beau into a steep dive to port. We obviously took the E-Boast by surprise because before they had time to fire a shot Tommy had loosed four rockets and was strafing the boat with our four 20-mm canon. The boat crashed into the rocks of a nearby island.

E - Boat crash

'Way to go!' I shouted.

'Yippee!' Tommy responded. 'The only thing that's more fun than this is sex.'

Foxley-Norris was handsome, charismatic, intelligent and had a great sense of humour. In 1935 he arrived at Oxford University to study law. Here he joined the University Air Squadron and obtained his wings. Awarded a scholarship to the Middle Temple for his finals, he then joined No 615 (Country of Surrey) Auxiliary Squadron. But war broke out before he could write his finals. I'm sure he would have been a great success as a barrister had he chosen that profession.

In 1972 I was startled to read in an aviation magazine that my former C.O. was now Air Marshal Sir Christopher Foxley-Norris, Chief of the Royal Air Force. He had reached the pinnacle of success in his chosen career.

In his autobiography 'A Lighter Shade of Blue', Foxley-Norris refers to Tommy Deck as: 'Short, thick-set, red-haired and noisy, he had a wonderful fighting record. Universally admired and liked, he was quite literally fearless. This is an overused and misused word but I genuinely believe that he never felt fear.' Right on!

Foxley-Norris adds: 'Very early one morning we managed to sneak into Andalsnes harbour and attack an anchored convoy before we were detected. For once we got away practically scot-free because we had caught the anti-aircraft defenses napping. This was not good enough for Tommy. He proceeded to fly round and round the harbour shooting up the anti-aircraft crews to encourage them to do better next time.' Didn't I know it!

Air Chief Marshal Sir C. Foxley - Norris

When the war in the Med was over, 603 Squadron returned home, re-equipped with Mosquitoes and flew out of Wick, Scotland for the balance of the war. (I had left by then). On one engagement there Foxley-Norris says: 'He (Tommy) was hit in his starboard engine during the attack and forced to feather one propeller. As we left the target area we heard with concern radio calls indicating that our rear sections, which Tommy was leading, had been jumped by Focke-Wulfs and were having a bad time. He turned back on his one engine and joined in the scrap. He got away with it - and apparently enjoyed it enormously.'

The remainder of July, 1944, was occupied by night intruder patrols without much success. One of our aircraft failed to return from an operation over the shipping routes north of Crete. We never found out why (enemy night fighter?) but later heard that the

Canadian pilot, F/O Soderland, and his navigator, F/S Nicol were taken POW.

Now that the OTU on Cyprus was running well, we were getting replacement crews on a regular basis although they sometimes had to wait for a Beau which had to come from the U.K.

During August the Germans realized that their hold on Greece and the Aegean Islands had become untenable because of air interdiction over the sea and partisan activity on the ground. They decided to evacuate as many troops and equipment as they could.

The RAF assigned two Beaufighter squadrons to hamper this withdrawal - 252 and 603. We got word that a large ship named 'Carola', which had just undergone repairs in Port Laki, Leros, was leaving there for Piraeus escorted by two flak ships. Our strike force consisted of eight Beaus from 252 Sqn with four Beaus of 603 Sqn for top cover, of which Tommy and I were one.

We caught the convoy nearing the Greek mainland, south-east of Athens. With rockets and canon fire, all of the vessels were hit and Carola so badly damaged that the Germans scuttled her in Piraeus harbour as a blockship. Two Beaus suffered some damage but all made it back to base.

On 14 Sept we made a strike on the harbour at Parockia on Paros where we had been briefed that German evacuation was in progress. A force of eight Beaus each from 252 and 603 Sqns was dispatched. The intelligence was wrong but we did sink a minesweeper named 'Nordstern' as well as two smaller vessels. It was amusing to see men on small vessels, if they were near the shore, jump overboard and start to swim when they saw a Beaufighter coming.

Led by W/C Foxley-Norris, 10 Beaus of 603 Sqn and two from 252 Sqn were briefed to find a minelayer named 'Zeus' off the Greek coast; it was a former Italian merchant ship named 'Francesco Morosini' which was playing a large part in the German evacuation. We couldn't find the 'Zeus' but came across a convoy of five small vessels escorted by three flak ships. Three of the freighters were set on fire and sunk and the other two badly damaged. But the flak was intense and two of our aircraft were shot down.

On the first the pilot, Sgt. Harrison, was killed but his navigator, Sgt. Bannister, survived to be taken POW.

The second, flown by F/Os Cas de Bounevialle and Potter, recently returned from their adventure through Turkey, had to ditch - not far from where they had done six weeks earlier. Neither man was injured and they were picked up by a U-Boat and taken to Piraeus. Under guard they then began a torturous trip which took them through Athens, Skopje, Zagreb, Vienna, Budapest and Frankfurt. They finally ended up in Stalag Luft III at Sagan in Upper Silesia where they remained until liberated by Russian troops in Jan 45.

Then, on 16 Sept 44, Tommy and I ran into trouble.

We were on a Rover near Naxos when I spotted an Arado-190, a single-engine float plane, going in an easterly direction.

'Tallyho!' I shouted.

'Where? What?' Tommy asked.

'Do a tight turn to port and you'll come up behind an Arado-190.'

'Good stuff!' Tommy was excited. He threw the Beau into a gut-wrenching turn.

But the Arado had seen us. The pilot opened the taps, dove for sea-level and headed for Leros harbour. So did Tommy. The Beau was a lot faster and we caught the Arado near the harbour entrance. A burst from our four 20-mm canons sent it crashing into the rocks.

Arado-190

'Good shooting!' I congratulated Tommy.

'Like shooting quail!' he responded.

We were now close to Leros harbour. 'There's an anti-aircraft site on that point of ground south of the harbour entrance,' I said, so that Tommy could take evasive action and avoid it. Stupid me!

'Let's wake them up!' Tommy shouted as he headed straight for the gun emplacement. He fired all eight rockets and we could see carnage below; he followed this with all four canon as he flew right over the site. There seemed to be nothing left intact but not all guns had been stilled. Just as we were pulling away the port side of the Beau was raked from stem to stern. The port engine began to vibrate, shrapnel careened around the inside as cordite and smoke filled the air.

'Get our of here!' I shouted. 'Fly south.'

'I am . . . I am. Are you okay?'

'Yeah . . . I guess so.' A shell had ripped through the fuselage right in front of me and ended up in canon magazines. 'How about you?'

'I'm not hit,' Tommy replied, 'but the port engine won't last long.'

'We'd better not try to fly across the Med,' I said. 'What say we hug the Turkish coast and try to make Cyprus?'

'All right.'

'We'll soon come to Rhodes, so stay low and very close to Turkey and maybe they won't see us.'

'Okay.'

Shortly after passing Rhodes, Tommy feathered the port propeller and said: 'Lee, we're losing fuel from the port gas tank . . . it must have taken a hit.'

'Damn! How much fuel do we have now assuming that tank to be empty?'

He gave me the number. I checked my fuel graphs for one-engine performance (with the good engine at nearly max) calculated our consumption, worked out our ground speed and measured the distance to Cyprus.

'We're not going to make it to Cyprus,' I said, sadly. 'We'll have to put down in Turkey.'

'Where?' he was quite casual.

'Give me a minute to look at my intelligence notes.' This I did. 'We are coming up to a large bay where there is a town called Antalya. It doesn't have an airfield as such but there is supposed to be a 2,000 - foot strip of Summerfeld Stripping.'

'That's those metal pieces strung together with holes that looks like a giant Meccano Set?'

'Yes.' I thought for a minute. 'Tommy, do you want me to lighten the aircraft by throwing things out?'

'No need,' he replied. 'I'll fire the canons to get rid of the spare ammunition.' This he did.

'I've got some stuff that I want to throw out . . . have you?'

'Just some let-down plates and recognition codes. I'll toss them out of my side window.'

'Well, I have quite a bit and I don't have a window so I'll have to jettison the canopy.'

'Go ahead.' Nothing ever fazed him.

My bubble canopy had two locking catches on the port side and two hinges on the starboard. The manufacturer's recommended procedure to jettison was to unfasten the two catches and give the canopy a sharp push upwards; the slipstream would then tear the canopy away. But we, and our sister squadrons, had found two flaws. One - the rear hinge would not always break and that left the canopy flapping in the wind. Two - the canopy was in danger of striking the tail plane, giving the pilot a severe problem.

So our technicians had installed explosive bolts at the two hinges. I released the port catches, lifted the red guard and pushed the button. There was a loud 'Bang' and the canopy sailed away. 'Eureka!' I shouted.

'Worked all right, did it?' Tommy asked.

'Like a charm . . . but it's sure draughty in here now.'

I tore up all my logs, intelligence notes and other papers and watched them fly away. There were two pieces of equipment that I didn't want to fall into the wrong hands.

One was the I.F.F. (Identification, Friend or Foe). I crawled forward. The unit was amidships. It was a black box about the size and shape of a box of kleenex tissues. I cut the wires to the antenna and then those to the front cockpit. Then I unscrewed the unit and threw it overboard.

The other was the radio transceiver. Try as I might, I couldn't get it out of its rack, so I drove the fire axe into it a couple of times. I also took the film out of the gun camera.

Antalya was easy to spot. It seemed to be a fair-sized town. The field with the metal stripping was to the east. Tommy made a pass to look things over. 'I don't think that anyone has ever used this strip,' he said. 'There's grass and weeds growing through the holes and alongside. It's hard to see where it begins and ends.'

'Are you going to lower the gear?' I asked.

'Yes.'

'Then give me a minute to cross-switch the generators. The port one lowers the gear and it's not working.' This I did.

We could see from smoke rising from the town that there was virtually no wind. Tommy said: 'I'll land going north . . . I can see that end of the stripping better. It may be rough so brace yourself.'

'Right.' I turned my seat around so that I was facing the rear and slumped down a little so that my head was resting against the seat back. 'Oh, shit!' I mumbled. 'Here we go again!'

Leros to Antalya

Chapter 12

Turkey

The jail cell in Antalya was crummy. The floor was cement. Three of the walls were concrete block; the fourth was bars with a gate locked on the outside. There were two cots, each with a skimpy mattress, two thin blankets and no pillows. Beside a small table were two wooden chairs. Overhead, a single light bulb drooped from a rod. In one corner there was a hole in the floor, with a foot-rest on either side, from which wafted a smell of crap and chlorine.

'All the comforts of home,' Tommy sighed.

'We'd be home,' I carped, 'if you hadn't decided to take on the German Army.'

'How did I know they were Germans? I though they were Italians who can't hit a barn door with a handful of peas.'

Just then a guard entered with two small trays of some unrecognizable food. While he put them on the table, I turned my back so that he wouldn't see my escape belt, which was under my shirt, and fished out a $5.00 U.S. bill. (I carried only American money these days). I held up the bill and said 'Raki'. The only word in Turkish that I knew. Then I pantomimed two glasses. He got the message and returned soon with a bottle of the anisette-flavoured liquor.

After our sumptuous meal, Tommy asked: 'What ever will we do to pass the time until these guys decide what to do with us?'

'How about some rummy?' I took a deck of cards from my escape belt.

'Well, I'll be . . . ! How did you ever think of that?'

'You're travelling with a man of great experience,' I replied, smugly.

Tommy, the eternal optimist, didn't have an escape belt. So we played rummy until it was time to go to bed.

The Turkish soldiers had not been unfriendly. It was more like they didn't know what to do with us and decided to keep us under lock and key until they found out.

Tommy made a perfect single-engine landing, holding the Beau inches off the metal stripping until all forward speed bled off and then touched down as softly as a baby's hand on its mother's cheek. However, the port tire blew- probably striking a sharp point in the metal - and the aircraft slewed to a halt. Before we could get out we were surrounded by soldiers with cocked rifles.

We shouted 'Englise' but it made no difference because no one spoke English. They sort of milled around; they had seen aircraft before but nothing like a Beaufighter. Then their leader, probably a Captain because he had two bars on his shoulders, clearly told them to put us in the truck and take us to the jail.

About noon the next day we heard voices, speaking Turkish, coming down the corridor. The guard opened our gate and ushered in a tall, broad-shouldered man wearing a bush jacket with many pockets, shorts and hiking boots. 'Hi, fellas,' he said, in broad American, 'how you doin'? I'm Keith Rankin from the U.S. Embassy.'

We introduced ourselves and shook hands.

'How did you know we were here?' Tommy asked.

Rankin chuckled. 'The whole town knows . . . they're talkin' about nothin' else.'

'What are you doing here?' I asked.

'I'm on a hikin' holiday,' he replied. 'Thought maybe I could help you boys out.' He paused. 'I speak the lingo.'

'Help us how?' Tommy asked.

'Do you know the procedure?'

We both shook our heads.

'Well, we've had American boys land in Turkey and here's how it goes. Officially, you are interned because Turkey is neutral. But they have no place to put you and, bein' pro-Allies, will agree to you bein' released provided certain financial arrangements are made. But this has to be done in Ankara because that's where the Embassies are.'

'How do we get there?' I asked.

'I'm comin' to that. Normally they would have a guard take you but they ain't got any who speak English. So I'm tryin' to talk them into me takin' you with a promise to turn you in to Army HQs in Ankara. My leave is over, anyhow.'

'Great stuff!' Tommy shouted. 'Can you get us out of this rat hole today?'

'Not today,' Rankin shook his head. 'Mebbe tomorrow. Just hang tight.'

He called to the guard to let him out and walked away. The guard locked the gate.

We resumed our rummy game. I was winning.

After breakfast the next morning - tea and two bread buns - we waited impatiently for our saviour to appear. Rankin arrived in the late morning with good news.

'Hi, fellas,' he said, as the guard opened the gate, 'you're free now . . . released in my custody until I turn you over to Turkish Army HQs in Ankara.'

'Hooray!' I shouted.

'Right on!' Tommy added. 'How do we get to Ankara?'

'By bus . . . tomorrow morning,' Keith replied. 'For tonight I have you a room at the Aspen Hotel where I'm staying. We can go there now, check in and have some lunch.'

We were delighted to leave that odious jail cell.

The Aspen Hotel overlooked the harbour and had nice rooms with balconies bedecked with flowers. Over lunch I asked Keith: 'What have you been doing around here? Are there some famous historic sites in the area?'

'A few,' he replied. 'Some remains of the Hittite Empire which date as far back as 1,500 B.C. But mostly Greek and Roman structures. I've been to Perge and Silge, west of here, and to a Roman amphitheater in Aspendos.'

'What is there to see in Antalya?' I asked.

'The thing to do,' Rankin answered, 'is to rent a horse-cab for the afternoon and I'll show you around.'

We were enchanted by our horse-cab. Pulled by a pair of sturdy Anatolian ponies it was called a 'payton' - from the English word 'phaeton'. The coach-work was a bright fire-engine red with brass lamps and hubcaps highly burnished. The driver was a middle-aged man with a magnificent moustache. He wore a cloth cap, a pink cotton jacket, a white shirt whose neck was fastened by a large gold stud and voluminous black baggy trousers. In his button hole was a scarlet rose and around his waist a cummerbund of green silk. His cab had an enormous 'hooter' which he used to great effect. He also carried a long whip which he cracked and flourished, although I noticed that he never actually hit his ponies; he had no aversion, however, in using it on passing donkeys.

'Drive around the harbour,' Keith said to the driver in Turkish, 'and then to Hadrian's Gate.'

We clip-clopped over the cobble-stone roads. The bay was formed by a deep notch in the rocky coast-line and held several caiques painted in brilliant colours. In the background were the snow-capped peaks of the Bey Mountains. Looking back to the city we saw a semi-circle of pinkish-grey cliffs, the slopes being dotted with houses.

'Hadrian's Gate,' Keith explained when our cab arrived there, 'was built to commemorate the visit of Emperor Hadrian in A.D. 130. You can see that the triple arcade marble has been restored. The interior of the arches are decorated with reliefs of fruits and cereals of the area.'

'Now,' Keith instructed the driver in Turkish, 'go to the Yivli Minare.'

We disembarked to look at the Fluted Minaret, a curious structure of pinkish brick partially inlaid with faience - decorated earthenware and porcelain - built about A.D. 1300.

Here we bought some nuts from a seller with a unique stall. He had a barrow, part of the top enclosed by a glass case in which the nuts were stored - peanuts, hazel nuts, cobs, pine kernels and pistachios. Beside it was a wood stove, complete with chimney, where the nuts were roasted and then kept warm. Incense wood was used and the smell was enticing.

On our return to the hotel we drove through the old quarter. Here, in a maze of cobbled and paved streets, were a variety of houses each with some feature to distinguish it from its neighbours. Most were of different colours. Many were wood with two stories and red tile roofs. Deep bay windows projected several feet over the narrow streets giving shade to passers-by.

On arriving back at our hotel we left Keith to settle with the horse-cab driver and went into the bar for a cool beer. It had been an interesting afternoon.

The bus ride from Antalya to Ankara was long and mostly boring with one-hour stops at Dinar and Afyon. The heat of the long summer - it was now September - had seared the countryside into a bleak and desolate landscape broken only occasionally by streams rushing through miniature ravines. Dwarf and scrub trees stood like lifeless sentinels on the low hills.

As we approached Ankara, Keith said to us: 'Before going to Turkish HQs, we must check in at the British Embassy so they know you are here, can notify Cairo that you are safe and start extradition proceedings. The Air Attache is Group Captain Sanders; I know him well and he'll take care of you.'

'We'll need some Turkish lira,' Tommy said.

'He'll fix you up.'

At the Ankara bus depot we took a taxi to the Embassy. We were ushered straight into the Air Attache's office.

'Hi, Sandy,' Keith said. 'I've brought you a pair of RAF flyers who force-landed in Antalya. I'm under bond to deliver them to the Turkish Army.'

'Well, I'm damned!' Sanders was a bulky man, about 40 years old, with wings and a row of ribbons headed by a DSO. He stood up to shake hands as we introduced ourselves. 'Have a seat . . . you too, Keith . . . and tell me your story.'

Tommy described our adventure and ended up with ' . . . and I understand that you can get us back home.'

'That I can . . . that I can,' Sanders mused.

'The first thing to do,' I said, 'is to notify our squadron that we are safe so that they can tell our families. This will be the second time that mine have received a telegram saying that I'm 'Missing in Action.'

'I'll see to that right away,' Sanders agreed.

'What will the Turks do with us now?' I asked.

'They'll put you up in a hotel. You'll need some civilian clothes and spending money . . . I'll alert the Paymaster.'

'How long will it take you to get us out of here?' Tommy asked.

'Between five and seven days.'

'And how will we get back to Egypt?'

'Civil air . . . Egypt Air has a flight from Ankara to Cairo.' Sanders turned to Rankin. 'Keith, give me an account of the money you've spent and I'll see that you are reimbursed.'

'Okay,' Rankin agreed.

So we got some Lira from the Paymaster and left with Sanders' parting words: 'Tomorrow, let me know what hotel they put you up in . . . either phone or come here. You must check with me every day.'

Keith Rankin took us to Turkish Army HQs. We thanked him profusely for his help, which he decried, saying: 'Glad to . . . Ah just happened to be in the right place at the right time. Good luck, fellas.'

An Army officer who spoke English was expecting us. With him was a Lieutenant named Matin Marsa who was to be our guard while we were in Ankara. He was about 30 years old, medium height, with a swarthy complexion and a heavy five-o'clock shadow. His English was only fair and his accent so thick that we sometimes had trouble understanding him. After a couple of days we found out that his French was good so we used both languages.

He escorted us to a seedy, second-class hotel in the city centre named the Hisarotel. The rooms were poorly furnished and the bathroom down the hall. We were very tired and after a skimpy meal in a nearby restaurant, fell into bed. As we were nodding off Tommy said: 'I wonder how much we are worth?'

'You figger the British will have to pay?'

'Yes.'

'I wonder, too.' We never did find out.

On the next day we asked Matin what there was to do and see in Ankara.

'Ankara is nothing,' he said, scornfully. 'Istanbul is the heart and soul of Turkey. I come from there,' he added, proudly.

'But Ankara is the Capital,' I said.

'Only because Ataturk decreed it in 1923,' Matin said. 'He thought that Istanbul was too vulnerable to his enemies.'

'Still,' Tommy said, 'there must be some history here.'

'There's Ataturk's Mausoleum and the Museum of Anatolian Civilizations.'

It seemed that we were not going to get to know much about

Turkey from our guard. 'Is there a book store with English books?' I asked.

'Yes . . . on Caddesi . . . I take you there.'

From a guide book we learned that Matin was quite correct in favouring Istanbul. In A.D. 200 the Romans conquered the Byzantines and in A.D. 330 the Emperor Constantine moved his capital there and renamed the city Constantinople. When Rome fell in 1261 the Byzantines returned briefly but in the 1400s Mahmet the Conqueror established the Ottoman Empire which was to rule for 500 years. During the reign of Sulyman the Magnificent the city was graced with many new buildings of great beauty and was the cross-roads for trade and diplomacy. The Ottoman Empire spread deeply into Europe, Asia and North Africa. Not until the end of W.W.I. was Turkey stripped of its conquests.

During this time Ankara was just a town on the bleak and barren Anatolian plain although claiming some history in the Hittites as far back as 2,000 B.C.

We bought some civilian clothes - shirts, trousers and sweaters; the latter because Matin told us that Ankara, at an altitude of 3,000 feet, got chilly at night. Since we had not had a bath or shower for almost a week, we asked about a Turkish Bath. He took us to one (taxis were plentiful and inexpensive) which had elaborate, marble hot and cold tubs. We sank gratefully into a hot one and stayed until our skin was wrinkled.

That evening we asked Matin to take us to a good restaurant for Turkish food which served drinks. Since Turkey was an Islamic country there were no bars and most restaurants did not serve drinks. But some did; we never found out why this was so. We went to one called Agora El Ve Balik Evi and had a sumptuous meal with an hors d'oeurve of Borek (flaky pastry stuffed with cheese and parsley); a main course of Dolma (lamb with vegetables, rice, and nuts) and wine; and a melon for dessert. In the late evening belly dancers appeared as the place became a cabaret.

On the following morning Matin asked us: 'What are your plans for the day?'

'We thought of going to Ataturk's Mausoleum this morning,' Tommy replied.

'And in the afternoon?'

'We hadn't got that far yet.'

'Would you like to go to the races this afternoon,' Matin asked.

'Horse races, you mean?' I queried.

'Yes. I wish to go.'

Tommy and I looked at each other and nodded. 'Okay,' I said.

'Good. You go and see sights this morning and I meet you here for lunch, then we go to race track.' He walked away.

'This internment is far too strict,' I commented, as we went in search of a taxi.

Anit Kabir - Ataturk's Mausoleum - is a colossal limestone building set in an entire hill with beautifully kept gardens and smartly uniformed guards. The stone sarcophagus weighs 40,000 kilos. The temple soars into the air, dwarfing all the surrounds. All signs were in Turkish and we were confused by some references to Mustafa Kemal while other said Ataturk. When we later asked Matin about this, he said: 'We used to have no surnames but only patronymics which was very confusing because there were so many people with the same name. Parliament decreed that all Turks must have surnames, so Mustafa Kemal chose Ataturk - Father of the Turks.'

Nearby was the Ankara Kalesi - the Citadel - with old foundations dating back to A.D. 300; some of the defensive walls are still standing. In the streets children were playing bare-footed in the dust.

The race track was at the Hippodrome. Matin had his spread sheet and was ready to make some bets. But the first race had only one horse, which cantered slowly around the track. The second race had two horses. All announcements were in Turkish and it was confusing to us.

'What do they do,' I asked Matin, 'add one horse to every race?'

'No . . . no,' he replied, 'there will be eight or ten now.' He left to place a bet.

'I wonder if Matin wins,' I mused. 'Should we give him a few lira to place for us?'

'Why not?' Tommy answered. 'It will make it a bit more interesting for us.'

So we gave Matin some money but by the end of the day it had vanished, along with his good humour. Matin did not have a good day.

On the afternoon of our fourth day in Ankara we had a most interesting time at the Hittite Museum. Matin did not come with us, saying: 'You two go . . . I have seen all that stuff.' He was no aesthete.

The building, set in a colourful, manicured garden full of statues and benches, is a renovated 15th century Ottoman 'Bedestan' - a covered market - which lends itself to a museum layout because one progresses chronologically around all four sides. In the central courtyard there is an Anatolian earth mother, grotesquely fat with bulging arms, legs, breasts, and belly. Female fatness was admired; an Ottoman saying was: 'She is so beautiful she has to go through the door sideways.'

Beside a wonderful display of Hittite objects of gold and copper, statuettes of stags and bulls, we were trying to decipher a sign in Turkish when we were approached by a man in his sixties, slim, a trim moustache and one of the few people we had seen wearing a Fez. He smiled at us and said, in perfect English: 'I see that you are having trouble with the Turkish language . . . you are English, yes?'

'Yes,' Tommy replied.

'No,' I said, 'Canadian.'

'Ah,' he said. 'I am the Curator. Let me tell you about the Hittites, one of the old civilizations dating back to about 2,000 B.C. They were an advanced people with a legal system and administration. Religious rites were complicated and obligatory. The wishes of the gods were promulgated by oracles or dreams.'

'They lived around here?' Tommy asked.

'Yes. Their capital was at Hoyuk, about 200 kilometres east of here. They were well known to the Old Testament writers. Bethseba, the lady who led David astray, was the wife of Uriah the Hittite. Solomon bought a number of Hittite women for his harem.'

'It's very interesting,' I remarked, 'to find out that these Old Testament people were real. I always have a slight feeling that some one made them up.'

'This is so,' the Curator remarked. 'Look at this tablet. It bears a message from the Egyptian Queen Nefertiti to her counterpart, Pudahape, the Hittite Queen. It was written after their husbands, Ramses II and Muwatallis II, fought one another.' He paused. 'Come into my office . . . we will have a coffee'.

This we did and had one of those little cups with the coffee so strong I was afraid the spoon would melt.

'We are still excavating remains of the Hittite Empire,' the Curator continued. 'The King was selected by a council of the Princes; his wife was the High Priestess. He could take a concubine if the Queen failed to produce a male child. It was a feudal system under which wives were obtained by purchase. A widow had to marry one of her late husband's brothers. Criminal law was strict, with named penalties for any serious offense.'

We had a second cup of coffee and chatted some more before taking our leave and thanking our host.

In the evening I made notes about the day, as was my habit. I remembered how Harry Deacon had made me the official recorder when we first landed in Africa and how I had kept up the habit ever since. Fortunately, I have an excellent memory, some times almost total recall.

The following day was warm and we decided to walk to the British Embassy (we had been checking in by phone) because we needed some more Turkish money. Matin came with us because he didn't want us to appear without him - after all, he was our 'guard'.

We discovered that Ataturk Bulvan was 'Embassy Row'. The U.S., German, and U.K. Embassies were lined up quite close to each other. As expected, the German Embassy was behind a high wall with an armed soldier in front of forbidding iron gates.

'I wonder,' Tommy mused, 'where they do their drinking at night?'

I knew exactly what my impulsive, red-haired pilot had in mind. Actually, I wasn't against the idea at all. 'Let's ask Sanders.'

We went to the Paymaster first. He gave us some lira, saying: 'You don't need much. I believe that G/C Sanders has you out of here the day after tomorrow.'

G/C Sanders confirmed this. 'I have you booked on Egypt Air to Cairo the day after tomorrow at 0900 hours. There are still a few loose ends so check with me in the late afternoon tomorrow. If all is well I'll have a car pick you up at your hotel at 0800 hours. The driver will have your tickets.'

'That's great!' Tommy enthused. 'By the way, do you know where the Germans go for nightlife, Sir?'

Sanders eyes narrowed. 'You're thinking of dropping in?'

'Well,' Tommy temporised, 'I thought we might show the flag.'

'All right, but don't get into trouble or you'll never get out of here. They favour the Time Cafe on Attar Sok.'

We thanked Sanders for his help and walked back down Ataturk Bulvan.

That evening we dressed for the occasion. We wore uniform shirts with rank tabs on the shoulders but covered these with a sweater. About 2200 hours we strolled into the Time Cafe. It was a western style club with a long bar, a small stage holding a piano, tables and chairs. Directly in front of the stage was a long table at which a dozen or so Germans were seated, four of them in Army Uniform. This obviously was 'their' table; its top was covered with bottles and glasses, indicating that they had been here for some time. The tavern was about two-thirds full.

We took a table nearby the Germans and ordered drinks loudly in English. We were rewarded with some dirty looks. Then we took off our sweaters to reveal that we were military and got some hostile comments.

The piano player appeared on stage. He was a tall, thin fellow of some indeterminate nationality who took requests from the audience. When he took his break, one of the Germans took his place. He played 'Lili Marlene' and they all began to sing. The song was so well known that Tommy and I knew the lyrics, at least to the first verse. So we joined in:
'Underneath the lantern,
By the barrack gate
Darling I remember
The way you used to wait.
T'was there that you whispered tenderly
That you loved me,
You'd always be,
My Lili of the lamplight
My own Lili Marlene.'

Our singing was too much for a German in Army uniform, so he picked up a bottle by the neck and started for our table. We got ready for a fracas but his friends grabbed him and held him back, while glaring at us. The German piano player returned to their table; he was not going to play any more if we sang.

We had one more drink and decided to leave before hostilities erupted into open warfare.

'At least,' Tommy commented, as we walked home, 'we ruined their evening.'

On the 28 Sept 1944, we flew civil air from Ankara to Cairo. We thanked Matin for his loose guardianship and gave him our lira. He seemed sad to lose his cushy job.

In Cairo we reported to RAF HQ and arranged for a flight back to Tobruk. There was a Canadian liaison office, headed by a Squadron Leader by the name of Taylor. I told him our story and we had a chat.

'The war in the Med is nearly over,' he said. 'The Germans are withdrawing as fast as possible. You've done quite a bit now . . . do you want to quit?'

'I can't leave Tommy without a navigator. What do you hear about the future of 603 Squadron?'

'That they will be stood down shortly and returned to England.'

'That's when I will leave,' I said. 'Can you pull me out when it happens?'

'Yes,' Taylor replied. 'I will do that.'

Chapter 13

Return to Tobruk

W/C Foxley-Norris insisted on hearing every detail of our adventure. He shook his head at our description of the jail cell in Antalya and laughed at our story of badgering the Germans in the Time Cafe. When we finished, he said: 'You've both done well. Tommy, I don't fault your attack on the gun emplacement; it's our job to strike at the Germans wherever we find them. It's just bad luck that you got shot up. You know, with three enemy aircraft shot down on your first tour, and now two on this one, you are an 'Ace'.'

'So what?' Tommy said.

Foxley-Norris turned to me. 'Lee, I've never seen anyone as well prepared for a mission as you are.'

'Thanks, Sir.' I replied.

He looked at us both fondly; I guess we were favoured. 'I'll put you both in for a bar to your DFC.'

'Thanks,' Tommy said. 'We heard in Cairo that the war in the Med is nearly over, with the Germans withdrawing rapidly.'

'True,' Foxley-Norris answered, 'but we'll have a few cracks at them yet.'

We flew a couple of Rovers but had no sightings. By day we flew in a VIC formation with us leading. At night we spaced the aircraft at 10-minute intervals. If one found a target he could direct the others towards it. There was little shipping of any size but our sister squadron, 252, found a warship at night. Unfortunately, it shot down the aircraft, killing the crew, and the others were unable to find it.

In support of the partisans we were often called upon to attack a specific target. There were problems with isolated enemy island garrisons, cut off and with no offensive capability, but still armed and entrenched. It was not easy to attack them since their installations were usually in the centre of the towns and we didn't want to kill any Greeks, who had had enough hardships. One such target was a three-story building in the town on Cos. We attacked it with rockets and canons. The building was left on fire with black smoke, debris and dust rolling upwards as our aircraft departed.

In mid-October Foxley-Norris took ourselves and one other aircraft to El Adem, a neighbouring airfield. He didn't tell us the reason; perhaps he didn't know. On arrival we found that we were to escort a transport bearing Anthony Eden, the Foreign Secretary, to Athens which had been newly liberated. Before leaving El Adem, Eden insisted that the aircrew have lunch with him. We found him to be gracious and entertaining.

Train Busting

The mood of the people in Athens was euphoric but with some sour overtones. One poor girl had her head shaved in public for collaborating with the Germans. There were many stories about the Greek resistance; some about successful operations and others about great suffering at the hands of the Gestapo. I doubt if any other occupied country in the war hated the Germans as much as the Greeks did.

We had an interesting discussion with a young Captain of the Greek Sacred Squadron, which we had never heard of. They were trained by the British Special Boat Squadron for guerilla operations against the Germans in the Aegean. We found that some of the targets that we had attacked were at their request. Their name in Greek was 'Eros Lokos', after the band of Spartans who had fought to the last man at Thermopylae against the Persians.

Unfortunately, Greek friendship with her wartime Allies didn't last very long as ELAS, ELAM and other noxious organizations began to kill foreigners and any others who didn't agree with them.

One of our missions had a touch of levity. The following is a quote from Foxley-Norris' biography, 'A Lighter Shade of Blue.' To wit:

'This situation provided for me one of the classic signals of all times. (I still preserve it). The target of the mission was a small German force in the island town of Kalymnos. The executive signal from Higher Authority to me as leader read: 'Pilots will not, repeat not, open fire but will fly in such a manner as to leave no doubt in the minds of the enemy that his fate is sealed.'
After some debate and tooth sucking, we finally interpreted this oracle by flying over the town at low level, upside down. Oddly enough, it did the trick!'

By the end of October the whole coast of southern Greece was in British hands although about 18,500 German troops were left in Crete, Rhodes, Leros, Cos and Melos, together with 4,500 Italians. These offered little danger to the Allies and were dealt with from the air or left to stagnate until they surrendered.

There was still a lot of action around Italy and I was delighted to read about my former squadron, No. 39. The beautiful Italian liner 'Rex' of 51,000 tons was spotted by Beaus of 272 squadron leaving Trieste. She was attacked and damaged. The 'coup-de-grace' was given to 39 squadron. Six Beaus, led by Flt Lt. Bob Pitman, approached from the land, through valleys and rainstorms, and down a hill. Surprise was complete. Every Beau claimed hits and Rex was left on fire along her entire length, listing to port. Photo recce showed her resting on her side with only about one-third above water.

I started to think about my return to England. I wrote Mary an

Air Mail Letter Card saying that I would likely be in Lytham before Xmas. I had saved quite a lot of money; there was nothing to spend it on in the desert and my small bar bills were taken care of by winning at bridge. The RCAF pay scale was always a bone of contention with the RAF; my pay was equivalent to that of the C.O.

I would have to get some clothes. I had one blue uniform, one blue shirt and one black tie. I had no coat of any kind. My civilian clothes consisted of a couple of sports shirts, one pair each of shorts and trousers, and two sweaters.

At the end of November a signal arrived from Cairo ordering 603 Squadron to 'Stand Down' from operations and prepare to return to England. I quote again from Foxley-Norris' autobiography:

> 'With the collapse of German resistance in Greece and the Aegean our job was completed and there was much speculation about our future, both as a unit and as individuals. I was much concerned, especially as other squadrons were being disbanded and their people dispersed in all directions. I need not have worried; the Royal Auxiliary Air Force 'Union' was very powerful. The Lord Provost of Edinburgh, then the great and good Sir Willy Darling, made forcible enquiries at high level about the whereabouts of, and plans for, 'HIS' squadron. No. 603 retained its entity and very shortly afterwards was on a troopship steaming home through the now secure Mediterranean. This also saved my own bacon; I had already been warned that I was to be given a ground appointment at last, as C.O. of a rather dreary Egyptian support base called Idku. I was very grateful to Sir Willy.'

On the following day a signal arrived ordering me to report to the RCAF Liason Office at RAF HQs, Cairo. It was hard to say goodbye to my friends on the squadron. The Brits do not like outward displays of emotion. Still, I gave Tommy a fierce hug and told him that he was 'The best Beaufighter pilot in the world.' I meant it.

I scrounged a lift to Alex to say goodbye to Susan. Although we both knew that parting was inevitable, it was still difficult.

Then I took a train to Cairo, checked in at Shepheards Hotel, and reported to S/L Taylor. He greeted me affably and said: 'I'm glad you made it. I can get you on a USAF Flight straight to North America.'

'No, thanks,' I replied. 'I have to go to England to collect my girl.'

He was a bit put out by this change to his plans but he rallied: 'All right . . . I'll see what I can do . . . check with me tomorrow.'

Taylor arranged a flight in an RAF DC-3. It wasn't fast. After stops in Malta and Sardinia, I arrived at Lyneham on 2 Dec 1944.

My war was over.

Chapter 14

Return to England

When I checked into RCAF HQs in London I was told that all personnel movements were handled at Warrington, about a two-hour train ride to the north, and that I was to report there. I spent a few days in London to replenish my wardrobe. The famous military tailors, Gieves Ltd, who were quite accustomed to panic orders, made me a blue uniform with all accoutrements in three days. They gave me a raincoat at once. After all, it was December and the rain was almost non-stop. Civilian clothes were bought at Marks and Spencers (always called 'Marks and Sparks' by Mary) since I had neither the time nor the inclination to visit another tailor.

The transition from the heat and dryness of the Western Desert to the rainy cold of England was difficult; I shivered for two weeks.

The officer in charge of movements at Warrington was an Admin type named F/L Kelly, middle-aged with dark Irish looks. We were to have some interesting discussions.

'The first thing I want,' I said, after introductions were over, 'is some leave. I must have months built up by now. Christmas is coming and I want to get married.'

'You do, eh? To an English girl?'

'Yes.'

'Where does she live?'

'In Lytham-St. Annes . . . that's near Blackpool.'

'I know where it is,' Kelly said, tartly. He picked up a sailing schedule and studied it for a few minutes. 'I have no space in December and not much in January . . . probably be February before I can get you away.'

'What about my prospective wife?'

'Certain ships have female quarters. She'll have to go on one of them. I'll tell you what . . . go on leave until the 21 Jan. Report back here then. Give my clerk your address and phone number in Lytham.'

'Okay, thanks.' I went to the Pay Office and drew many pounds. Then I phoned Mary and caught a train for Lytham on which I barely got a seat.

Mary met me at the station. My heart turned over when I saw her. Had this lovely, intelligent girl really waited for me for three years? How lucky could a guy get?

We fell into each other's arms. She held me at arm's length and said: 'Look at you . . . you're so brown . . . and your hair is almost white. Why are you carrying that cane?'

'And you're as beautiful as ever!' I gave her another hug. 'The cane is a keepsake . . . I'll tell you about it.'

Instead of going straight home we went to the Railway Hotel where we had a beer and talked non-stop for an hour.

Mary's two sisters, Joan and Veronica, greeted me with hugs and kisses. But her parents had reservations. Up until now I had just been some 'fly-by-night' affair of Mary's that would probably never materialize into anything serious. Her girl-hood sweetheart lived nearby and the two families had taken it for granted that they would marry. Worse, I was not a Catholic. Now it looked as if their youngest daughter would not only marry outside the faith but be lost to them forever by emigrating to Canada.

The family had only skimpy reports of my adventures in Malta, Elba and Turkey, and other operations, so I was kept busy for many hours with many questions. Mr. Fletcher was very interested in Malta because of some connection, never quite clear to me, with the organization of the Masons of which he was a member.

I was again given that cold-storage bedroom. The definition of a split-second is the time that it took me to shed my clothes, put on my pyjamas and dive under the covers.

If Mary and I were to be married in the Catholic Church, which both we and the family wanted, it would be necessary for us to obtain a 'Dispensation'. We got an application form, spent some time filling it in, and took it to the church in Lytham. Shortly after, Mary and her mother were asked to a meeting with the Parish Priest. He rejected the application!

Father was furious! While he was not enamoured about our marriage, he was livid at this rejection. 'What did that young idiot have to say?' he asked.

'He said,' mother replied, 'that Mary was young and pretty and would have no trouble finding a good Catholic boy to marry.'

'That damn black-robe!' father stormed. 'The church is here to serve the people, not vice versa. I've supported them for 30 years and the first time that I ask for anything, they turn me down! Well, I know the Bishop personally . . . we'll see what he says!'

Mr. Fletcher paid a visit to the Bishop, whose seat was in Preston, about a half-hour on the train from Lytham. But the Bishop upheld his Parish Priest's decision and father was crosser than ever.

Mary was also mad. She said to her parents: 'We'll get married in a Registry Office if we have to.'

Now Xmas was upon us and we put our trouble aside for a week or so while we got involved in buying presents, decorating a tree and finding food for Xmas dinner. This was my first Xmas celebration for three years and I enjoyed it greatly. Of course, we went to Mass on Xmas day, through which father glared at the Priest.

It was on Boxing Day that Joan had her inspiration. 'Why don't we get in touch with Donald Proudfoot?' she suggested.

I well remembered the Proudfoot brothers, Donald and Brian, both RC Priests, and spending enjoyable hours with them singing around the Fletcher piano. Brian was now a missionary in Africa (where he died of some obscure African disease) but Donald had a parish in Greenford, a London suburb.

When Mary called Father Donald on the phone, he was immediately cooperative. 'Come and see me,' he said.

It turned out that Mary had an aunt, her mother's sister, who lived in this same parish. Her name was Agnes Tudor. She and her daughter, Angela, lived alone in a good-sized house and would welcome our arrival.

So early in the new year of 1945, Mary and I set off by train for London.

Aunt Agnes was in her sixties, thin, grey hair and glasses, took no notice of her clothes, usually had a cigarette dangling from one corner of her mouth and was a living example of why the people of London had survived the blitz. All through the bombing, with nearby houses and streets destroyed, she had never gone to an air raid shelter. Under the stairs leading to the upper story of her house, she had placed an arm chair, table and lamp. "'itler will never get me 'ere,' she said.

I can see her now, in a shapeless dress and bedroom slippers, grey hair askew, pushing a manual carpet sweeper around the living room and singing:

'I'm gonna dance with the dolly
With a hole in her stockin'
While her knees keep a-knockin'
And her toes keep a-rockin"

Nor was the danger over. London was now being attacked by V-1s. These small, unmanned rockets were a terror weapon designed to fall indiscriminately. Fuel to the rocket engine was cut off when over the city. When one heard the engine sputter and die it was time to dive for shelter because its bomb would explode as soon as the V-1 crashed.

In later years her daughter, Angela, also a free spirit, emigrated to Canada and stayed with us for a while. We happened to be in Toronto at the time. She married a farmer from London, Ontario, and raised a brood of children.

We walked from Aunt Agnes' house to Father Donald's church - 'Our Lady of the Visitation.' The Rectory was behind the church. When we knocked he appeared quickly and greeted us with open arms. 'Aye . . . it's great to see someone from my home town!' He gave Mary a hug and me a firm handshake.

Father Donald was a tall, good-looking man in his thirties; an extrovert with more than a touch of 'ham'. He missed a career as an actor.

Seated in his study he asked: 'Now, Mary, what do your parents think of you marrying a non-Catholic?'

'Mother has always been in favour. Dad was against it at first but now he's so mad at the Church hierarchy in Lancashire that he wants us to get married just to spite them.'

Donald smiled and turned to me. 'Lee, what religion are you?'

'We attend the United Church in Canada. It's fairly close to

Anglican. My mother is very religious and so I've attended regularly.'

'Have you thought of taking instruction to become a Catholic?'

'Mary and I have discussed it but I don't want to be rushed into it and there's not much time now.' (Many years later I did convert).

'I see. You realise that any children will have to be raised as Catholics?'

'Yes . . . I've agreed to that.'

By this time Mary was perched impatiently on the edge of her chair. 'Will you give us a Dispensation, Donald?'

'Aye, my dear . . . that I will.'

Mary and I beamed at each other so widely that he had to smile also.

'Will you get into trouble with your Bishop?' Mary asked.

'No,' Donald replied, 'because he's very sick and won't be back at work for many weeks.'

(The Heide luck still at work?)

'Let me see,' he looked at his calendar. 'I need two Sundays to proclaim the Banns and then the best date for the wedding would be the 31 Jan.'

'That's fine,' Mary confirmed.

'Who will be your bridesmaid?'

'My sister Joan will come.'

'And to give you away?'

'I guess my Aunt Agnes will have to do that.'

'Lee, do you have a best man?'

'No.'

'No matter.' Donald stood up. 'Come and see me a few days before the wedding and we'll go over things.'

'We'll do that,' Mary said.

'And I expect to see you both at Mass on Sunday,' he added.

We assured him that we would be there and left on Cloud Nine.

The end of the war was in sight and many of the severe restrictions placed on Londoners were eased. Nobody carried gas masks now. The black-out was still in effect but not so strictly enforced. Some people still took shelter in the underground tube stations but they were not nearly as crowded as they had been during the blitz. But food was still scarce.

I was keen on the theatre so we saw two stage plays and the revue at the Windmill theatre. This theatre had never closed during the war and girls could be 'sans clothes' as long as they didn't move; Mary didn't appreciate them as much as I did. Of course we took in such sights as the Tower of London, British Museum and other London historic places.

On 19 Jan 1945, we paid a visit to Canada House which was the domain of the High Commissioner to England, Vincent Massey. My reason for going was to buy some food at their canteen. I knew that Aunt Agnes would be delighted with some real coffee (vice chicory) real butter (vice oleo) and other delicacies such as tinned salmon. I particularly wanted some peanut butter; unknown to the British.

As we were leaving I was stopped by a young man whom I knew was Massey's secretary. 'Ah,' he said. 'Just the man I want to see . . . you're Fl/Lt Heide, aren't you?'

'Yes.'

'Good. I was just on the phone to Fl/Lt Kelly at Warrington. He said you were in Lancashire.'

'Ah, yes. I was about to check in with him.'

'The reason that I wanted to get in touch with you is that I have here an Invitation from St. James Palace for you to attend an Investiture at Buckingham Palace for your DFC on 2 Feb.'

I was stunned. 'How did that come about?'

'Don't know. Anyhow . . . here it is . . . I assume you'll attend?'

'You bet!' I turned to Mary: 'Stick with me, doll, and you'll be consorting with King George!'

I phoned F/L Kelly.

'Good,' he opened, 'just the man I wanted. I have a sailing date for you on 31 Jan. You'll have to . . .'

'Hold it,' I interrupted. 'I have to attend an Investiture at Buckingham Palace on 2 Feb.'

'Oh.' He was clearly put out. 'Well, in that case, come here on 4 Feb.'

'I can't. I'm getting married on 31 Jan.'

'How does it happen, Heide, that every time I make an arrangement for you it isn't satisfactory?' Kelly was clearly disgruntled. (He would be more so later).

'Not my fault.'

'When do you think you could spare the time to come to Warrington?' he asked sarcastically.

CENTRAL CHANCERY OF
THE ORDERS OF KNIGHTHOOD,
ST JAMES'S PALACE, S.W.1.

18th January 1945

CONFIDENTIAL.

Sir,
        The King will hold an Investiture at Buckingham Palace
on Friday, the 2nd February, 1945, at which your attendance is
requested.
        It is requested that you should be at the Palace not
later than 10.15 o'clock a.m. (Doors open at 9.45 a.m.)
                DRESS:—Service Dress; Morning Dress; Civil Defence
                        Uniform or Dark Lounge Suit.
        This letter should be produced by you on entering the
Palace, as no further card of admission will be issued.
        I am desired to inform you that you may be accompanied
by two relations or friends to witness the Investiture, but
I regret that owing to the limited accommodation available
for spectators, it is not possible for this number to be
increased. The spectators' tickets may be obtained on
application to this Office and I have to ask you, therefore,
to complete the enclosed form and return it to me immediately.

                        I am, Sir,
                            Your obedient Servant,

Flight Lieutenant Cecil L. Heide,   Secretary.
                D.F.C., R.C.A.F.

'Well, I need ten days for a honeymoon,' I replied. 'How about
10 Feb?'

'I'll see you then.' He cut off sharply.

Mary's sister, Joan, arrived from Lytham. She was excited to hear
of our invitation to Buckingham Palace and ecstatic to learn that I
could get an invitation for her as well.

I paid a visit to RCAF HQs to give them my temporary address
in Greenford and was given an invitation to a dance at Grosvenor
House, Park Lane, being put on by Air Marshal Breadner.

Mary bought a new blue-on-white dress that showed off her

excellent figure to perfection. Her shining blonde hair hung to her shoulders; her sky blue eyes sparkled; she exuded health and vivacity. She was the 'Belle of the Ball.' The orchestra played tunes that I was familiar with. Mary never missed a dance and only half of them were with me.

ROYAL CANADIAN AIR FORCE OVERSEAS HEADQUARTERS.

Officers' Dance

GROSVENOR HOUSE, PARK LANE,
Friday, January 26th, 1945
::   8.30 ⎯ 1.30   ::

By kind permission of
Air Marshal L. S. BREADNER, C.B., D.S.C.,
Air Officer Commanding-in-Chief.

Music by R.C.A.F. Overseas Dance Orchestra.

I wore one decoration that very few Canadian airmen had. This was an African Star with a Bar. The Bar indicated early service in the Western Desert in support of the Eighth Army's breakout at El Alemein. This medal provoked several discussions on my time in Malta and the desert. I also met a pilot who had married an English girl and he told me that he and his bride were going to Canada on the same ship. This set me thinking.

We had a wedding rehearsal at Father Donald's church. He had asked a friend to be my best man and had arranged for an organist. Aunt Agnes was so delighted at the whole affair that she rarely stopped talking.

The weather co-operated on the 31 Jan and it didn't rain although it was overcast. Mary looked splendid in a new suit; I was in uniform. As we walked down the aisle I found it hard to believe that it was really happening; that this lovely girl was mine and that she loved me so much that she was prepared to leave her family and friends and come with me to Canada.

Aunt Agnes put on a nice 'tea' with some of the 'goodies' that I had brought from Canada House. I had reserved a room for a week at the Russell Hotel where Mary and I made love, ate peanut butter sandwiches and watched the Buzz Bombs over London.

Lancashire papers picked up our news.

Miss Mary Fletcher and Flt.-Lt. C. Heide, D.F.C.

One of the R.A.F.'s daring fliers who in January received from the King at Buckingham Palace, the Distinguished Flying Cross, was married at Greenford, Middlesex, to Miss Mary Fletcher, youngest daughter of Mr. and Mrs. R. S. Fletcher, 26, Park View Road, Lytham.

The bridegroom is Flt. Lieut. Cecil Lu Heide, D.F.C., of the Royal Canadian Air Force, eldest son of Mr. and Mrs. A. F. Heide, of Vancouver, B.C. Attending the bride was Miss Joan Fletcher, sister.

Flt. Lieut. Heide was in Malta during the worst period of the "blitz," and he, as a navigator, along with a companion torpedoed a large enemy tanker in the Mediterranean.

Both engines of their plane gave out and the couple were "ditched" in the sea. They eventually reached the Island of Elba, but it was in German occupation. Flt. Lieut. Heide and companion got away in an old boat.

The bride was formerly employed at the District Bank, St. Annes.

The couple are spending a few weeks in London, before taking up residence in Vancouver.

LYTHAM GIRL MARRIES CANADIAN D.F.C.

The marriage (of interest to many people in Lytham and St. Annes) of Miss Mary Fletcher, youngest daughter of Mr. and Mrs. R. S. Fletcher, 26, Park View Rd., Lytham, was solemnized at the Church of Our Lady of the Visitation, Cranford, Middlesex, on January 31st. The bridegroom was Flt.-Lieut. Cecil Leroy Heide, D.F.C., R.C.A.F., eldest son of Mr. and Mrs. A. J. Heide, of Vancouver, B.C. Canada. The bridesmaid was Miss Joan Fletcher (sister of the bride).

Flt.-Lieut. Heide was invested with the D.F.C. on Friday last, by H.M. the King at Buckingham Palace. During operations in Malta at its worst period, Flt. Lieut. Heide as navigator, torpedoed a large enemy oil tanker in the Mediterranean and when both engines of the plane "gave out" he and his pilot were in the open sea in their dinghy for several days. Eventually they managed a landing on Elba which then was being evacuated by the Germans. After gaining valuable

On the following day I sent a telegram to my favourite Grandparents in Saskatoon:

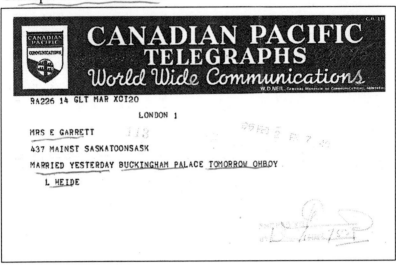

Buckingham Palace is very impressive and familiar to most people from pictures, if not in person. There were many people outside taking pictures of the 'Changing of the Guard.' We showed our invitations to an Army Captain at the Gate. Inside, the gracious front hall is wide with many paintings and carvings. We were ushered into a large Drawing Room. The walls were covered with paintings of previous Royalty and the ceiling held figurines in gold leaf. There was a low dais in front of which were about 75 folding chairs. I guessed that about 25 persons were to receive awards and about 50 were spectators.

We all stood up when King George VI entered, flanked by two aides. A slight man, he was dressed in the uniform of an Admiral in the Royal Navy. This of course was the man who never wanted to be King. Shy, nervous, with a bad stutter, he was forced into the role when his brother abdicated to marry the American divorcee, Wallis Simpson.

The King stood in the centre of the dais. The aide on his left, from which direction we filed, read out the citation while the aide on his right gave him the medal to be pinned on.

3792

BUCKINGHAM PALACE.

Admit one to witness the

Investiture

(at 10.15 o'clock a.m.)

Lord Chamberlain.

I was near the end of the presentations. There were DSOs, DSCs, DFCs and two George Cross' given to civilians. King George looked tired by the time that I got there. He perked up a bit when his aide mentioned that I had been in Malta during the blitz and asked two questions about the island. His stutter was evident.

Mary and Joan were thrilled at the occasion and we even found a good restaurant afterwards. Over dinner I told them the story about King George that was making the rounds:

'It was the end of a long day of presentations and the King was dead on his feet. The last award was a DFC to a fighter pilot who had shot down five Focke Wulf-190s. The King said: 'You may have shot down f-f-five F-F-Fockers but you're only getting one f-f-fucking medal.'

On 10 Feb we said our good-byes and thanks to Aunt Agnes, Angela and Father Donald and boarded a train for Lytham, with a stop in Warrington. I left Mary with a shandy in the lounge of the Railway Hotel, saying: 'There's no need for you to traipse out to the base . . . wait here . . . I'll only be about an hour.'

'All right,' she agreed.

'I have a plan,' I added.

'What is it?'

'I'm not telling you.' I left her with a bemused smile on her face.

'Hi,' F/L Kelly said, as I entered his office. 'How was the Investiture?'

'Very interesting . . . especially for my wife and her sister.'

'Good. I haven't been able to find a spot for your wife yet but I have one for you. You leave from . . . '

'Hold it!' I interrupted.

'What now?' Kelly sighed.

'When I was at a dance at Grosvenor House I got talking to Air Marshal Breadner. When he heard that I was about to be married, he said to tell you to get my wife and myself on the same ship.'

I looked Kelly straight in the eye - the picture of honesty. In fact, it was a blatant, bare-faced lie. I had not spoken to the AOC at all.

There was a strained silence.

Kelly was trapped. He couldn't very well call me a liar. On the other hand, he wasn't about to stick his neck out by calling the Air Marshal for verification.

He gave in. 'Are you on your way back to Lytham now?'

'Yes.'

'All right,' he sighed. 'I'll get you both on the same ship . . . I'll send you a telegram.'

'Thanks.'

'Don't mention it,' he said, sarcastically. 'I'll sure as hell be glad to see the last of you.'

Back on the train, I told Mary what I had done. 'Oh, you liar!' she laughed.

'Well, it worked, didn't it?' I gave her a hug.

Back in the Fletcher house we were given the deep-freeze bedroom but it wasn't so cold this time - Mary and I generated our own heat. I had now been on leave for over two months and was quite satisfied to have it continued indefinitely. Although the weather was a bit rainy and chilly, we still biked around the lovely Lancashire country-side.

Early in March the expected telegram arrived from Kelly. We were to sail from Liverpool on 11 March. Since Liverpool was close to Lytham, the whole family came to see us off. There were hugs, kisses and tears as we boarded the Vic Ingram, a passenger liner of 9,000 tons.

Once on board we were separated. There were about 50 wives, some with babies, who had their own quarters with a guard at the end of the corridor. I was given a hammock above the engine room; this was the first time that I had experienced this device and I found it quite comfortable once I mastered the technique of getting in and out.

We found ourselves in a convoy of some 20 ships. There was now little or no danger from U-Boats and the convoy proceeded at the agonizingly slow speed of ten knots. The sea was rough and many were seasick.

On the second day Mary and I were standing by the rail when one of the ship's officers came along. He had two stripes of the 'Wavy Navy'. 'I know him,' Mary whispered. 'He's from Lytham.'

'Well, say something then,' I ordered.

'Denis,' Mary called. The man turned around; he was in his early thirties, not handsome but with pleasant features.

'Well, I'll be . . . ' he said. 'Mary Fletcher!'

'Mary Heide now. This is my husband, Lee.'

We shook hands.

'I want to hear all about this,' Denis said. 'Come along to the Wardroom for a coffee.'

This we did while we told Denis our story. For the rest of the voyage we made use of the Wardroom which made a great difference to our comfort. (Fletcher luck at work?) Especially since the crossing took two weeks.

We were informed that the ship would dock at Halifax and that we would proceed from there by train. 'How long will it take to get to Vancouver?' Mary asked.

'About a week,' I replied, casually.

'A week!' she exclaimed. 'We have to spend a whole week on a train?'

'Well, there are bunks or beds. If we get a roomette, we can spend the whole week in bed,'

'Oh, you . . . '

Chapter 15

Return to Canada

On the CPR train Mary and I were squeezed into an upper bunk; but we didn't mind. It took six days to reach Vancouver. 'How can a country be this big?' she asked.

We were met at the station by my family: father, mother, brother Ray - age 19, sister Diane - age 17, and a new arrival, sister Lynne - age 3, whom I had not met before. Also on hand were a reporter and a camera man from the Vancouver Province newspaper.

HOME—-Flt.-Lt. Cecil L. Heide, D.F.C., and his bride, the former Mary Fletcher of Lytham, Lancashire, smile happily as Mrs. Heide gets her first look at Vancouver—her future home. Flt.-Lt. Heide and his English bride arrived in the city today from Britain.

They all adored Mary whose infectious smile and good humour put them at ease. They all had many questions for her about England and for me about my adventures on Malta, Elba and Turkey.

My father wanted desperately to get into the fight. He was too old for the Armed Forces so he joined the Merchant Marine as a cook. Since he had never so much as boiled an egg in his life, I always felt sorry for his shipmates. He survived several trans-Atlantic crossings.

After the war, disgusted by the Government's shabby treatment, he formed the Merchant Navy Veteran's Association to fight for their rights. These seamen were not entitled to housing or education grants, civil service employment preference or medical and dental treatment. Yet the death rate for them was the highest in the war at one in ten; the Air Force was one in 16; the Army one in 32; the Navy one in 47.

I remember my father making several trips to Ottawa to appear before one committee or another. All of his efforts failed. Not until 1999 did parliament give quasi-status to merchant seamen. By this time they were mostly dead, including my father.

My brother Ray was also in uniform, having joined the Navy, but he was too young to see any action.

Ray   Dad   Me

It was mid-March, 1945, when I was discharged from the RCAF. Mary and I now had to think about our future. We decided that I would return to UBC in the fall on the skimpy government grant of $60 a month. But I still had some savings and quickly found a job in a sawmill for the summer. Mary also found a job - with BC Tel.

We needed a place to live and found a new apartment block of three stories being built right next to Sylvia Court on English Bay. The rent was steep at $65 a month but we couldn't resist the location. (The building was later torn down for an addition to the Sylvia hotel).

Open window - our apartment

The flowers and the lush greenery of Stanley Park were a tonic to me after so long in the desert. Mary was pleased at the variety of food and fruit for sale, especially meat which had been rationed for so long in England.

We had no sooner settled into our civilian routine when in May two momentous things happened. Mary got pregnant and the RCAF offered me a permanent commission with no reduction in rank. It didn't take us long to make up our minds - I still loved to fly and Mary was quite willing to live the nomadic life of an Air Force wife.

Then followed 18 wonderful years until Paul Hellyer destroyed the RCAF that I knew with his abortive attempt to integrate the Services and I resigned.

But that's another story!

Epilogue

On returning to the RCAF I was sent to the Search and Rescue Squadron at Sea Island - across the airport from the present Vancouver civil terminal. They flew a mixed bag of aircraft - Hudson, Canso, DC-3 - and I got to know well the beautiful but treacherous B.C. coast.

In July, 1945, I was selected to go to Mountainview, Ontario, for a course in aerial gunnery. This was the last thing I needed. I had been firing machine guns for years and now the war was over. I protested but to no avail. In the Service one learns to follow orders even if some of them are assinine.

Since the course was only six weeks long, I left Mary in Vancouver.

The aircraft used at Mountainview was the Bolingbroke - a twin-engine cousin of the Blenheim. Waiting my turn one day to go in the rear turret for drogue-firing, I was standing behind the radio rack with my parachute at my feet. Unbeknownst to me, I was standing on a hatch. It fell open.

I fell out to my waist before grabbing the rack in front of me. My heart stopped as I saw my parachute spinning to the ground 6,000 feet below. Nobody came to help. By sheer will and determination I hauled myself back into the aircraft where I lay on the deck and cursed the Bristol Aircraft Company, the ground crew, the air crew and anyone else I could think of.

Still lucky, eh?

CPSIA information can be obtained at www.ICGtesting.com
Printed in the USA
BVOW042117230512

290864BV00002B/1/A

John A. Burgess
5801 W Bethel Ave Apt 216
Muncie, IN 47304